Publications of the Pennsylvania–Yale Expedition to Egypt
Number 6

Inscribed Material from the Pennsylvania-Yale Excavations at Abydos

The Pennsylvania–Yale Expedition house in the desert at Abydos

Publications of the Pennsylvania–Yale Expedition to Egypt

William Kelly Simpson and David B. O'Connor

Co-Directors and Co-Editors

Number 6

Inscribed Material from the Pennsylvania-Yale Excavations at Abydos

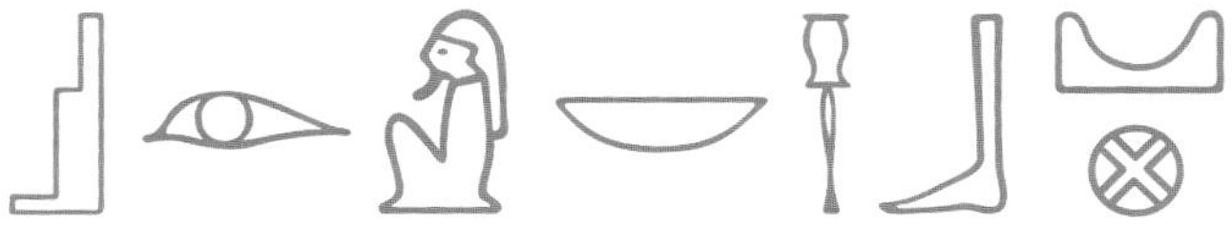

by William Kelly Simpson

The Peabody Museum of Natural History of Yale University

The University of Pennsylvania Museum of Archaeology and Anthropology

New Haven and Philadelphia

1995

Jacket illustration: General view of the Pennsylvania–Yale excavations, looking south, with the facade of the "Portal Temple" of Ramesses II in the foreground and Middle Kingdom cenotaphs behind

Frontispiece: The Pennsylvania–Yale Expedition house in the desert at Abydos

Front endpaper: The "Portal Temple" of Ramesses II and the Middle Kingdom cenotaph area at Abydos, looking southwest, before the Pennsylvania–Yale excavations

Back endpaper: The "Portal Temple" of Ramesses II and the Middle Kingdom cenotaph area at Abydos, looking south, during the Pennsylvania–Yale excavations

Manuelian DESIGN

Typeset in Garamond and Syntax
Edited, typeset, designed and produced by Peter Der Manuelian

ISBN 0-912532-39-4

Manufactured in the United States of America
by
Henry N. Sawyer Company
Charlestown, Massachusetts

Contents

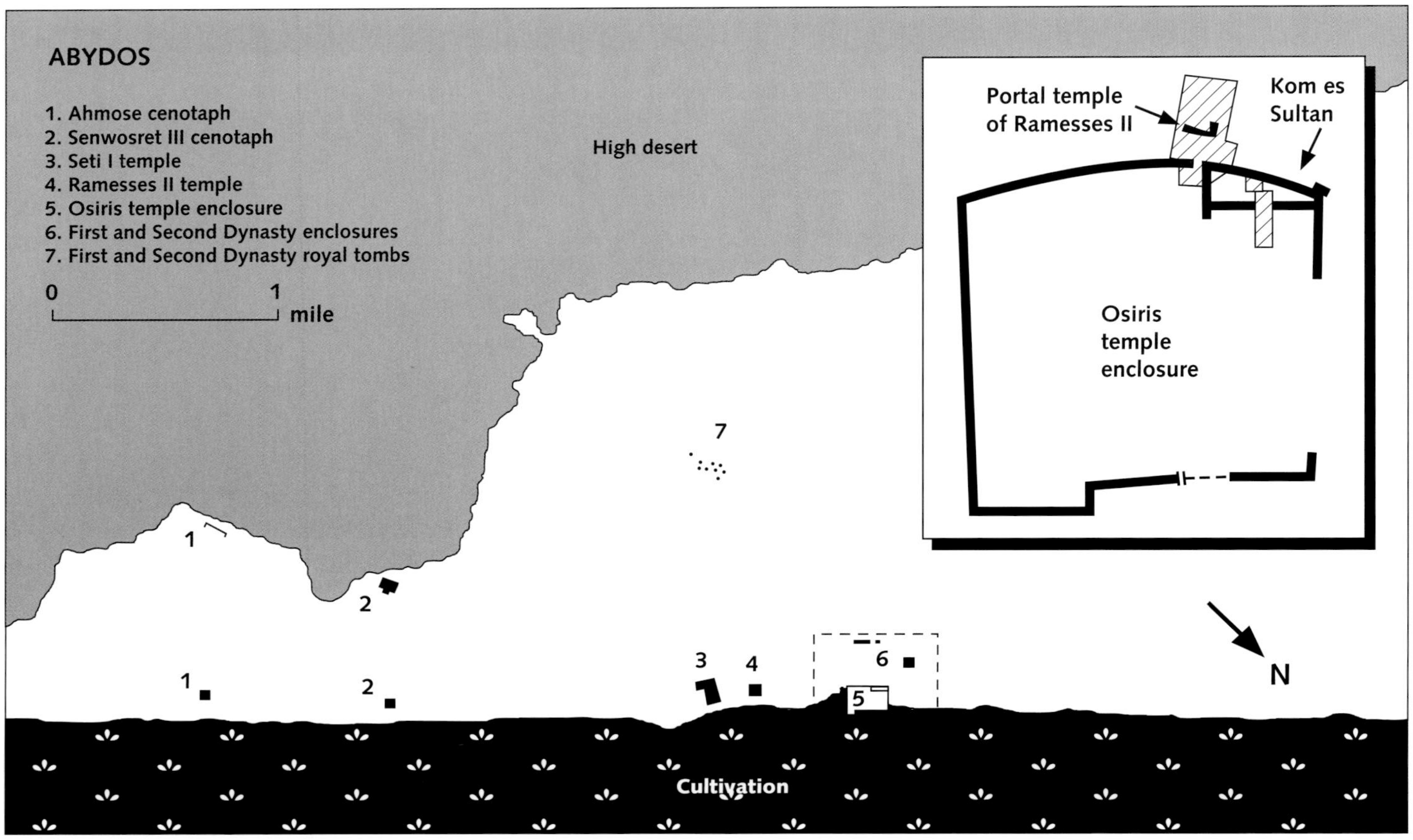

Fig. 1. Overview map of Abydos, with the area of Pennsylvania–Yale excavations discussed in this volume shown in the enlargement

Preface

The inscriptions published in this volume derive from the Pennsylvania–Yale Expedition to Egypt, a joint project of the University of Pennsylvania Museum of Archaeology and Anthropology and the Peabody Museum of Natural History of Yale University, in continuation of the Nubian salvage program conducted by the same expedition at Toshka and Arminna from 1960 to 1963. The Abydos project has been jointly directed by Professor David B. O'Connor of the University of Pennsylvania, and Professor William Kelly Simpson of Yale University, and the recording of the inscriptions is in the charge of the latter. It was originally planned to combine the archaeological, architectural, and textual material in a single study or series of studies. This has proved impractical, and the inscriptions presented here will be noted in their archaeological context in the volume(s) on the excavation proper. The scope of the expedition has increased dramatically since the seasons of 1967–69, which are covered in this volume. Professor O'Connor has examined the Second Dynasty structure known as the Shunet el Zebib and the First and Second Dynasty structures in front of the Shunet.

Several graduate students from the University of Pennsylvania have also conducted their own projects at Abydos: Janet Richards, Diana Craig Patch, Matthew Adams, Stephen Harvey, and Josef Wegner. The nature of their contributions is indicated under their names in the attached bibliography.

Financial support for the 1967–69 seasons was provided by the continuation of the United States Department of State Grant of Public Law 480 funds initially assigned to the excavations in Nubia, as well as the Eckley B. Coxe Jr. Fund of the University Museum (University of Pennsylvania), and a grant to the Peabody Museum (Yale University) from the Andrew W. Mellon Foundation. The publication has been made possible by a grant to Yale University from the Marilyn M. Simpson Charitable Trust, and funding from the Mellon Foundation.

Over twenty-five years having passed since the excavations, it is difficult to list the members of the staff and thank the members of the Egyptian Antiquities Organization without committing the error of omission. We are indebted to Dr. Gamal el Din Mukhtar, Director-General of the Egyptian Antiquities Service, Dr. Zahi Hawass and Mr. Abdullah el Sayid, our Inspectors, and to the able crew of excavators from Quft and their local assistants. For assistance in the Egyptian Museum, Cairo, we thank Dr. Mohammed Saleh and the curators and photographers. Among expedition staff members, we were fortunate in having Dr. Barry J. Kemp of Cambridge University, Lanny Bell, Gulbun O'Connor, Vincent Pigott, Elizabeth Dowman, William Potts, John Stengelhofen, and Gayle Wever of the University Museum, and David Sims and Douglas Connor of Yale University.

In the preparation of this volume I wish to acknowledge the major contribution of Ms. Jennifer Houser in undertaking the index of names, autographing texts, and replying to countless questions about the objects in the records and storerooms of the University Museum in Philadelphia. Mr. André Soldo aided in setting up the Macintosh computer system and preparing the cross-index of publication numbers with expedition and museum numbers. Mr. Mark Stone autographed many of the texts, inked drawings made in the field, and in particular autographed my hieroglyphic text of stela C 1, traced the Middle Kingdom lintel of Amenemhet III, and autographed my copies of some of the building ostraca.

Lastly, Dr. Peter Der Manuelian of the Museum of Fine Arts, Boston, has undertaken the editing, typesetting, design, and production of the monograph. To all, my thanks and admiration.

WKS
New Haven, Connecticut
April 5, 1995

List of Abbreviations

AL	*Année Lexicographique*
ASAE	*Annales du Service des Antiquités de l'Egypte*
BdE	Bibliothèque d'Etude
BIFAO	*Bulletin de l'Institut Français d'Archéologie Orientale*
CdE	*Chronique d'Egypte*
GM	*Göttinger Miszellen*
JARCE	*Journal of the American Research Center in Egypt*
JEA	*Journal of Egyptian Archaeology*
KRI	Kitchen, *Ramesside Inscriptions*
LÄ	*Lexikon der Ägyptologie*
MDAIK	*Mitteilungen des Deutschen Archäologischen Instituts, Abteilung Kairo*
MÄS	Münchner Ägyptologische Studien
NARCE	*Newsletter of the American Research Center in Egypt*
n.	note
no.	number
PN	H. Ranke, *Die ägyptischen Personennamen*
RdE	*Revue d'Egyptologie*
Rec Trav	*Recueil de Travaux relatifs à la philologie et à l'archéologie égyptiennes et assyriennes*
SAK	*Studien zur altägyptischen Kultur*
Urk.	*Urkunden des ägyptischen Altertums*
Wb.	*Wörterbuch der ägyptischen Sprache*
ZÄS	*Zeitschrift für ägyptische Sprache und Altertumskunde*

List of Figures

List of Plates

Introduction and Numbering System

The objects in this catalogue derive from the expedition finds in 1967–69, at which time there was a division between the expedition and the Egyptian Museum in Cairo. All these finds, whether or not inscribed, were registered with University of Pennsylvania, University Museum, numbers in the sequence from 69–029–001 to 69–029–1021, whether the objects are in Cairo, Philadelphia, or New Haven. During excavation, all items received a field number, composed as follows: i) the year of excavation (67, 68, 69); and ii) a sequence number within the year (67.1, etc.; 68.1, etc.; 69.1, etc.). There are also the Egyptian Museum Journal d'Entrée number (JdE) for objects retained by the Egyptian Museum. For objects in the Peabody Museum at Yale, the Peabody numbers are provided in the Division of Anthropology registers. UC, or "uncatalogued," refers to some objects, such as stamped bricks, not individually catalogued in the expedition register or fragments of temple relief of Ramesses II or earlier. With few exceptions the blocks from the Ramesses II temple and the blocks reused from earlier structures at the site or brought to the site for use in the temple remain at the site either in the storerooms or at the temple site itself.

Transliterations and translations are provided, but not infrequently one or the other is given, since the offering formula and phrases such as *Wsỉr ḫnty-ỉmntyw* are not translated each time as "Osiris, foremost of the westerners," or vice-versa.

For convenience of presentation in *this* volume alone, the objects are designated with letter and number sequences as follows:

A	Literary or religious texts on ostraca (limestone flakes)
B	Building construction accounts on ostraca (limestone flakes)
C	Middle Kingdom texts, from the memorial chapel area: "Cenotaphs" (see figs. 4–5)
D	"Dockets." Texts on potsherds, such as wine labels, etc.
FO	Figured ostracon with text. Other figured ostraca not included
LP	Late Period
NK	Texts of the New Kingdom and later
OK	Texts of the Old Kingdom
SBS	Stamped bricks and seals
TIP	Texts datable to the Third Intermediate Period

To give a few examples of this system:

OK 1 = Cairo JdE 91218 = Expedition 69.9

C 10 = U(niversity)M(useum) 69–29–56 = Expedition 69.203

Middle Kingdom Lintel = Peabody Museum (Yale), Anthropology Division 7227 = Expedition 67.97, 128; 69.165

Among inscribed objects *not* included are demotic ostraca (mostly non-literary); stamped Greek amphora handles; Old Kingdom jar sealings from the project conducted by Matthew Adams; some reused blocks of the Amarna Period; the blocks from the Ramesside "Portal" Temple, both those *in situ* and in debris; large temple blocks from earlier stages of the same temple; a series of votive texts of a homogeneous character on pottery bowls such as those in the Rijksmuseum, Leiden; from previous work at Abydos; the Ahmose area inscriptions from the project conducted by Stephen Harvey (1993–); and the Sesostris III area inscriptions from the project conducted by Josef Wegner (1994–).

Location is indicated by the following pattern:

D 9 (a wine label on a potsherd):
RP 5 F (W) 15 indicates a location in the R(amesses) P(ortal) temple area, Square 5 F (W)estern quadrant, object 15. When the archaeological record is published this indication pinpoints the area in which the inscribed object was found. See fig. 3 (redrawn by Joseph Wegner)

C 19 (a stela):
RP T. 28 indicates R(amesses P(ortal) temple area, Tomb 28

Photographs reproduced are either those taken in the field (expedition photographs); or a large series taken by the late Felix Korsyn, a volunteer in the University Museum, which are designated as UM storage photograph with roll and frame number (for example 15–32); and several taken by the photographer of the Egyptian Museum in Cairo in 1994, where expedition photographs were not of requisite quality, especially in cases where the object had been subsequently cleaned.

For ease of use, all citations to parallels and other reference materials are given in the narrative text accompanying each object, rather than in footnotes. All abbreviated references occurring in the following pages may be found in full in the Bibliography at the end of the volume.

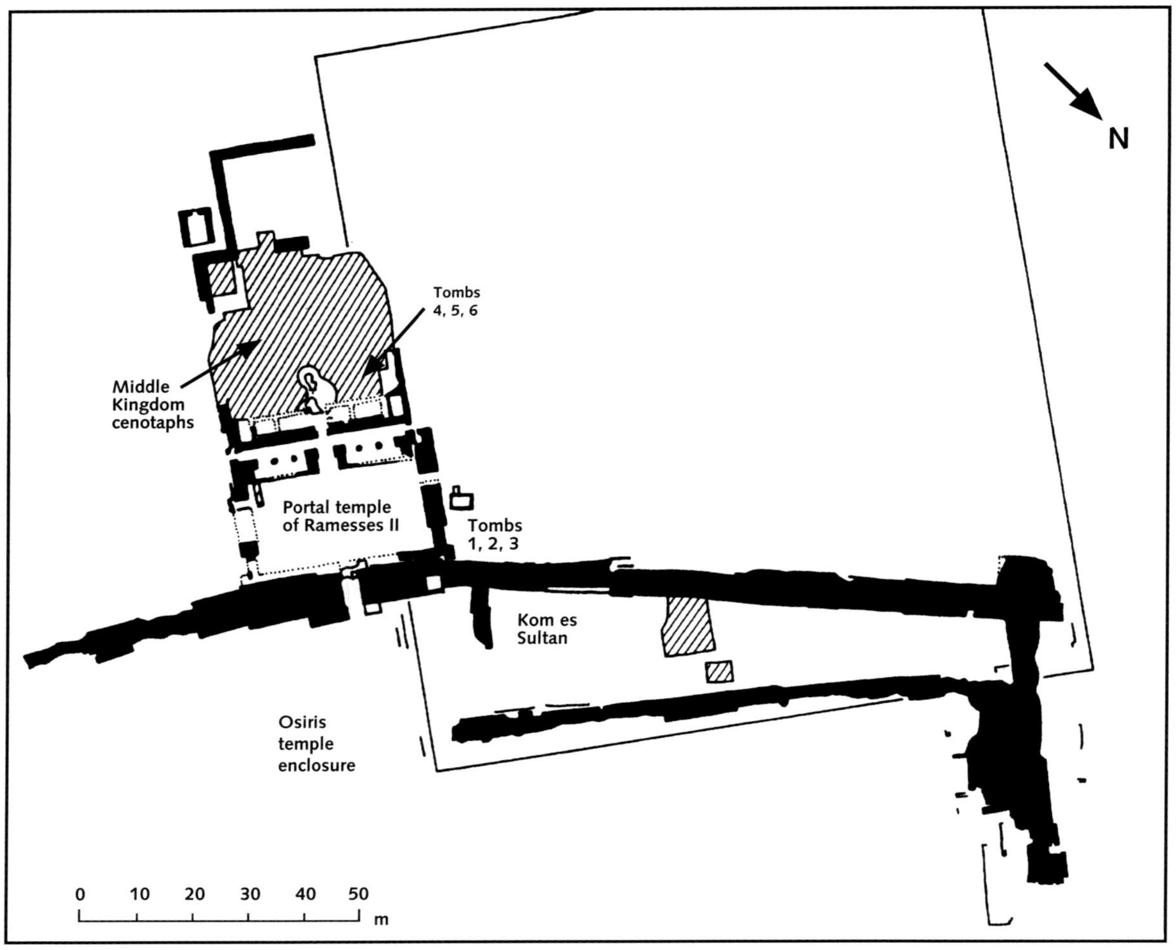

Fig. 2. General plan of the Pennsylvania–Yale excavation area

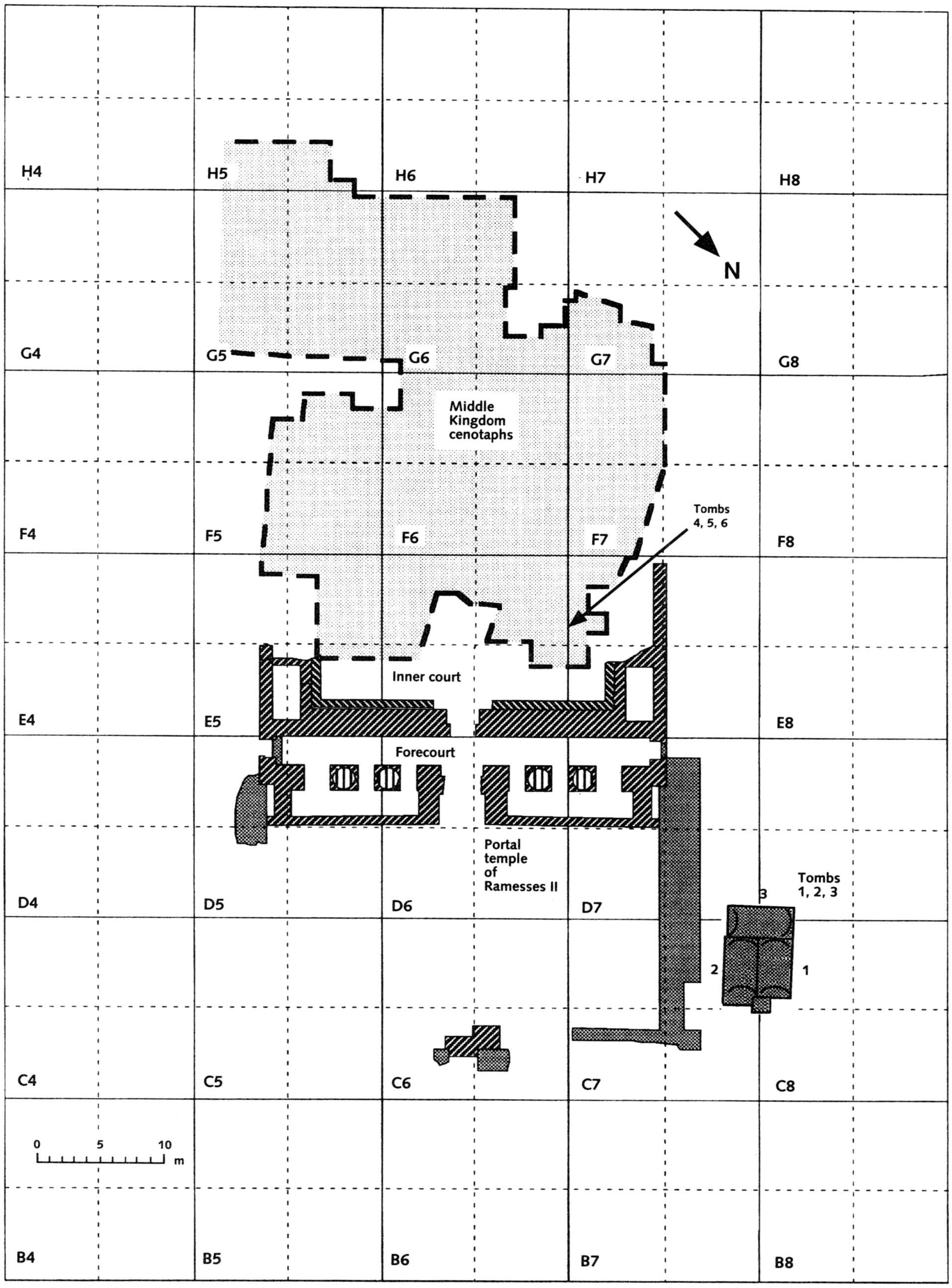

Fig. 3. Detail plan of the Pennsylvania–Yale excavation area, showing quadrant designations

Old Kingdom Objects

For a detailed discussion of Abydos in the Old Kingdom, with extensive bibliography, see Edward Brovarski, "Abydos in the Old Kingdom and First Intermediate Period, Part 1," in *Hommages à Jean Leclant* (Cairo, 1994), pp. 99–121; "Part 2" in David P. Silverman (ed.), *For His Ka: Essays Offered in Memory of Klaus Baer* (Chicago, 1994), pp. 15–44.

OK 1 (fig. 4, pls. 2–3b)

Cairo JdE 91218. Expedition 69.95 (also designated as 889)
Thrown into fill to local west of the Ramesside Portal Temple
RP J 7 (N)
Limestone
1.30 x 54 x 26 cm
Doorjamb (right side) of Pepy-nakht. Dynasty 6. Inscribed on two adjacent sides. Traced by Lynn Holden and inked by Suzanne E. Chapman. Collated by Simpson in Cairo with revisions traced by Nicholas Thayer. I am indebted to my predecessor at Yale, Dr. Henry G. Fischer, for useful comments and references. The block is pitted and difficult to read.
Museum of Fine Arts, Boston, negative of drawing: EG 4611.

Front. A column of text with large hieroglyphs, upper part missing, with the text *[iry pꜥt ḥꜣty]-ꜥ imy-rꜣ Šmꜥw mꜣꜥ smr wꜥty imy-rꜣ ḥmw-nṯr Ppy-nḫt.* Below this is a standing figure of the owner facing left with hands raised in adoration wearing a shoulder-length wig, broad collar, projecting kilt, and bracelets. The figure with hands raised is a feature of the late Old Kingdom. Beneath this is a second register on a smaller scale with a similar figure with a diagonal on the kilt. There are two columns of text in front of the figure and one above and behind it, with some of the signs difficult to make out:

> (1) *smsw hꜣyt wꜥb n zꜣ 200*(?) *Ḫnzw rn.f nfr Ḥtp* (2) *imꜣḫw*
> (3) *nḫt-ḫrw ḥwt wrt wꜥ m mḏ*(?) *m wꜥbt*(?)
>
> (1) Elder of the portal, *weeb*-priest of a phyle of 200, Khonsu, his good name Hetep (probably Khonsu-hetep), (2) the vindicated, (3) tallyman of the lawcourt, one in ten in the workshop.

The transliteration and translation is particularly questionable in the last column. Perhaps read: *wꜥ m smt,* "one (alone) in the (house) of judgment," a tentative suggestion of Henry Fischer. For the title, *nḫt ḫrw,* see the references in Simpson, *The Offering Chapel of Sekhemankhptah in The Museum of Fine Arts, Boston* (Boston, 1976), p. 15, n. 61, and Fischer in L. Limme and J. Strybol, eds., *Aegyptus Museis Rediviva. Miscellanea in Honorem Hermanni de Meulenaere,* (Brussels, 1993), p. 98. For the judicial context, see Fischer, *Orientalia* 30 (1961), p. 174. For *wꜥb 200* (only, without *n zꜣ*), references, which I owe to Henry Fischer, are: T.G.H. James and M.R. Apted, *The Mastaba of Khentika called Ikhekhi* (London, 1993), pl. 13; CG 1438 (*wꜥb n 200*), 1455, 1551, 1634, 3; G. Daressy, *Le mastaba de Mera* (Cairo, 1898), pp. 562, 567; G. Jéquier, *Tombeaux de particuliers contemporains de Pepi II* (Cairo, 1929), fig. 124; H. Junker, *Giza* 7 (Vienna and Leipzig, 1944), fig. 8. *CCG* 1455 belongs to the Thinite noble *Ggi.*

Side. Three registers, each with two main figures facing left, followed by a shorter fourth register with a smaller figure facing right. The left side is rough and blank, as it was covered by the door frame.

Register 1: Two standing offering bearers face left, the first with a fowl in each hand, his right hand raised, the second with a tray of offerings in his upraised right hand and a knife and pail (situla) on a cord in his left. Both wear a projecting kilt, the second with diagonal, and broad collars. The first wears a shoulder-length wig, the second a short wig. Above them are the remains of a text in two lines, possibly two names, one above the other, the second *In-it.f*(?).

Register 2: Two standing figures face left, both with shoulder-length wigs, broad collars, bracelets, beards, and projecting kilts with diagonal, the second also with a diagonal band from right shoulder to under left armpit. The first holds an incense vessel with his right hand and tosses a pellet into it with his left hand. The second extends his right hand in a gesture while holding a papyrus roll in his left hand. Over the first is the caption *zš wt(w),* "scribe of the embalmers," a title not represented in W.A. Ward, *Index of Egyptian administrative and religious titles of the Middle Kingdom* (Beirut, 1982), and conceivably a name, and over the second *ḫry ḥꜣb smsw Mṯty,* "the elder lector priest, Methethy." In front of the first figure is the name *Mmy* (*PN* 1, p. 149.25). Between the figures are two smaller figures, one above the other, each with right hand crossed over to the left shoulder. The top figure is captioned *smsw hꜣyt Ḫnzw-ḥtp,* "the elder of the portal, Khonsu-hetep," possibly the same individual represented in the lower section of the adjacent side of the jamb, while the text for the second figure is so abraded it cannot be made out, but possibly begins with *imy-ḫt . . . ,* "under-supervisor. . . ." To the rear of the second main figure are also two small standing figures facing in the same direction in the same attitude, the top figure captioned *smsw hꜣyt Ḫnzw-ḥtp,* "the elder of the portal Hetep-Khonsu (or more likely Khonsu-hetep)," perhaps again the same individual between the figures and on the adjacent surface of the jamb. The lower small figure is captioned *imy-ḫt sꜣ pr Ḥmi*(?), "the under-supervisor of police-officers Hemi(?)." For the police titles, see Jean Yoyotte, "Un corps de police de l'Egypte pharaonique," *RdE* 9 (1952), pp. 139–51; Andreu, *LÄ* 4 (1982), col. 1069.

Register 3: Again, two standing men face left, the first bearing a foreleg of an ox with both hands, and the second dropping a pellet with his left hand into an incense vessel held in his right hand. Both wear short wigs, beards, broad collars, bracelets, and the same kilts as

Fig. 4. OK 1

above. Above them are respectively *smr wꜥty Spt,* "the sole companion, Sepet," and *smr wꜥty ꜥnḫ nb.f,* "the sole companion, Ankhnebef." The name *Spt* is attested with the same determinative (Sign List Aa 2, pustule or gland) in the feminine form *Sptt* in the Old Kingdom (*PN* 1, p. 306.14). As a masculine, the name *Spt* determined by the eye occurs on a Dynasty 5/6 relief of Iny seen on the art market in Paris in June 1991. In front of the first figure is a small, badly formed figure facing right with the caption *ỉmy ḫt M* ... , "the under-supervisor, M ...." Following the first main figure is a small figure facing left and captioned *ỉmy ḫt* ..., "the under-supervisor ...," perhaps the same individual as in the lower center of the register above. Following the second main figure is another small figure facing right with a long kilt and captioned *smsw hꜣyt Ḫnzw*(?)-*ḥtp*(?), "the elder of the portal, Khonsu-hetep(?)," perhaps again the same individual encountered three times before. These subsidiary figures have the right arm bent at the elbow with the hand on the body.

Register 4: A single small figure with upraised arms faces right, this time, with shoulder-length wig and longer kilt. He is captioned *ỉmy-ḫt sꜣ pr ... w*(?), "the under-supervisor of police officers, ...u(?)."

The secondary figures and the texts related thereto are crudely executed. It is possible that they were added later in the Middle Kingdom, especially since some of the names or their spellings are unattested in the Old Kingdom and some of the titles are better attested in the Middle Kingdom. *Ḫnsw-ḥtp, PN* 1, p. 271.12, Middle Kingdom and New Kingdom (frequent). *Nmỉ,* not in *PN. ꜥnḫ-nb.f* is attested in *PN* 1, p. 64.26, *PN* 2, p. 271.12, and *Abu Sir Papyri,* pl. 68, d2 (5, 8); A.-M. Abu Bakr, *Excavations at Giza 1949–1950* (Cairo, 1953), fig. 95 A, C (references courtesy of Henry G. Fischer).

A false door evidently from the tomb (CCG 1573) was discovered by Mariette at Abydos and published by Borchardt with references to several earlier publications by Mariette and de Rougé (L. Borchardt, *Denkmäler des Alten Reiches* 2 [Cairo, 1964], CCG 1573, pp. 51–52, pl. 75). Important additional titles on the false door are those of the vizierate (*ỉmy-r niwt, ṯꜣty, zꜣb ṯꜣty*), as well as *ỉmy-rꜣ kꜣt nbt nt nswt,* "overseer of all the works of the king," *ỉmy-rꜣ wꜥbty,* "overseer of the double *wabet,*" *ỉmy-rꜣ zš ꜥ nswt,* "overseer of king's document scribes," *ḫtmty bỉty, ḫry ḥꜣb ḥry tp, sm, ḫrp šndyt nb,* "sealer of the king of Lower Egypt, chief lector priest, *sem*-priest, controller of every kilt." The style of the false door and jamb differs, but the height is the same (jamb 1.30 m, false door, 1.26 m); the jamb was set up on the right side of the false door, if they belong to the same monument.

OK 2 (fig. 5, pl. 4a)

UM 69–29–50. Expedition 69.165 or 166
RP G 6 (W)
Limestone
25 x 21 x 10 cm
Dynasty 5. Temple block in incised relief with cartouche of Djedkare. Top of the white crown, indicating a standing figure of the king, above which a winged falcon holds an ankh sign. In front of the king is the cartouche Djedkare followed by *nṯr ꜥꜣ*. In front of the

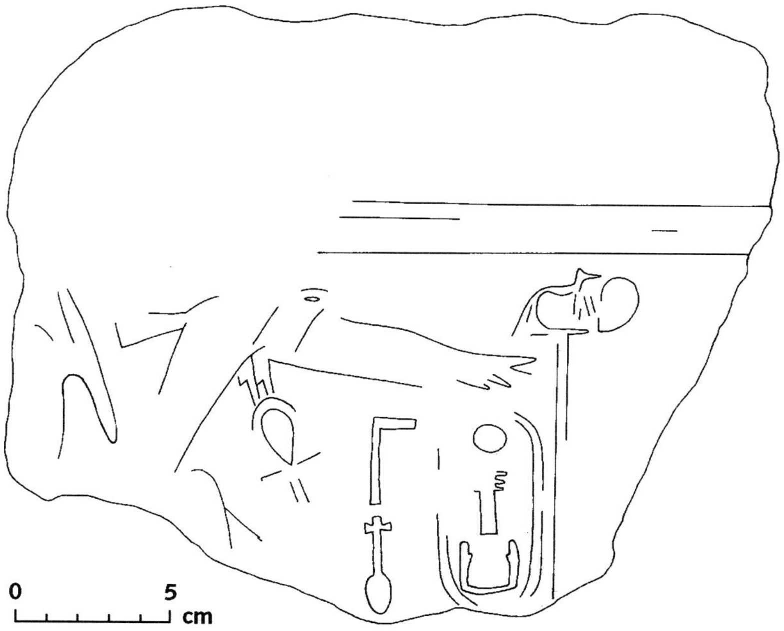

Fig. 5. OK 2

cartouche is a Wepwawet standard, and a large *wꜣs* scepter on the extreme left. Above the scene is a border.
UM storage photograph 22–22.

OK 3 (fig. 6, pl. 4b)

UM 69–29–178. Expedition 69.164
RP G 7 (N)
Limestone
38 x 24 x 8 cm
Column of text on right, signs facing left: ... *rmṯ.f r rḏit i[š]t r i* ..., "... his people, in order to give property for ...." On left, diagonal lines, perhaps part of rigging of a large ship.
UM storage photograph 17–35.

OK 4 (fig. 7, pl. 4c)

UM 69–29–48. Expedition 69.163
RP
Limestone
25 x 20.5 x 13 cm
Incised relief of two men facing left, one in short kilt standing and holding rigging with both hands, the second in front of the latter sitting and similarly holding rigging with both hands. Body parts with traces of red, upper part of rope yellow, upper right traces of alternating black and yellow bands. Possibly part of same scene as OK 3.
UM storage photograph 22–21.

OK 5 (fig. 8, pl. 4d)

UM 69–29–119
Expedition 69.67
RP J 7 (N)
Limestone
16 x 10 x 3 cm

Fragment of relief with foot in upper register facing right and vertical cartouche facing right, beginning with *Mry-Rʿ* below, possibly part of personal name. Dynasty 6 or First Intermediate Period.
UM storage photograph 16–10.

Fig. 7. OK 4

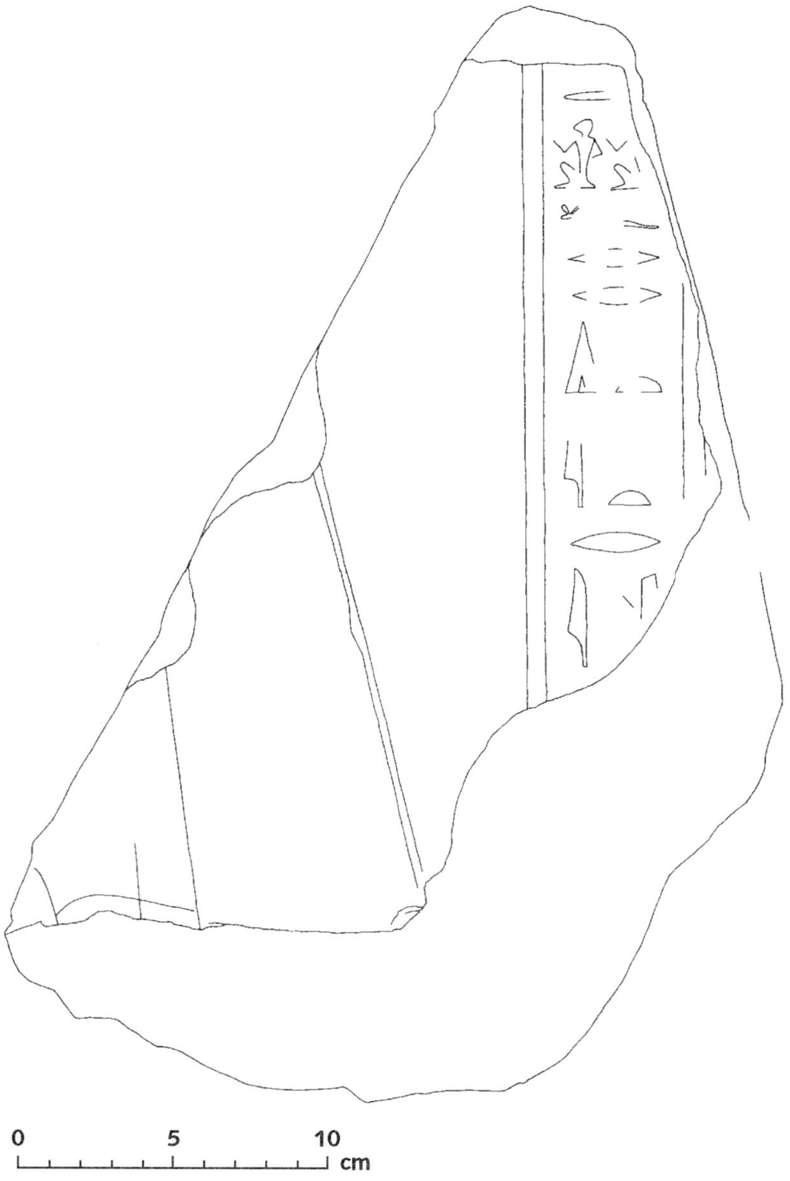

Fig. 6. OK 3

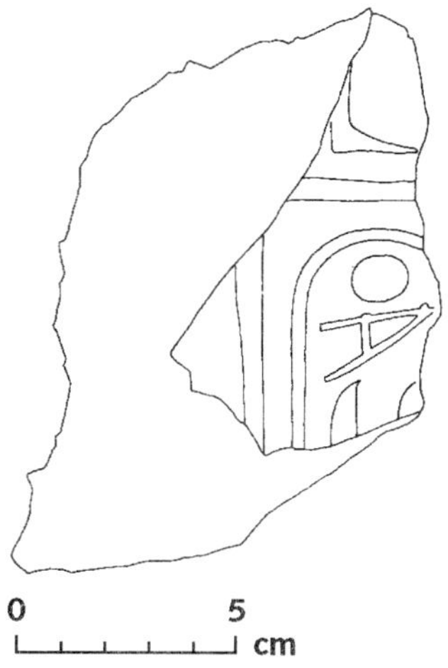

Fig. 8. OK 5

Dynasty 12 Lintel

(FIG. 9, PL. 5A)

Peabody Museum Yale: Anthropology Division, Egypt 7227
Expedition 67.97, 128; 69.165
RP 5 E (W), (W+S), RP 5 F (S), (N), (E+W); RP 6 E, (S+E), (S)
Limestone
Preserved height .84 m x preserved length 2.04 m = 4 cubits
Fragments of lintel in raised relief of Amenemhet III; Dynasty 12. The king is shown in two parallel scenes offering to a god. Both inner columns of text are identical and represent the words of the god: *Ḏd mdw di.n.i n.k irt ḥbw sd ꜥšꜣ wrt,* "Statement: I grant you the accomplishment of very many *Sed* festivals." The references to the (first) Sed Festival in this reign are gathered in Simpson, *JARCE* 2 (1963), pp. 62–63, and E. Hornung and E. Staehelin, *Studien zum Sedfest,* Aegyptiaca Helvetica 1 (Geneva, 1974), pp. 29, 45, n. 22. The hieroglyph for the palm of the hand shows the internal markings noted elsewhere in contemporary and other relief. Cf. Simpson, *RdE* 24, (1972), pp. 171–75; Claude Sourdive, *La main dans l'Egypte pharaonique* (Berne, 1984), passim.

Left half. The king on the left facing right offers two milk jars to a god on the right facing left. Over the king are four short columns with the text: *nṯr nfr nb irt ḫt Ny-mꜣꜥt-Rꜥ di ꜥnḫ ḏd wꜣs mi Rꜥ ḏt,* "the good god Nymaatre, master of performing ritual, given life, stability and dominion like Re forever." Below the text, the king is represented standing and offering the jars with their distinctive stoppers. He wears the nemes with uraeus and with a lappet partly covering a broad collar. There is a bracelet on the left wrist and presumably on the missing right. He wears a projecting triangular kilt with sporran terminating in uraei, one preserved. Behind him is the text: *sꜣ ꜥnḫ ḥꜣ nb [di ꜥnḫ],* "all protection and life around [given life]." Facing the king is a god standing with a long staff in his right hand and an ankh sign in his left. He appears to wear a headdress with lappets, although the face is missing. He wears a short wraparound kilt with the "knot of Isis." Of the columns of text above him only the last is preserved: *[s]nb nb ḏt,* "and all heath forever." The section with the identity of the god is missing. Between the king and god are fragmentary signs with the identification of the offering as *i[rṯt],* "milk."

Right half. The corresponding scene shows the king, similarly costumed, standing and facing left and presenting two *nw*-jars to the god. Over him were four columns of text of which the last two are missing: *nṯr nfr nb irt ḫt [Ny]mꜣꜥt[rꜥ] [di ꜥnḫ ḏd wꜣs mi Rꜥ ḏt],* "the good god [Ny]maat[re], master of performing ritual, [given life stability and dominion like Re forever]. Behind the king is the same text as in the left section. Facing right toward the king is the standing figure of the god wearing a headdress with lappets and broad collar. In his left hand he extends the *wꜣs* staff combined with the ankh toward the king and holds an ankh sign in the right hand to the rear. Of four columns of text above the god, indicated with column separators, only the second and third are well preserved: *[Ws-ir ḫnty] imntyw nb ꜣbḏw di.f ꜥnḫ wꜣs nb [mi Rꜥ] ḏt,* "[Osiris Khenty]-amentyu, lord of Abydos, may he give all life and dominion [like Re] forever." Between the king and god in the same orientation as the king is the identification of the offering: *ir[p],* "wine." A misplaced fragment has the word *wsr,* and it is difficult to see how it can be properly placed, if it belongs to the same scene; perhaps it belongs to another part of the building.

Ostraca

The relative rarity of ostraca from sites other than Thebes has been noted by scholars (B. van de Walle, *ZÄS* 90 (1963), p. 123, n. 4). Those from the Pennsylvania–Yale Expedition include not only a few with literary texts, indicating that there was a school here (or at least an interest in literature), but also several with building construction memoranda, including the delivery of materials (stone and gypsum) as well as the mention of sources and the designation of parts of the building involved.

Since the initial transcription of the facsimiles prepared in the field were made as long as thirty years ago, I have taken the opportunity of reviewing them with my former professor, the late Georges Posener, with Edward F. Wente, and recently with Jac. Janssen, all of whom made valuable suggestions and saved me from errors. I wish to acknowledge my debt to them without ascribing any faults, which are my own.

Literary Ostraca

All are in Cairo JdE 91283 (included with other ostraca).

A 1 (fig. 10)

Expedition 67.560
From dump. RP 8 C (S) 6
Black ink on limestone flake
20 x 13 x ? cm
Three lines of Text: Satire on the Trades 5, 5–5, 6.

A 2 (fig. 11)

Expedition 69.43
RP J 8 E
Black ink on limestone flake
10 x 14.5 x 3 cm
Washed, erased, and reused for text, faded
Six lines of text, poorly preserved: Teaching of Amenemhet (Millingen 1, 11–2, 2). Note line-by-line division of clauses. Identified by E.F. Wente.

A 3 (fig. 12)

Expedition 67.457
RP 7 E (S) 76
Black ink on limestone flake. Verse points in red
15.5 x 20.5 x ? cm
The other side is smoothed with an erased text, probably indicating an exercise stone.
Five lines of text: Unidentified story. Cf. ll. 2–4 in part: "Let there be brought to me the gods who are in Djedu, the judges of Rehorakhty who are in the barque."

A 4 (fig. 13)

Expedition 67. 266
RP 6 F (N) 29
Black ink on limestone flake, smoothed and washed several times for exercises
14.5 x 21 x 4.3 cm
Five lines of very badly preserved text with beginning of literary text. Cf. G. Posener, *RdE* 6 (1951), p. 46, nos. 30, 31, for *ḥꜣty-ꜥ m mdt,* for which reference I am indebted to Prof. Posener.

A 5 (fig. 14)

Expedition 67.32
RP 5 D (S+E) 2
Limestone with two lines in black ink
8 x 17 x ? cm
(1) *ỉr nfr ỉr nꜥ Ḏḥwty* (2) *m ỉr dit* . . . .
Cf. M. Marciniak, "Quelques remarques sur la formule IR NFR, IR NFR," *Etudes et Travaux* 2, Travaux du Centre d'Archéologie Méditerranéenne de l'Academie Polonaise des Sciences 6 (1968), pp. 26–31; idem, *BIFAO* 73 (1973), p. 109.

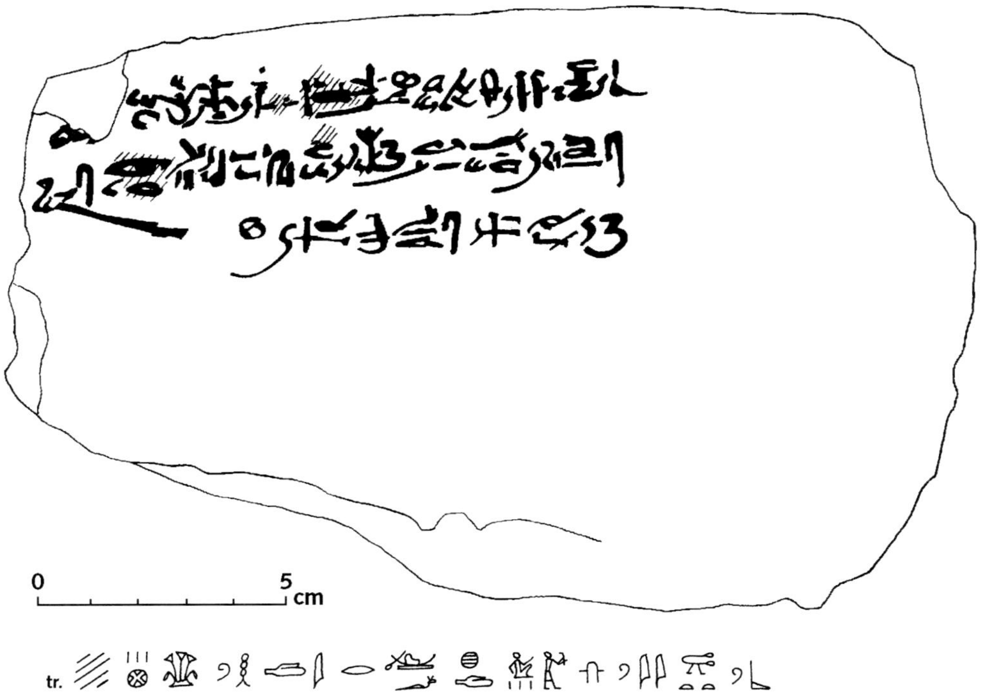

Fig. 10. A 1, facsimile drawing and transcription

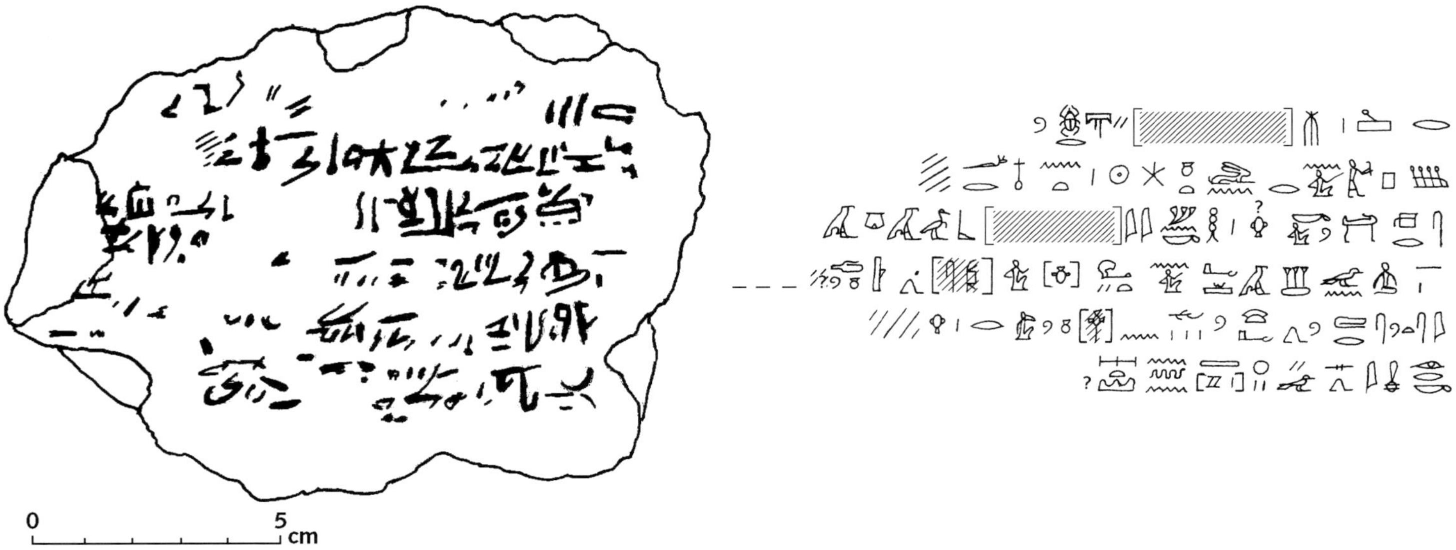

Fig. 11. a 2, facsimile drawing and transcription

Fig. 12. a 3, facsimile drawing and transcription

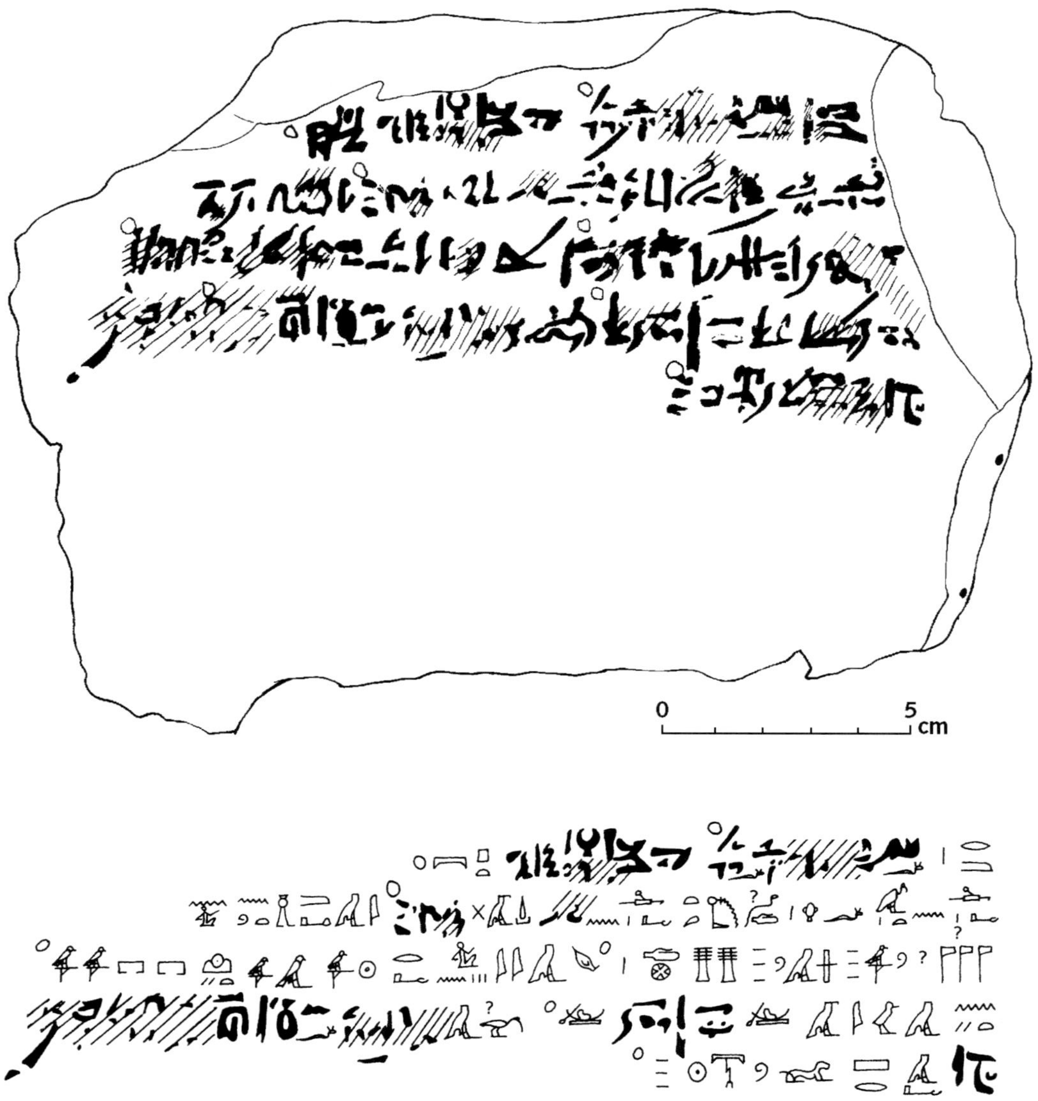

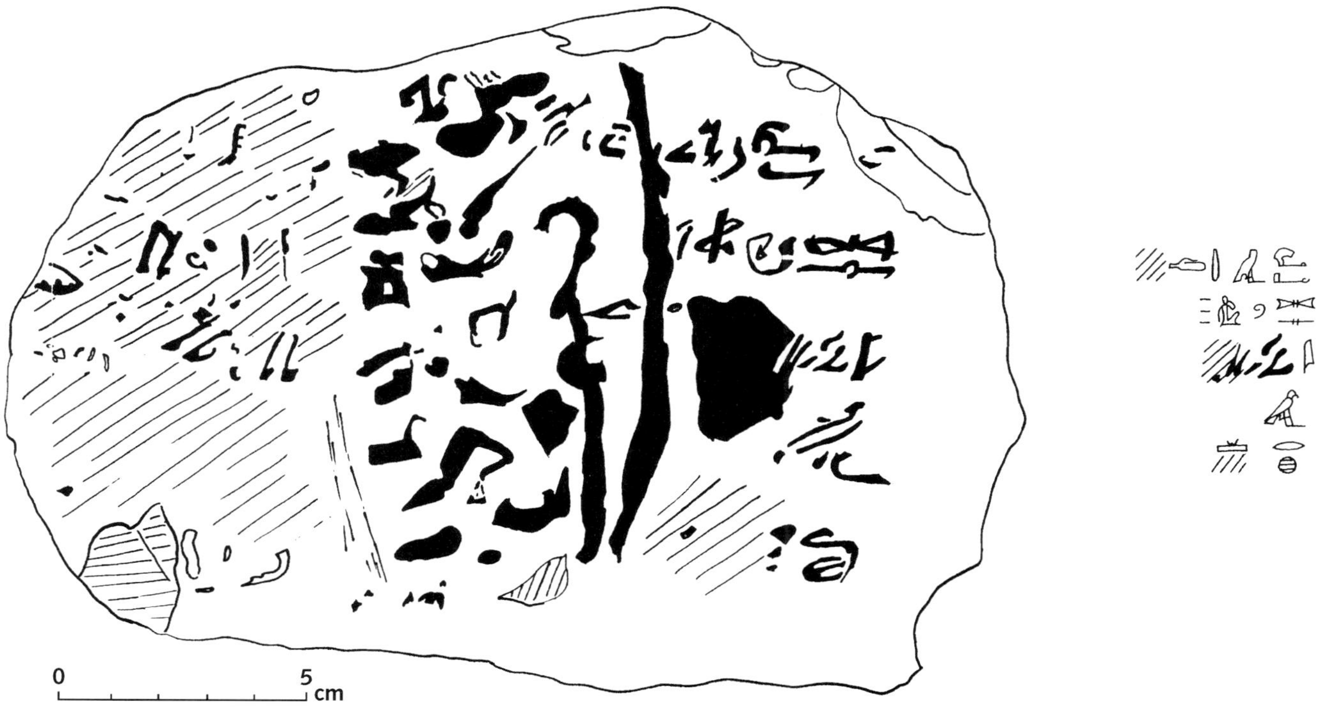

Fig. 13. A 4, facsimile drawing and transcription

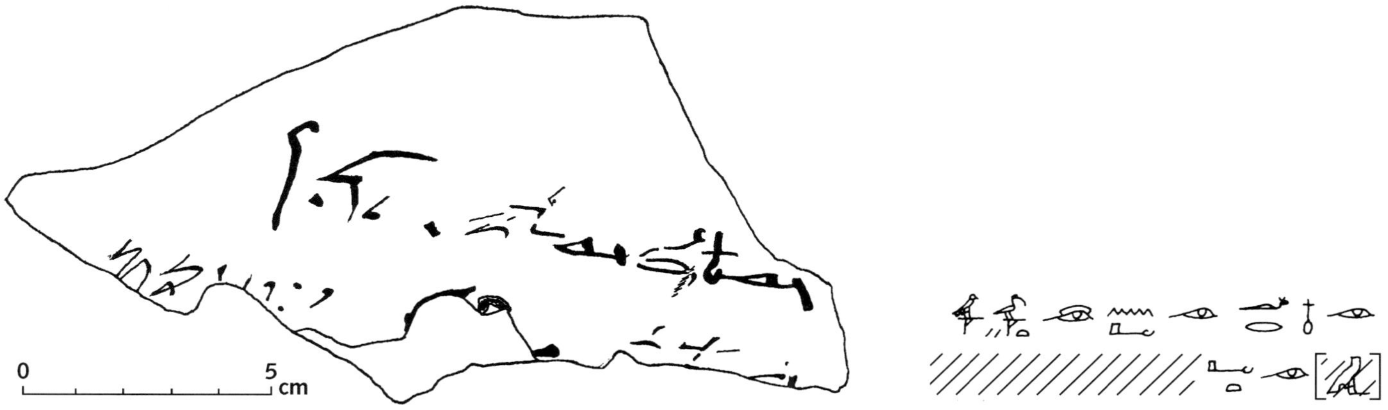

Fig. 14. A 5, facsimile drawing and transcription

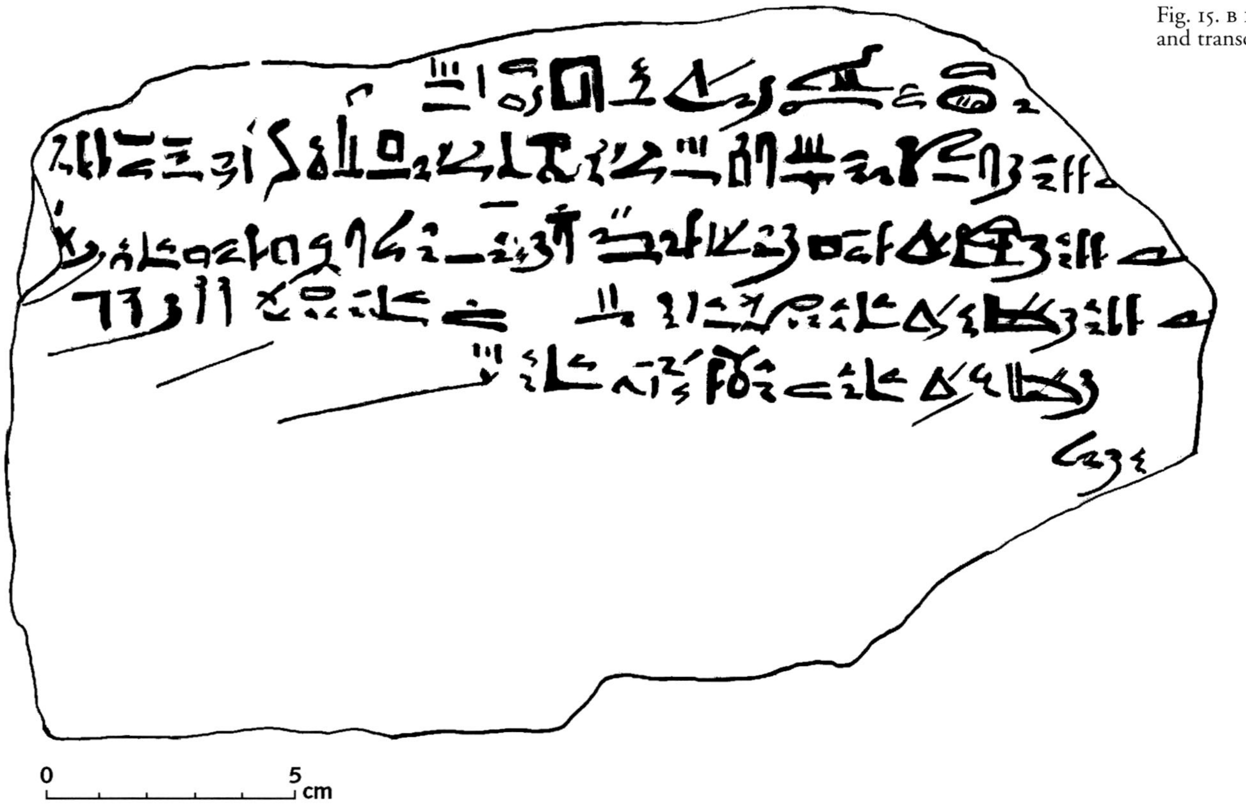

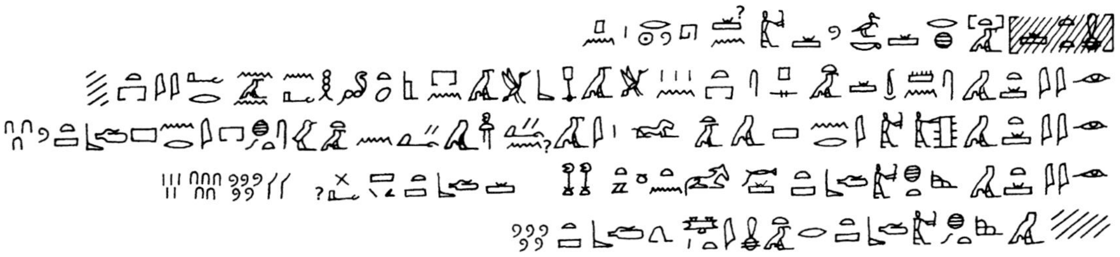

Fig. 15. B 1, facsimile drawing and transcription

CONSTRUCTION ACCOUNTS FOR THE TEMPLE

These accounts evidently relate to the building in which they were found, as indicated above, and provide designations for various parts. There are ostraca from the Ramesseum which indicate deliveries of stone by boat crews, specifying the three dimensions of the blocks (W. Spiegelberg, *Hieratic Ostraka and Papyri found by J.E. Quibell, in the Ramesseum, 1895–6* [London, 1898], pls. 16–18); for a recent discussion, see D. Arnold, *Building in Egypt: Pharaonic Stone Masonry* (Oxford, 1991), pp. 65–66). A series of building accounts is represented in Dynasty 18 in the Deir el Bahri material studied by W.C. Hayes, *JEA* 46 (1960), pp. 29–52. In Hayes, no. 19, rt. (pl. 12 A), *ḏbt* is used for blocks of stone, as in these ostraca, whereas the usual meaning is brick; it can also be used for blocks (bricks) of natron. A series of ostraca relating to construction is conveniently gathered in Daressy, *CCG Ostraca* (Cairo, 1901), pp. 61–86. I wish to acknowledge again the aid of Professor J.J. Janssen, who kindly reviewed my transcriptions and comments and made several suggestions and corrections, for which I am indebted.

Unless otherwise noted, all of these ostraca (limestone flakes) are in the Egyptian Museum, Cairo, included under JdE 91283.

B 1 (FIG. 15)

Expedition 69.128.
RP G 7 E <922>
Black ink on limestone flake
15 x 25 x 4 cm
Six lines of copy of daily work on stone and brickwork in the open court of the temple of Isis, the western side of the *webkhet*, and the causeway.

B 2 (FIG. 16)

Private Collection
Purchased by a colleague in Cairo in 1972, but almost certainly from the excavations at Abydos
Black ink on limestone flake
12 x 22 x ? cm
Four lines of text dated Year 52 (evidently Ramesses II) II *Shomu* 19. Daily account of construction on temple, stone and gypsum, and transport of stone.

Fig. 16. B 2, facsimile drawing and transcription

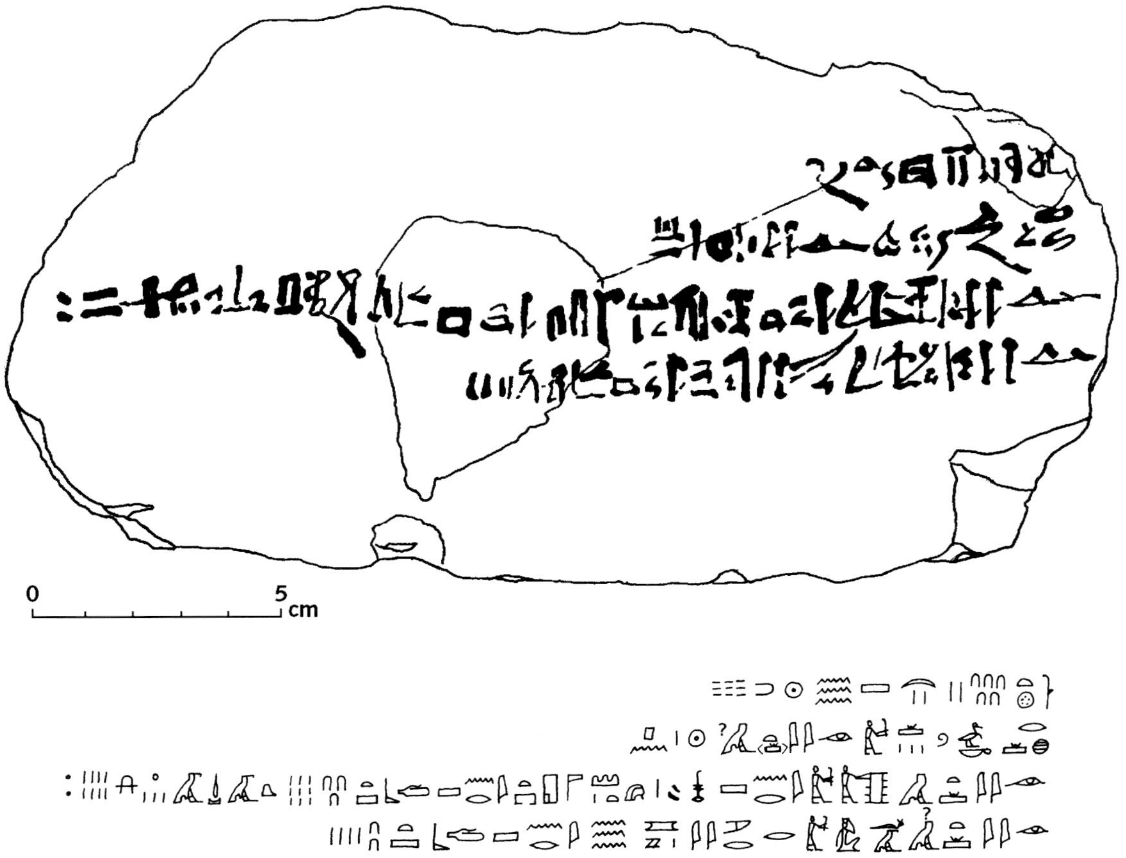

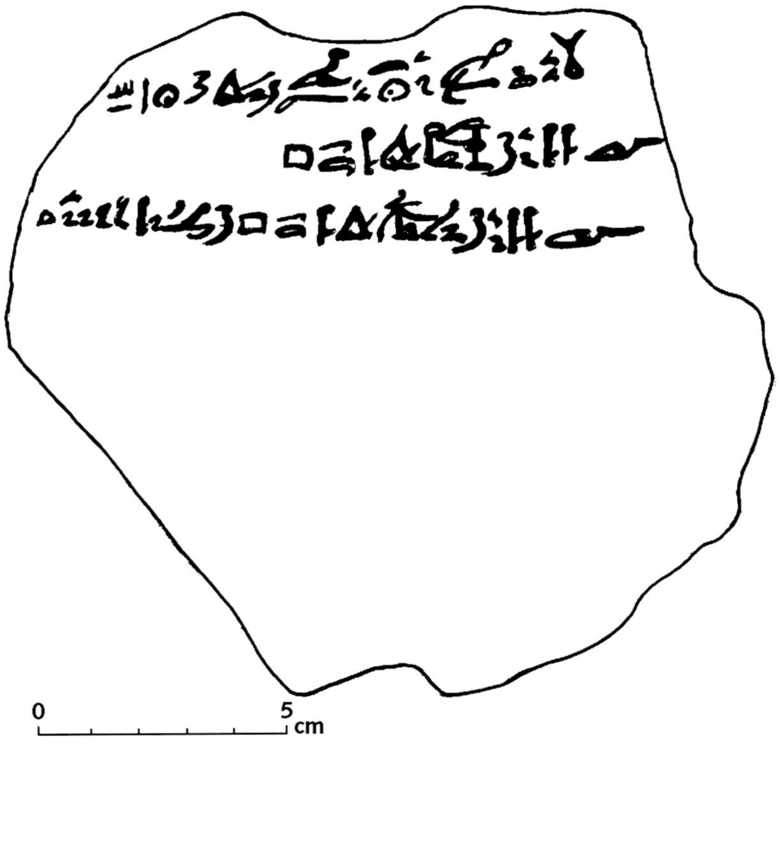

Fig. 17. B 3, facsimile drawing and transcription

An ostracon with construction accounts and names of officials illustrated by Mariette, *Description des fouilles d'Abydos* 2 (Paris, 1880), pl. 60 b = *Catalogue général des monuments d'Abydos* (Paris, 1880), no. 1500, p. 590, is similarly dated (without year) in II *Shomu* 19, conceivably the same day as this ostracon. It cites *pꜣ wḫꜣ n pꜣ wbꜣ* (twice). Professor Janssen provides additional references to this ostracon: Daressy, CCG 25241; Spiegelberg, *OLZ* 5 (1902), cols. 319–20, Černý, *Notebook* 101, p. 42; Kitchen, *KRI* 7, p. 7 (dated to Seti I after Spiegelberg). Černý believed the ostracon 25241 may have come from Deir el Medina, since the verso has names known from the workmen's community at Thebes. There seem to be three possibilities regarding Cairo CG 25241: a) the ostracon comes from Thebes and is erroneously assigned to Abydos by Mariette and Daressy; b) the ostracon comes from Abydos and reflects Thebans working at Abydos; c) the names are similar to Theban workmen but the individuals are not identical and the ostracon comes from Abydos and reflects Abydene workers. Of these possibilities I favor b or c.

B 3 (FIG. 17)

Expedition 69.167
RP G 6 (W) <961>
Black ink on limestone flake
15 x 15 x 2 cm
Three lines of text with account of stonework and transport. The source of the stone is the mountain (*iꜣdt*).

B 4 (FIG. 18)

Two adjoining fragments separately found
Right portion: 69.48. RP G 7 (W) <842>; 11 x 13 x 4 cm
Adjoining left portion: 69.215. RP T 8 <1009>; 11 x 9 x 4 cm
Black ink on limestone flakes
Nine lines of text with account of stonework, stone transport, and gypsum, with previous balances, mention of the festival hall (*wsḫt ḥbyt*), fetching gypsum from the mountain (*ḏw*), carrying stone from the bank of the neshmet-barque to the south of [...], smoothing (stone?) in the *šṯyt*, laying brick, etc.

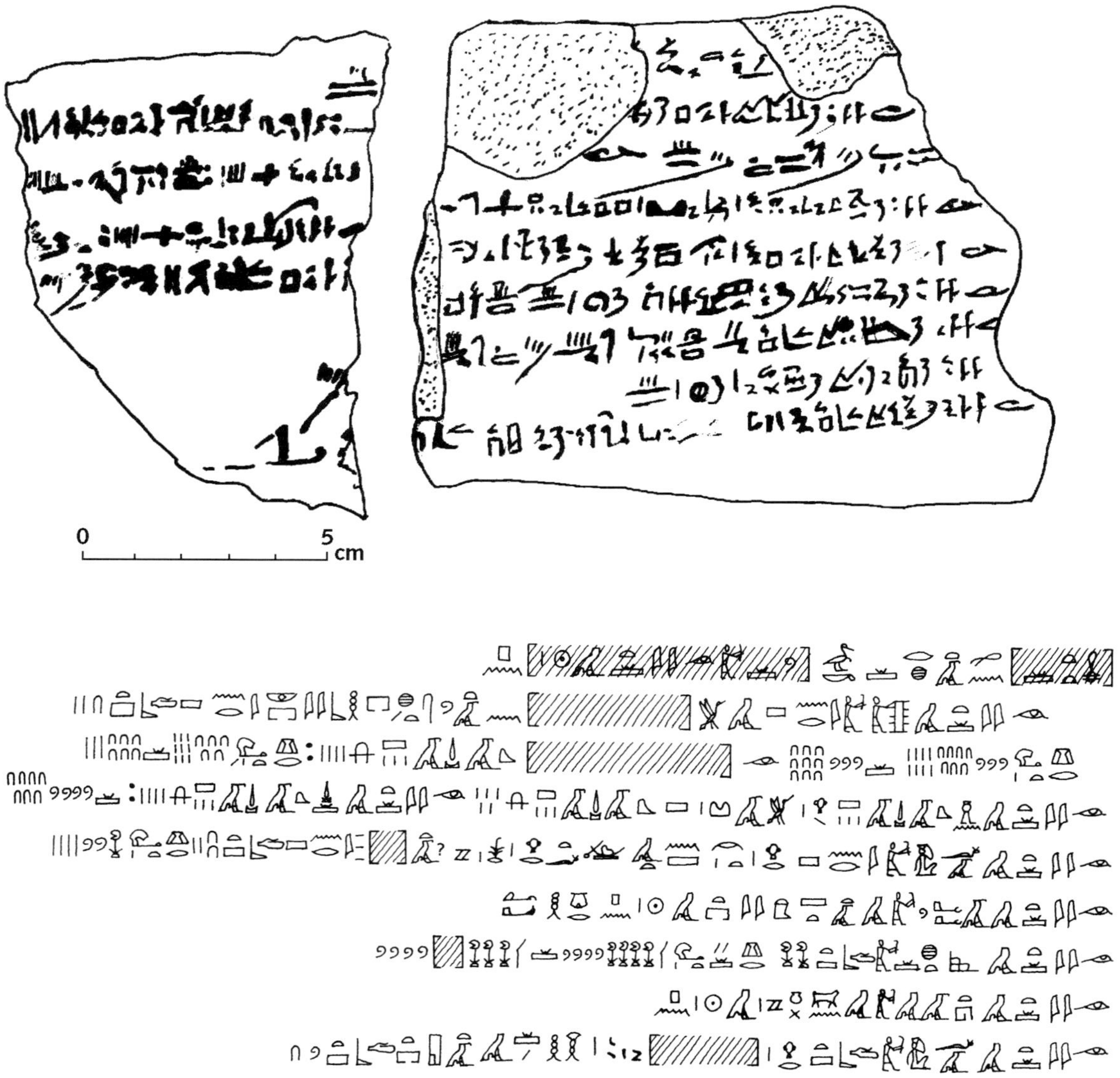

Fig. 18. B 4, facsimile drawing and transcription

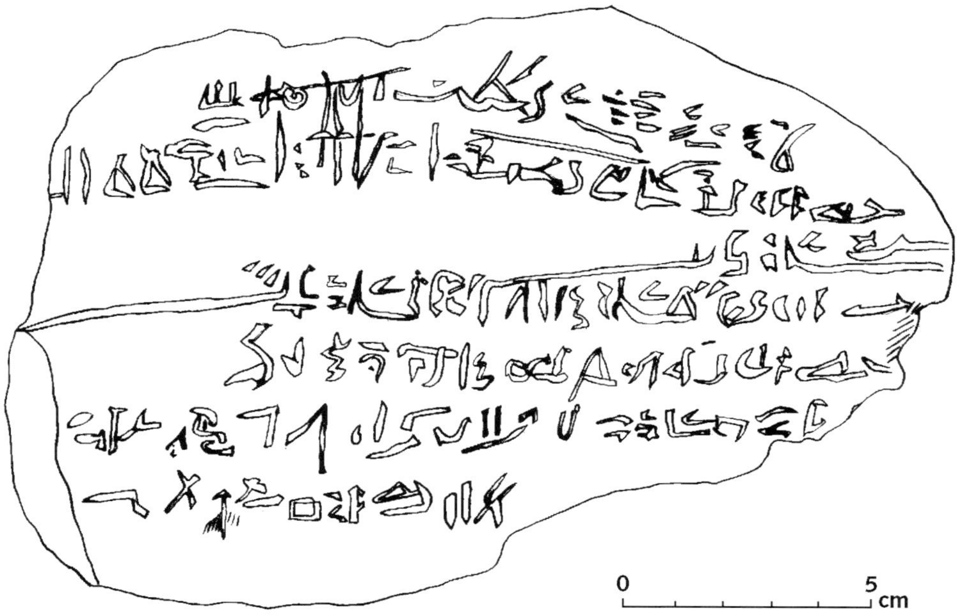

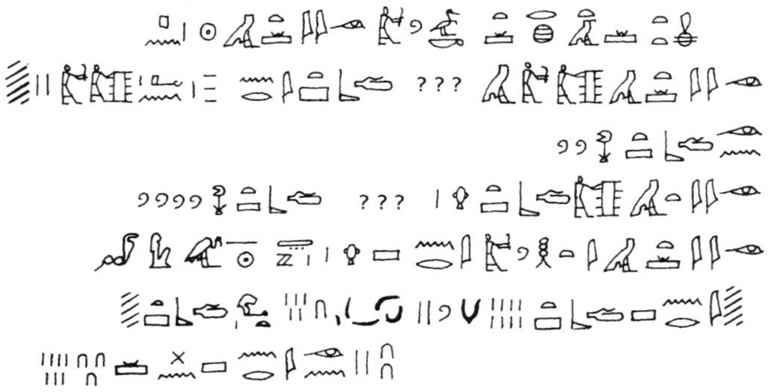

Fig. 19. B 5, facsimile drawing and transcription

Fig. 20. B 6, facsimile drawings and transcriptions of recto (left) and verso (right)

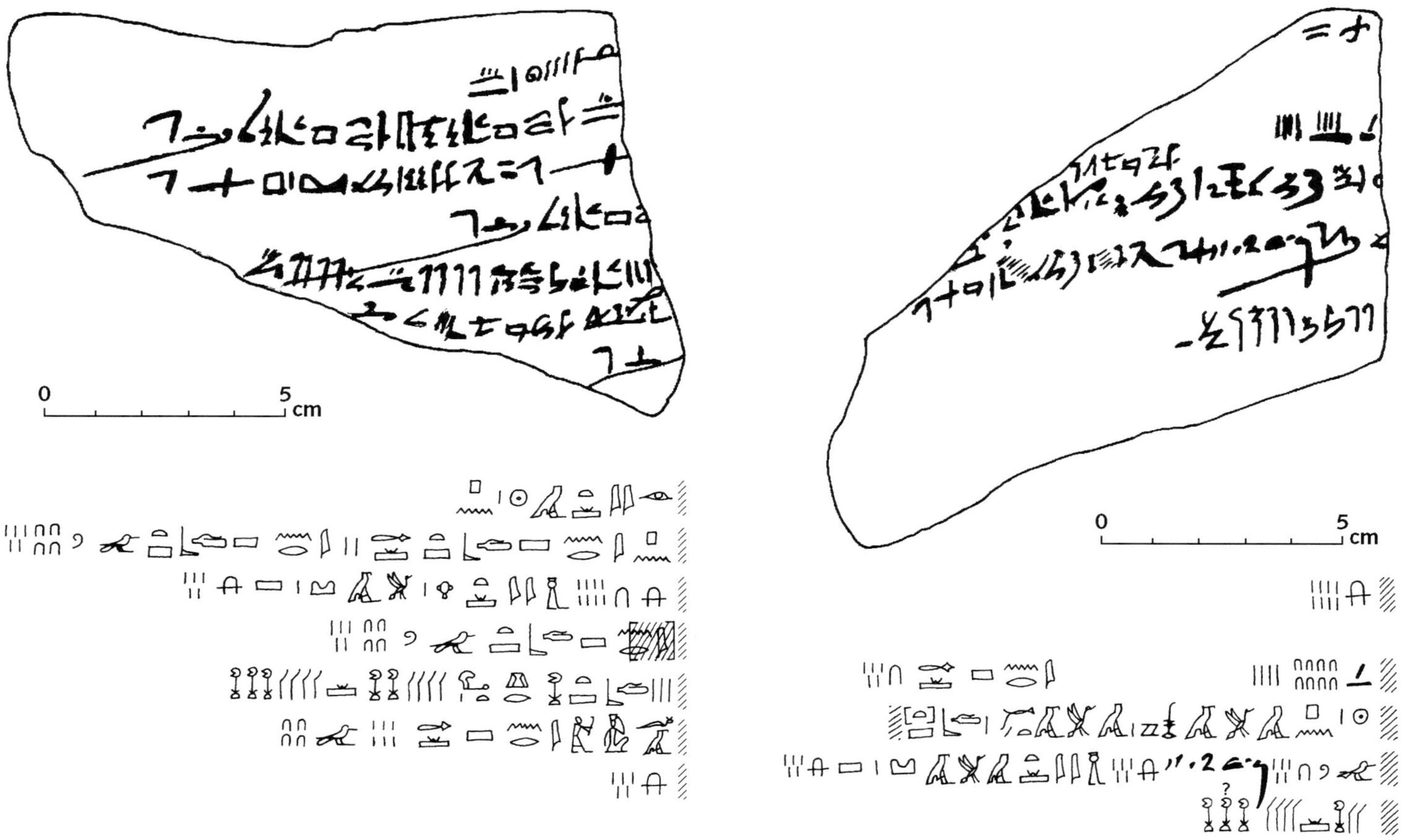

B 5 (FIG. 19)

Expedition 67. 530

RP 7 F (N+W) 60 <530>

11.6 x 19 x 4.2 cm

Seven lines of incised text. Construction account of blocks of stone utilized and hauled on the ground.

B 6 (FIG. 20)

Expedition 69.26

RP J 8 (E) <820>

8 x 13 x 3 cm

Seven lines of text in black ink on recto, six lines on verso. The beginning of all lines missing. Construction account of delivery of large and small stone blocks, some from the south and north and gypsum(?) brought from the mountain.

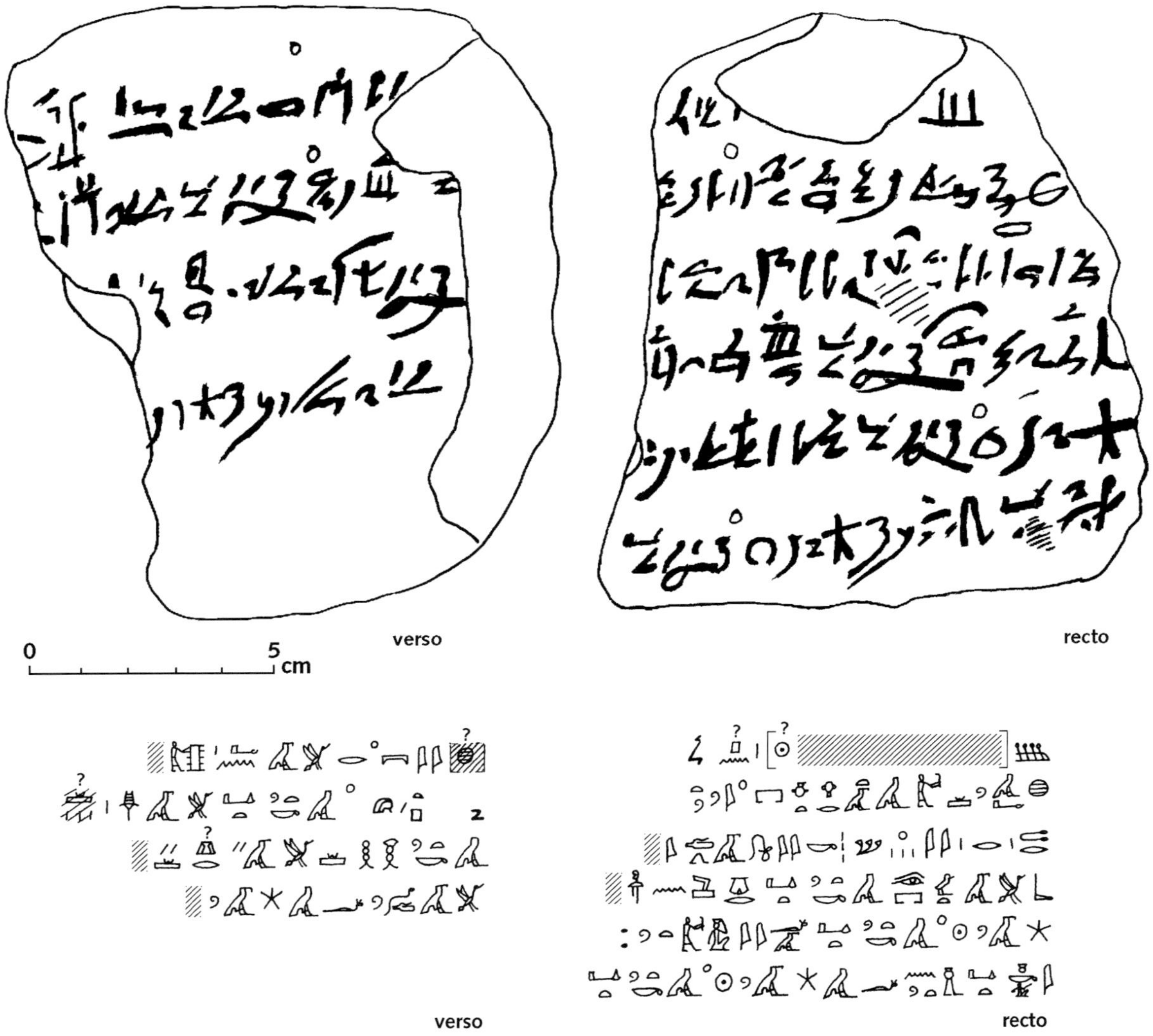

Fig. 21. B 7, facsimile drawings and transcriptions of recto (right) and verso (left)

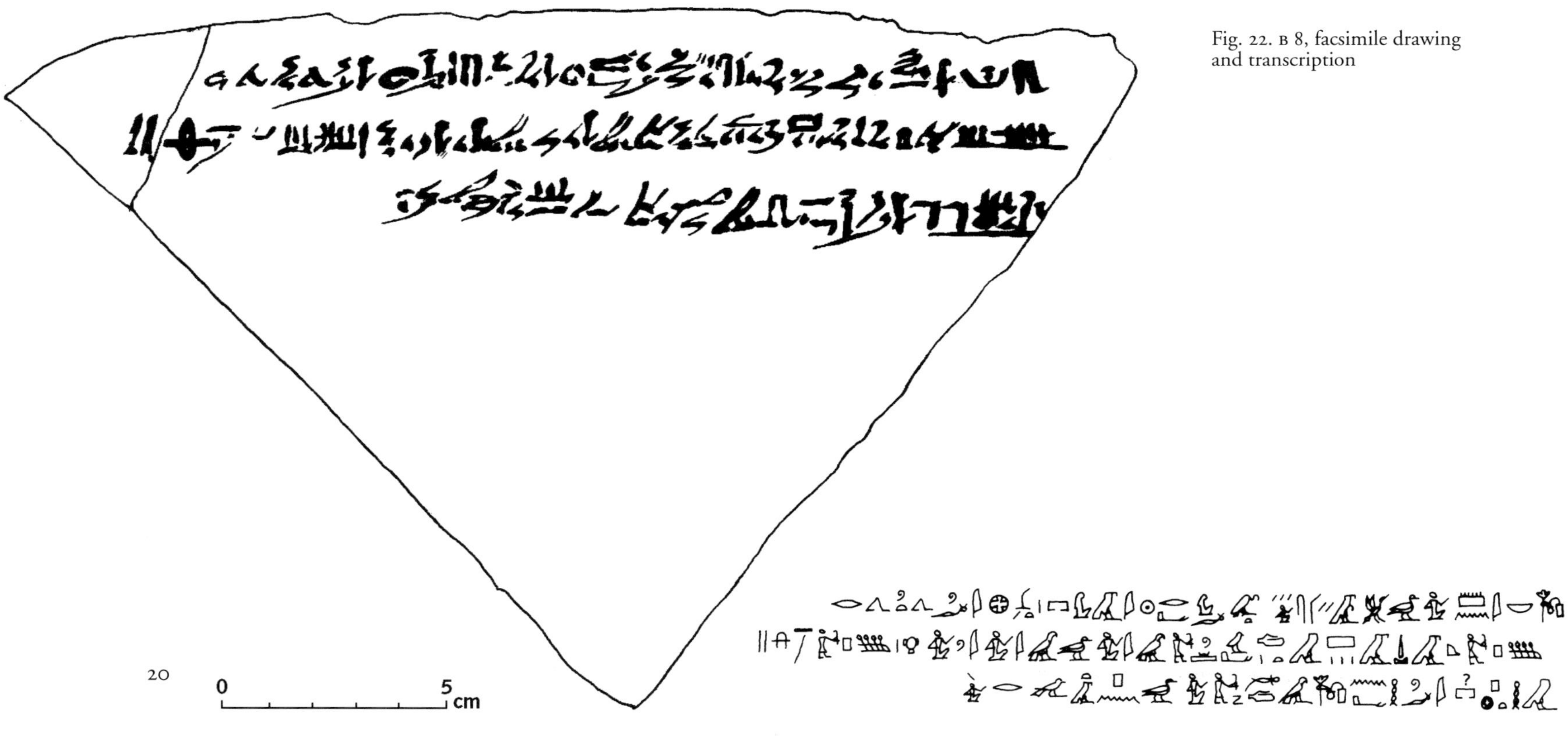

Fig. 22. B 8, facsimile drawing and transcription

B 7 (fig. 21)
Expedition 69.42
RP H 7 (E) <836>
12.5 x 11.5 x 4 cm
Six lines of black ink on recto, four lines on verso, with red verse points. Letter (or model letter?) from a superior regarding construction work for the following day, beginning and end of lines lost on verso. Mention of destruction or fill (*ḥmꜥw*) in the central hall (*ḥrit-ib*); cf. R. Stadelmann, *MDAIK* 34 (1978), p. 177, n. 54 = D. Meeks, *AL* 2 (1978), p. 256) and mention of the open court (*[w]bꜣw*). Cf. P. Spencer, *The Egyptian Temple: A Lexicographical Study* (London, 1984), pp. 4–13.

B 8 (fig. 22)
Expedition 67.65
Data incomplete
Three lines of text in black ink. Letter regarding construction:

> The accountant Neb-Amun son of Pa-Nehesy, whose mother is Reja, of Per-Anty. He went to accept the gypsum from the officer Hori, son of Hori, I accepted [...] two sacks in Hepet(?) He is with the accountant Shed-Hor the son of Pentawer[t].

Another ostracon of *Nb-Ỉmn sꜣ Pꜣ-Nḥsy* is B 9.

B 9 (fig. 23)
Expedition 67.639
RP 4D (S) 11
22 x 27 x 5 cm
Four lines in black ink on large flake of limestone

> (1) *sš Nb-Ỉmn*(?) (2) *sš Nb-Ỉmn sꜣ Pꜣ-Nḥsy* (3) *mwt.f Rꜥiꜣ* ...
> (4) *Wnn-nfr*

See B 8 for same individual.

B 10 (fig. 24)
Expedition 67.446
RP
Limestone
6.5 x 5.5 cm
Six lines of black ink. Gypsum account.

B 11 (fig. 25)
Expedition 67.437
RP 74 (N+W) 56
Limestone
8.5 x 19.5 cm
Two lines in black ink of incomplete construction account.

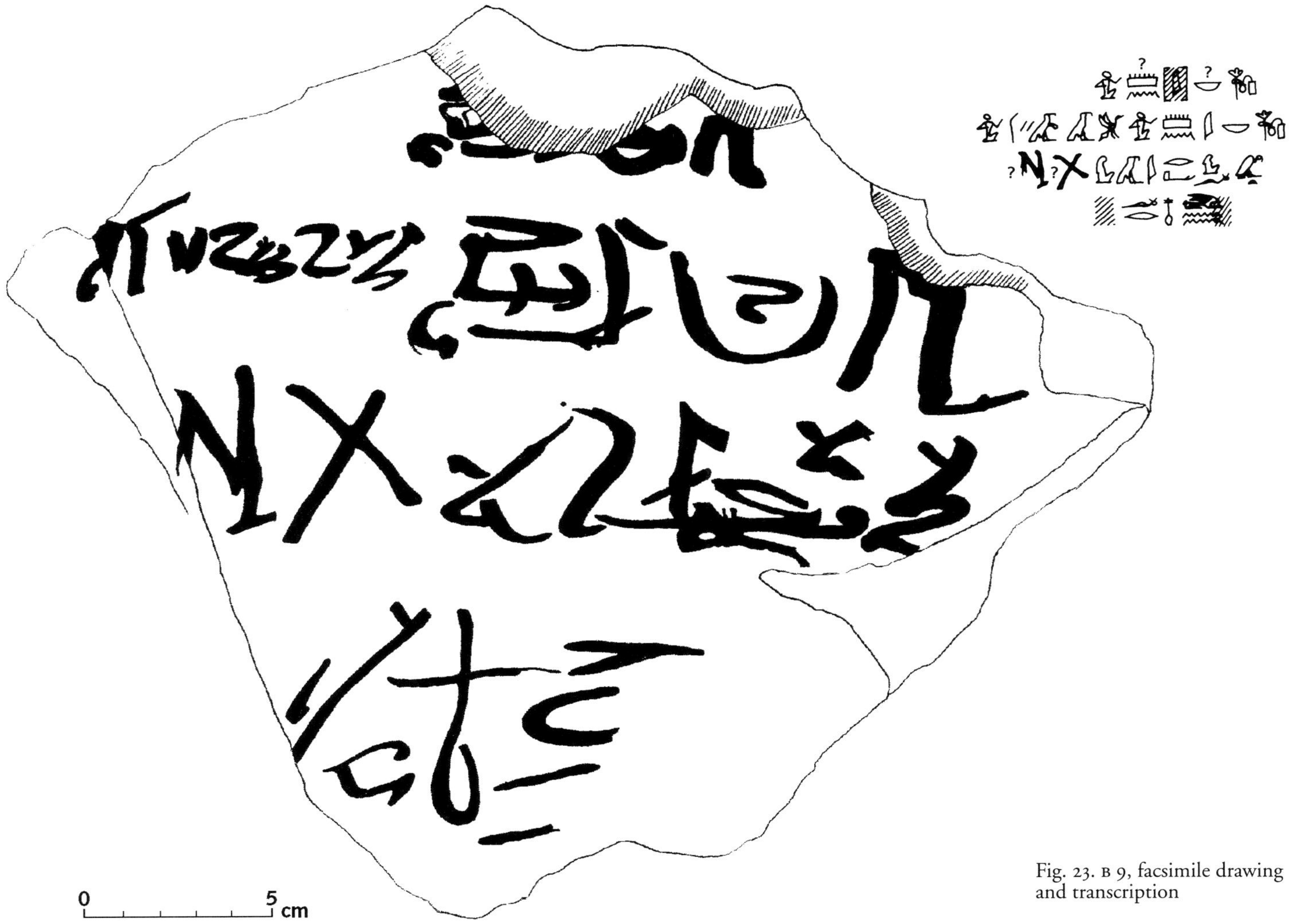

Fig. 23. B 9, facsimile drawing and transcription

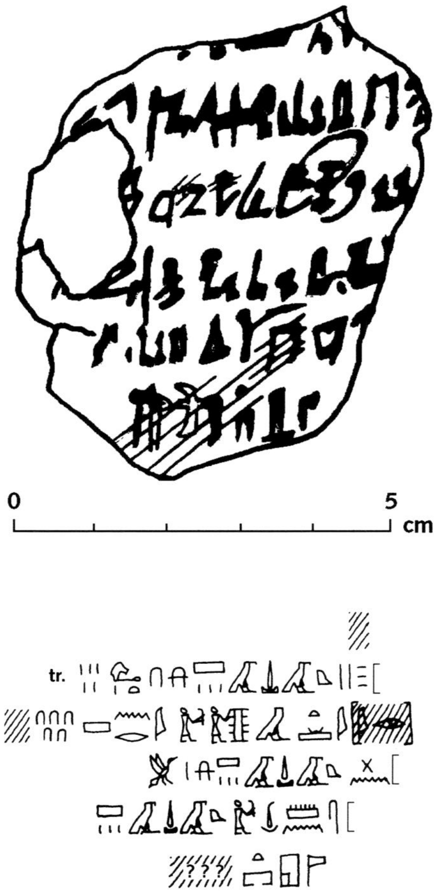

Fig. 24. B 10, facsimile drawing and transcription

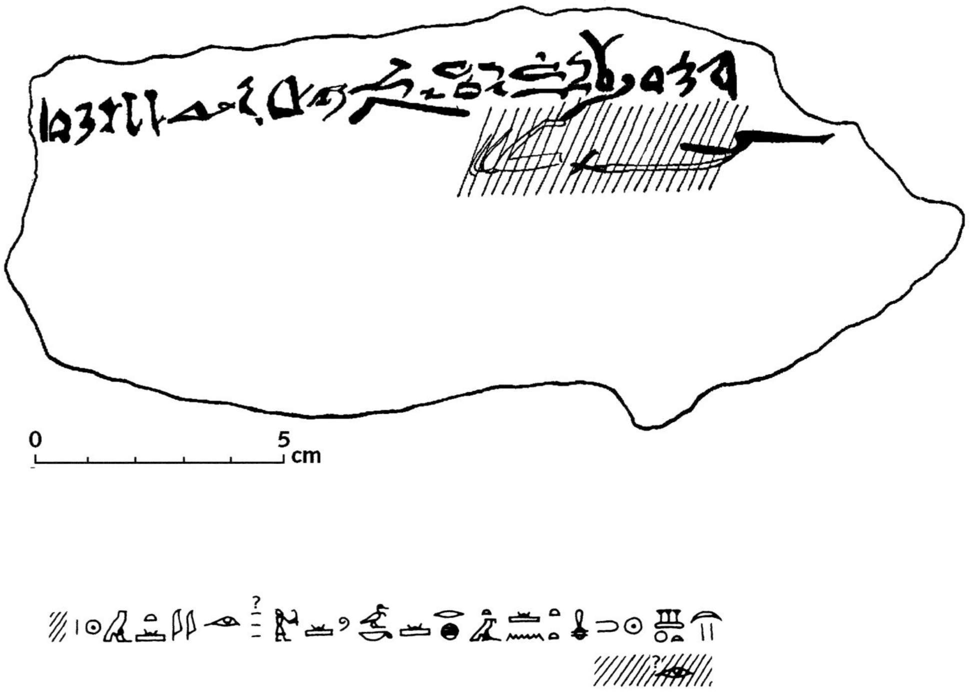

Fig. 25. B 11, facsimile drawing and transcription

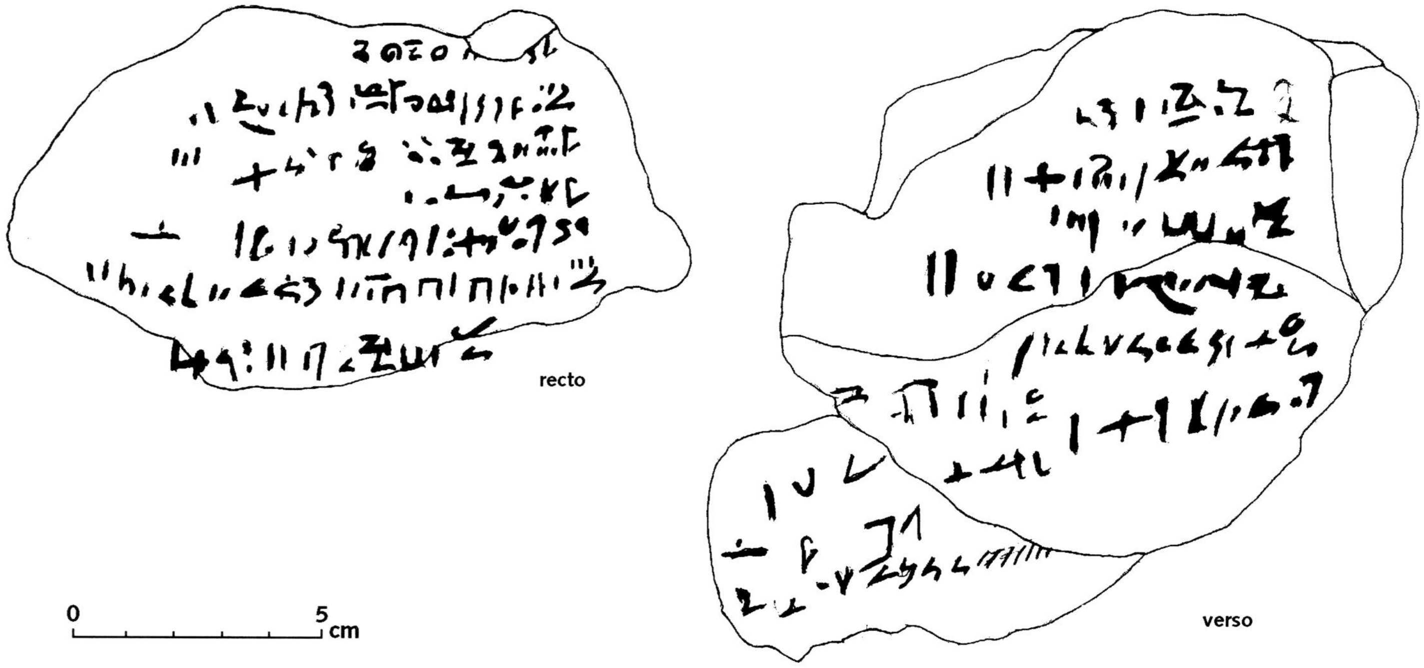

Fig. 26. B 12, facsimile drawings of recto and verso

B 12 (FIG. 26)

Expedition 69.156 (also numbered 950)
RP G 7 (E)
Limestone
14 x 8 x 5 cm
Two sides, seven lines in black ink on recto, eight on verso. Mention of *wsḫt rst* on recto, line 5. Not transcribed.

B 13 (FIG. 27)

University Museum 69–29–231. Expedition 67.529
RP 7 F (N) 59
Limestone
13 x 1 5 x 17.5 cm
Two lines of text in black ink:

(1) *tꜣ ḥwt nt ḥḥw n rnpwt n nsw bity*
(2) *tꜣ ḥwt Rꜥ-ms-sw mr(y)-Ỉmn*

Cf. Helck, *Materialien zur Wirtschaftsgeschichte des Neuen Reiches* 4 (Wiesbaden, 1963), p. 731.

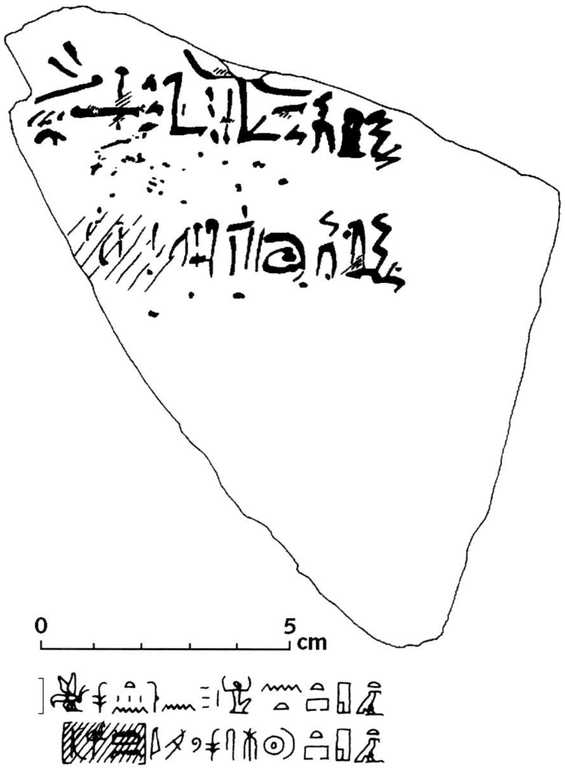

Fig. 27. B 13, facsimile drawing and transcription

B 14 (FIG. 28)

Expedition 67.688
RP 5 (F)
Limestone
11.5 x 12 cm
Five lines, not transcribed.

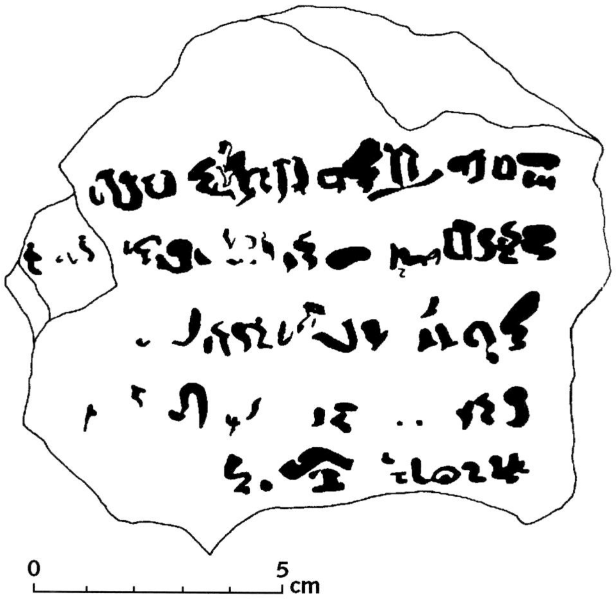

Fig. 28. B 14, facsimile drawing

B 15 (FIG. 29)

Expedition 67.380. RP 7 (C)
Limestone
9 x 15 cm
Two lines on recto, three lines on verso, not transcribed.

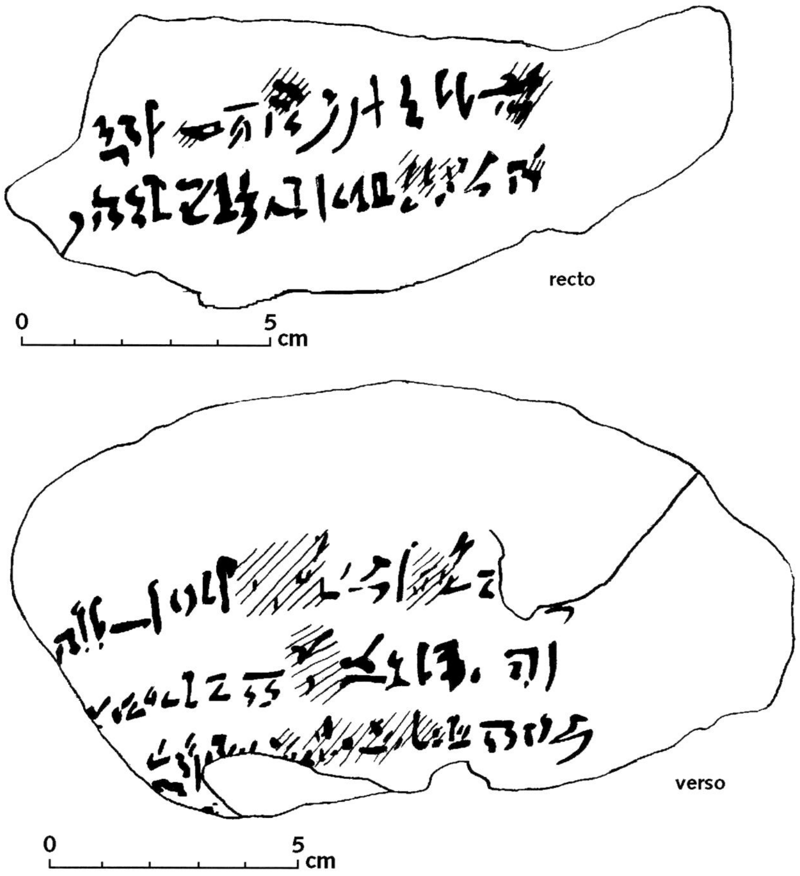

Fig. 29. B 15, facsimile drawings of recto and verso

B 16 (FIG. 30)

Expedition 69.115
Location not recorded
Limestone
8.5 x 13 x 3 cm
Two lines, not transcribed.

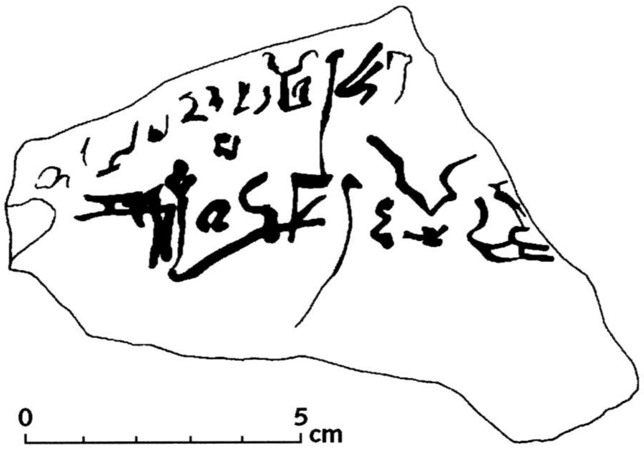

Fig. 30. B 16, facsimile drawing

B 17 (FIG. 31)

Expedition 69.137
RP 5 FCT?
Limestone
5 x 7 cm
Two lines, not transcribed.
sš ḥꜣt

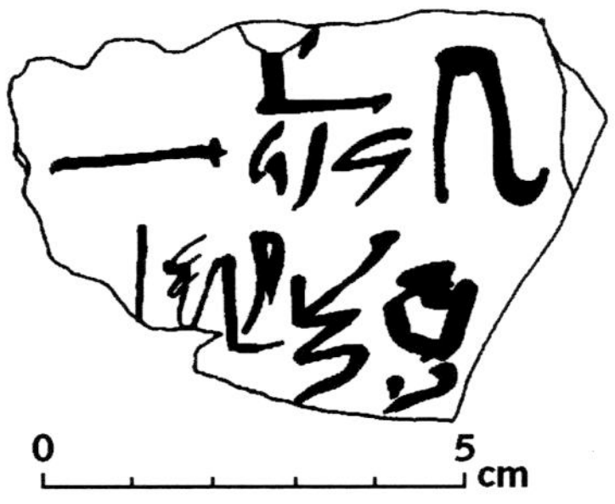

Fig. 31. B 17, facsimile drawing

B 18 (FIG. 32)

Expedition 67.170
RP 6 (C)?
Limestone
9.5 x 6 x 2 cm
Six lines, not transcribed.

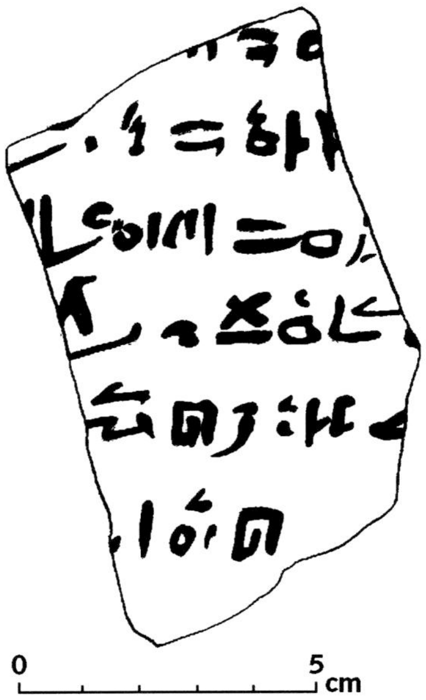

Fig. 32. B 18, facsimile drawing

Dockets

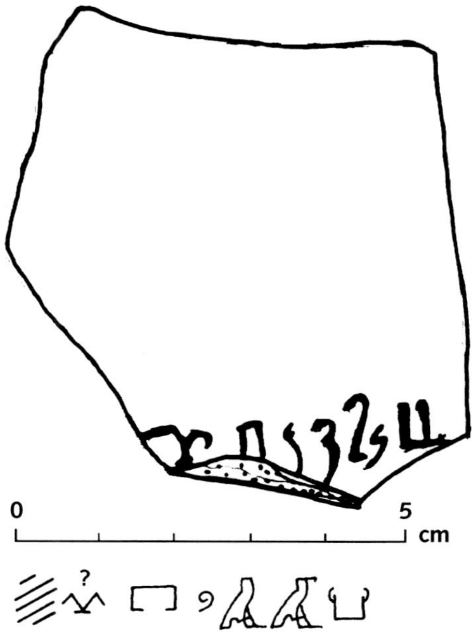

Fig. 33. D 1, facsimile drawing and transcription

Under this heading, hieratic labels in black ink on pottery are included. Except when otherwise noted, all are included under Cairo JdE 91282. There is also a series of ex-voto bowls with figures of deities and occasional hieratic texts in black or white (see O'Connor, *Expedition* 10, no. 1, (1967), pp. 16–17, illustrated, and *Expedition* 21, no. 2 (1979), p. 46, fig. 2). Similar bowls were discovered through earlier work at Abydos and are represented in various museum collections, particularly the Rijksmuseum, Leiden. These will be presented by O'Connor, who has studied the series, in his archaeological report, and are omitted here.

D 1 (fig. 33)
UM 69–29–442
Expedition 69.83
RP TT 2, 10 cm below temple floor level
Keneh ware
7 x 6 x .8 cm
One line in black ink from just below neck of jar. Text: *Kꜣmw ...*, "Vineyard ...."

Fig. 34. D 2, facsimile drawing

D 2 (fig. 34)
Expedition 67.447
RP 7 E (W) 66; 7 F (N) 84
Pottery type, dimensions not recorded
Honey delivery. Potsherd with two lines of text in black ink.
(1) *wbḫt wꜥb* (2) II *ꜣḫt 20 bit*

D 3 (fig. 35)
Expedition 67.444
RP 7 E (S+W) 63
Potsherd, light red ware
18 x 7 cm
One line of text: (cartouche of Ramesses?).

D 4 (fig. 36)
Expedition 69.161
RP G 6 E, general level on top of tombs
Pottery, light brown ware
8 x 7 x .7 cm
Wine label: (1) *Mn-mꜣꜥt-Rꜥ mꜣꜥ-ḫrw ḥr wḥꜣt* (2) ... *ẖn*

D 5 (fig. 37)

Expedition 68.65
RP 4 E (W)
Pottery base
9.5 x 9 cm
Inscribed on outside of base: *Ỉmn ỉw.k m ꜣbḏw*(?), "O Amen, may you come in Abydos(?)."

D 6 (fig. 38)

Expedition 69.15
RP H 7 (S)
Potsherd, brownish red ware
7 x 6 x .4 cm
Two lines of text. (1) *Ḥwt Rꜥ-ms-sw mr* … (2) *m ḏrt ḥry kꜣmwy* ….

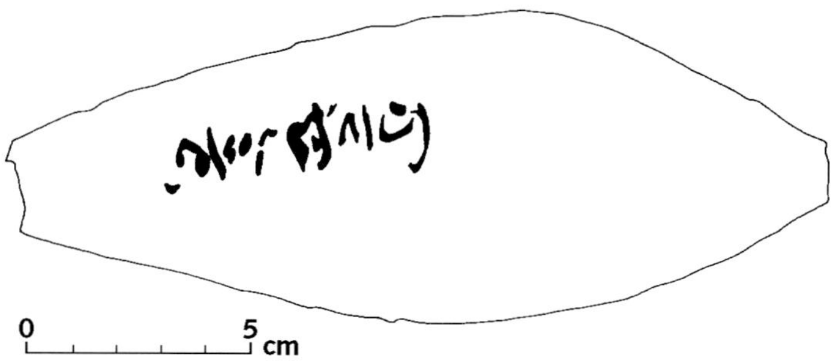

Fig. 35. D 3, facsimile drawing

Fig. 37. D 5, facsimile drawing

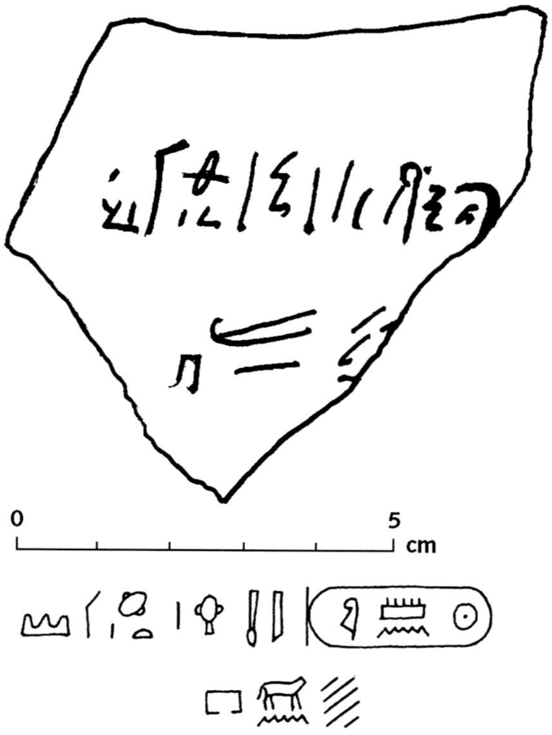

Fig. 36. D 4, facsimile drawing and transcription

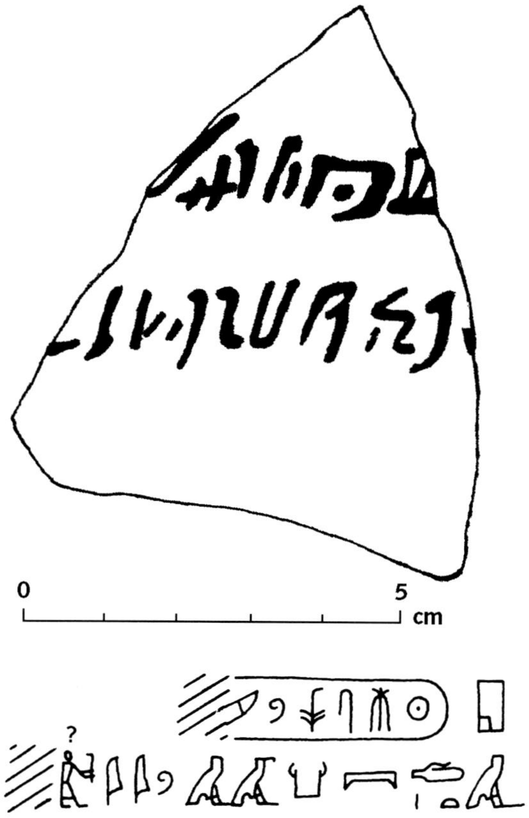

Fig. 38. D 6, facsimile drawing and transcription

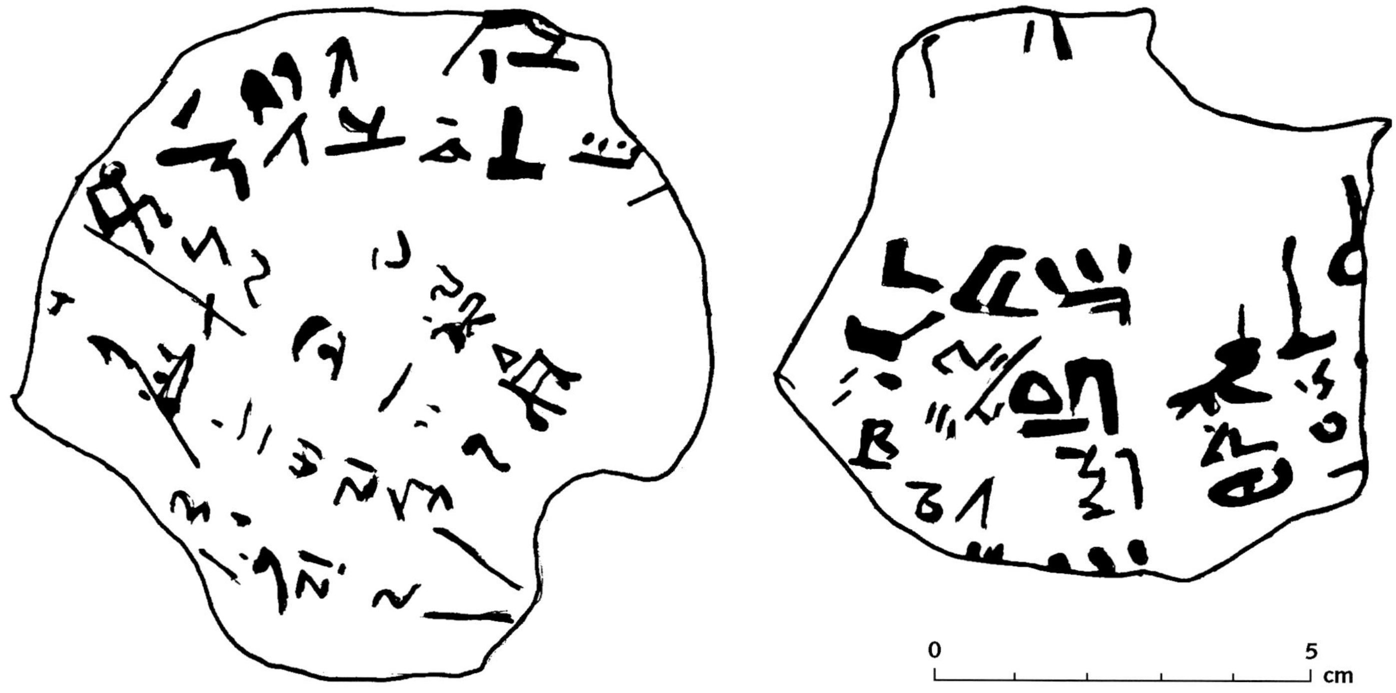

Fig. 39. D 7, facsimile drawing

D 7 (FIG. 39)
Expedition 69.79
Kom Sultan TR 1
Potsherd, red-brown ware
9 x 9 x 1 cm
Inscribed indistinctly on both sides. Not transcribed, citation of *ꜥqw*, "rations."

D 8 (FIGS. 40–43)
a) Expedition 67.452
RP 7 E
18 x 11 cm

b) Expedition 67.595
RP 8 D 9
11.5 x 11.5 cm

c) Expedition 67.596
RP 8 D 7
7.5 x 4 cm

d) Expedition 67.641
RP
7.5 x 4 cm

All RP 7 E
Potsherds from same vessel, once adjoining, red-brown ware with thick gray core. Confusing (overwritten?) text, not transcribed.

D 9 (FIG. 44)
Expedition 67.112
RP 5 F (W) 15
Potsherd, white slip over pink fabric
6 x 5.5 cm
Text: wine label *[itrw] ꜥꜣ n Mn-mꜣꜥ(t)-Rꜥ*
Cf. W. Spiegelberg, *ZÄS* 58 (1923), pp. 125–36.

D 10 (FIG. 45)
Expedition 69.105
RP J 8 (S)
Potsherd, red-brown ware
9.5 x 5 x .7 cm
Two lines of text relating to fruit contents, of which the first reads *. . . bꜥ išd.*

D 11 (FIG. 46)
Expedition 69.116
Kom Sultan TR 1
Potsherd, light ware (Keneh ware?)
10 x 7 x 1.2 cm
Inscribed both sides, recto with text *sš qd Ꞽqr,* verso citing *sš n tꜣ* . . . .

D 12 (FIG. 47)
Expedition 69.70
RP H 7
Potsherd, red-brown ware
11 x 7.5 x .7 cm
Four partial lines, list of foodstuffs.

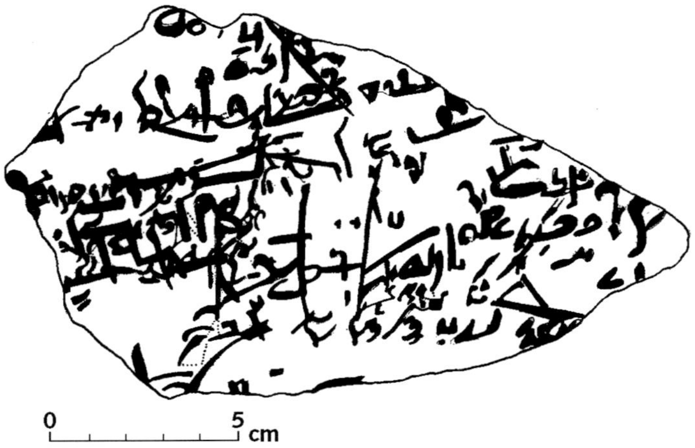

Fig. 40. D 8a, facsimile drawing

Fig. 41. D 8b, facsimile drawing

Fig. 42. D 8c, facsimile drawing

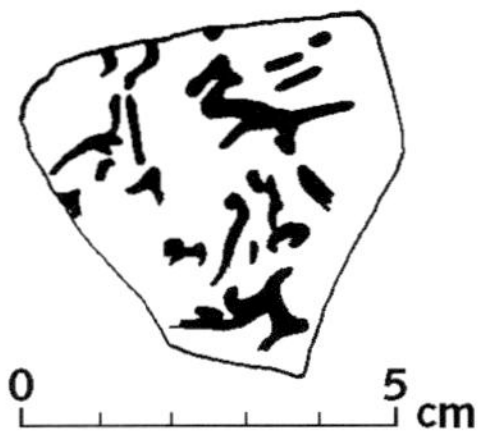

Fig. 43. D 8d, facsimile drawing

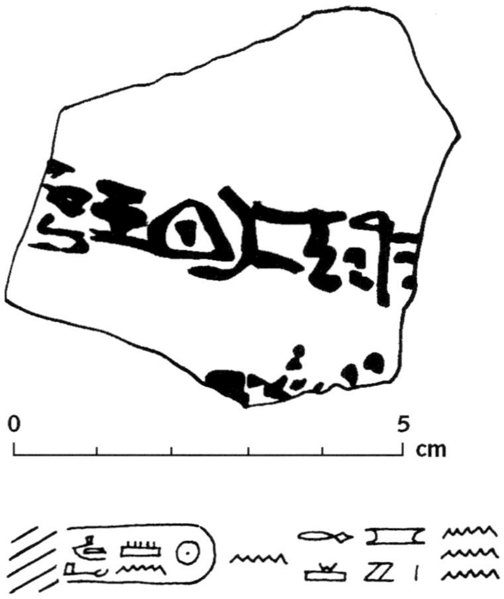

Fig. 44. D 9, facsimile drawing and transcription

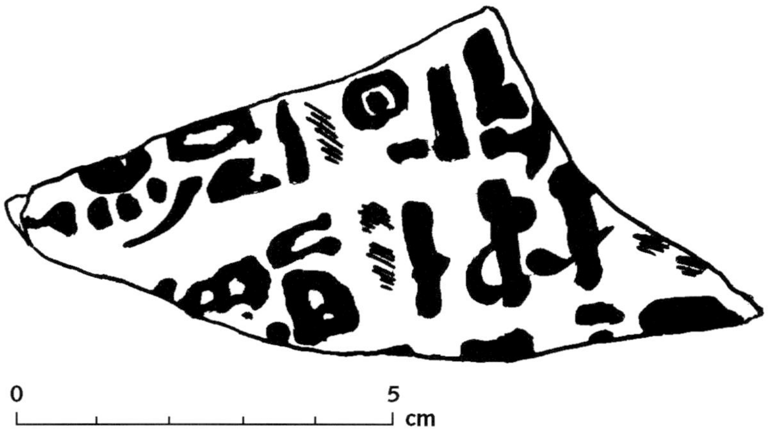

Fig. 45. D 10, facsimile drawing and transcription

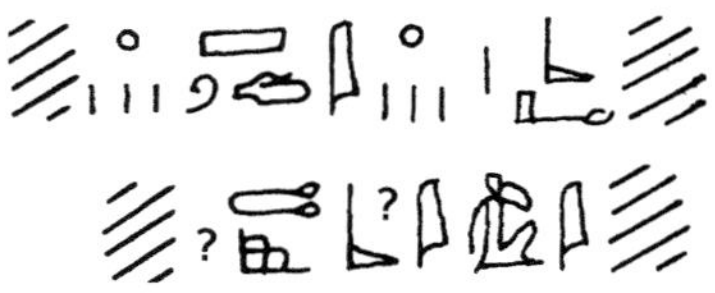

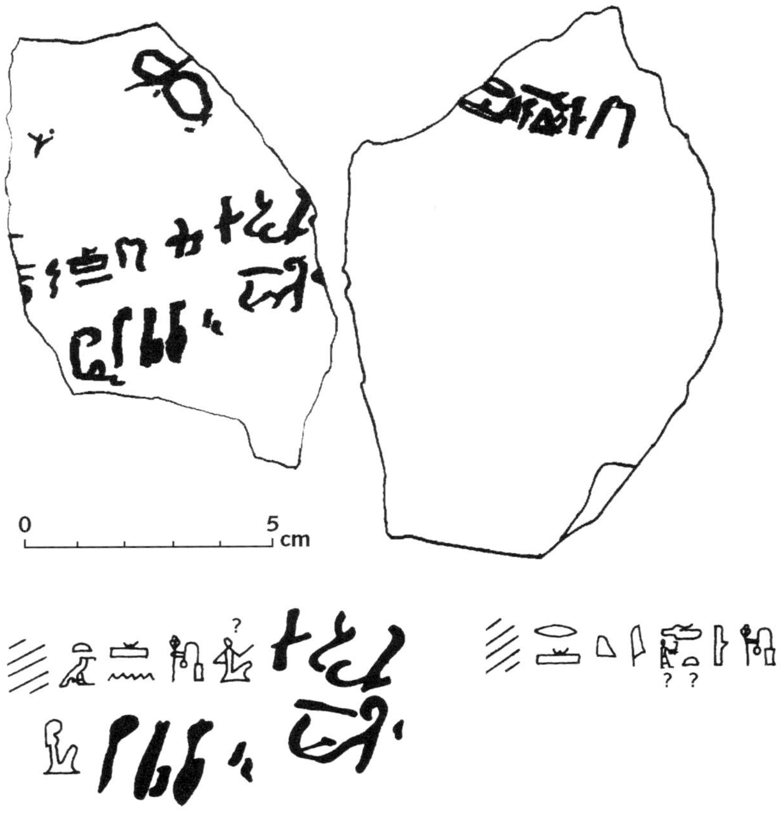

Fig. 46. D 11, facsimile drawing and transcription of verso (left) and recto (right)

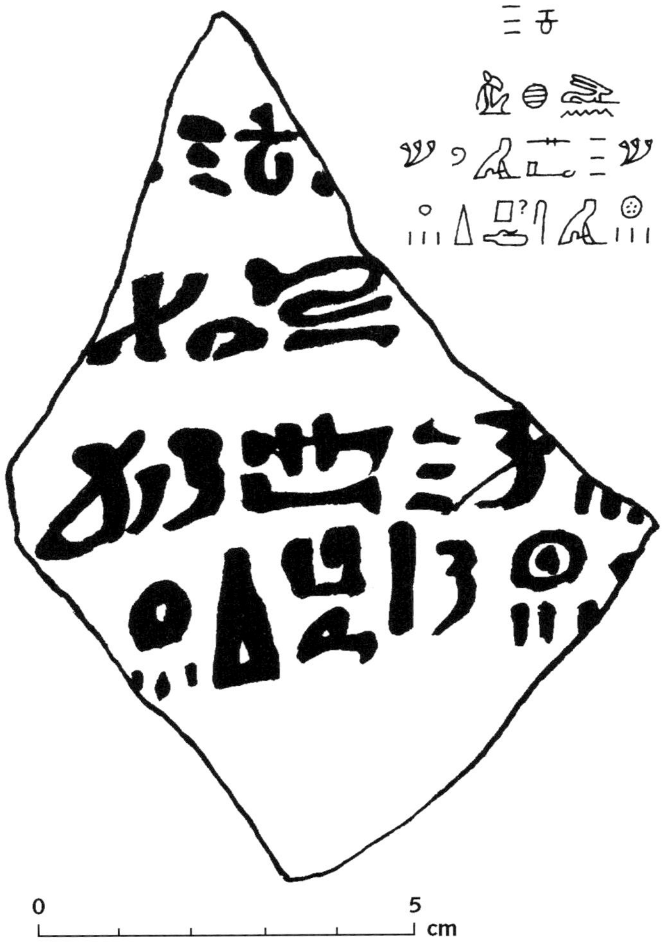

Fig. 47. D 12, facsimile drawing and transcription

D 13 (FIG. 48)
Expedition 67.523
RP
Bowl fragment, wheel made, brown fabric
9 x 11.5 x .7 cm
One line of inscription on inside below lip: *ḫsbd*(?)

D 14 (FIG. 49)
Expedition 67.354
RP 7 D (N+W) 41
Bowl fragment, wheel-made, reddish-brown gritty fabric with brownish-gray core
Diam. 26 cm., preserved to height 7 cm
Inscribed below inner lip: *ḫsbd*(?)....

D 15 (FIG. 50)
Expedition 67.349
RP 7 D (N+W) 36
Bowl fragment, wheel-made, reddish-brown gritty fabric, gray core
Text 9.5 cm. wide
Inscribed below inside lip: *ꜥkp nfr 2* (reading questionable).

D 16 (FIG. 51)
Expedition 67.355
RP 7 D (N) 42
Bowl fragment, wheel-made, reddish-brown fabric with gray core
12 x 5 x .9 cm
Inscribed below inside lip: *ḏꜣrm: 2.*

For this plant material, attested in Hellenistic times, see *Wb.* 5, p. 603.7: "bei der Kyphibereitung verwendete Pflanze;" not indexed in R. Germer, *Flora des pharaonischen Ägypten* (Mainz am Rhein, 1985), p. 259. It is probably not the same term as the *ḏrm* cited by Lesko, *A Dictionary of Late Egyptian* 4 (Providence, 1989), p. 165, with reference to I.E.S. Edwards, *Hieroglyphic Papyri in the British Museum* 4 (London, 1960), vol. 1, p. 21, n. 38, for which the sense "papyrus, book," is indicated by the context; the determinatives differ as well.

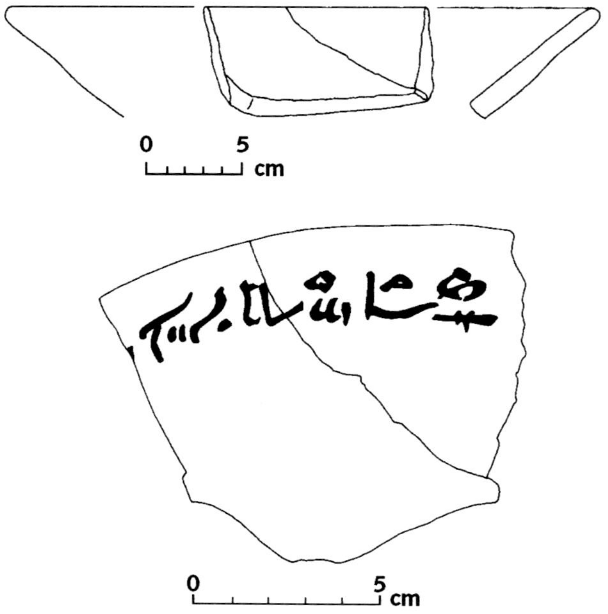

Fig. 48. D 13, profile and facsimile drawing

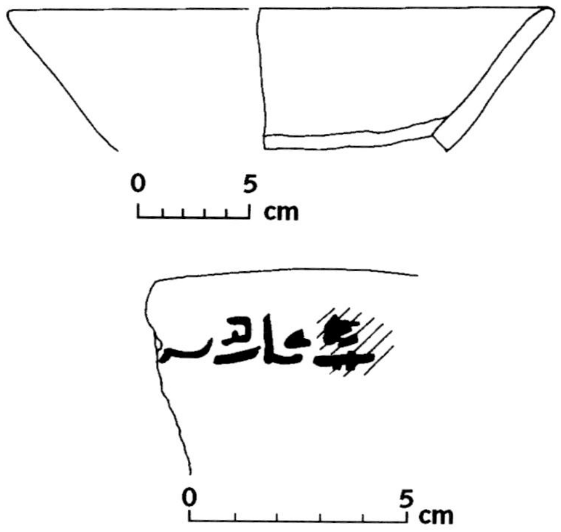

Fig. 49. D 14, profile and facsimile drawing

D 17 (FIG. 52)

Expedition 67.343
RP 7 D (N) 30
Five lines in black ink on gray, gritty pottery fragment with buff surface. Account of plant material or foodstuffs dated in II Shomu 25(?).

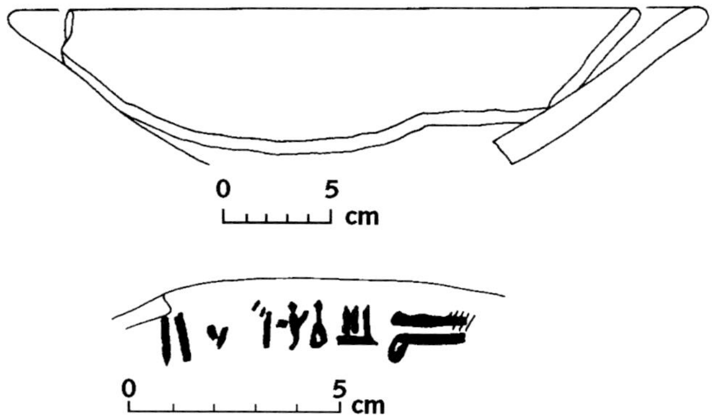

Fig. 50. D 15, profile and facsimile drawing

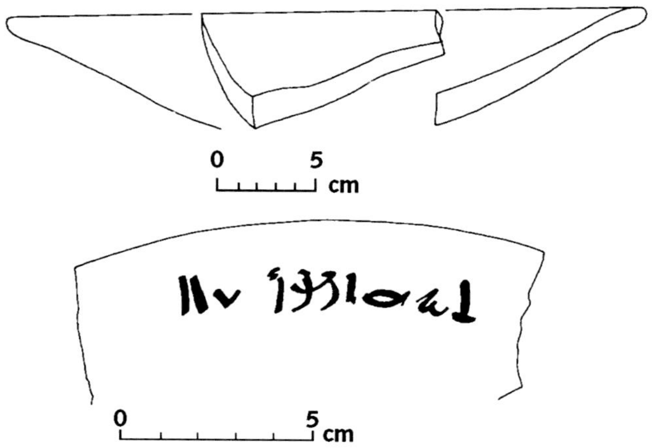

Fig. 51. D 16, profile and facsimile drawing

Fig. 52. D 17, facsimile drawing

Figured Ostracon

FO (FIG. 53)

Cairo JdE 91286. Expedition 67.6

RP 4 D (N+W) 2

10.25 x 11.25 x 2.8 cm

Figured ostracon in faded black ink on a limestone flake in two registers.

Upper register: diagonally supine male with extended phallus administered by two females and a seated figure on the left. Label above: *wʿb,* "washing(?)."

Lower register: On left, two females fighting. On right: two confronting wrestlers or erotic figures (male?) with texts above. Text above right figure *wʿb* ..., text above left *sš*(?) .... To the left of both pairs of figures an ox-head and foreleg with three circles. This highly curious scene deserves more study. The main figure is strangely unsupported by a seat of any kind. One attendant appears to tend his head (shaving, hairdressing?), another his feet (pedicure?), and the central one holds something (food or incense) before his face. Is the context a treatment or preparation of a dead body? Dr. Emma Brunner-Traut has kindly communicated her views on the subject and points to a similar scene in the Turin Erotic Papyrus. In it a male figure, also shown at a diagonal, is tended by three women, one at the head, one at the feet, and the central one supporting him (J.A. Omlin, *Der Papyrus 55001 und seine satirisch-erotischen Zeichnungen und Inschriften* (Turin, 1973), pls. 7, 11, 12, and 17 (lower section, center), 19 (middle row, left), Bild 7, p. 35). Omlin titles the scene, "the exhausted man is carried away by the woman and the two maidens." Thus the ostracon is probably to be understood as a scene in a brothel. The pairs of men and women in the register below, if not wrestling, may then be possibly regarded as erotic or as brawlers. Scenes of wrestling on ostraca are rare according to B. Peterson, *Zeichnungen aus einer Totenstadt* (Stockholm, 1973), no. 65, p. 89, p. 120, n. 76.

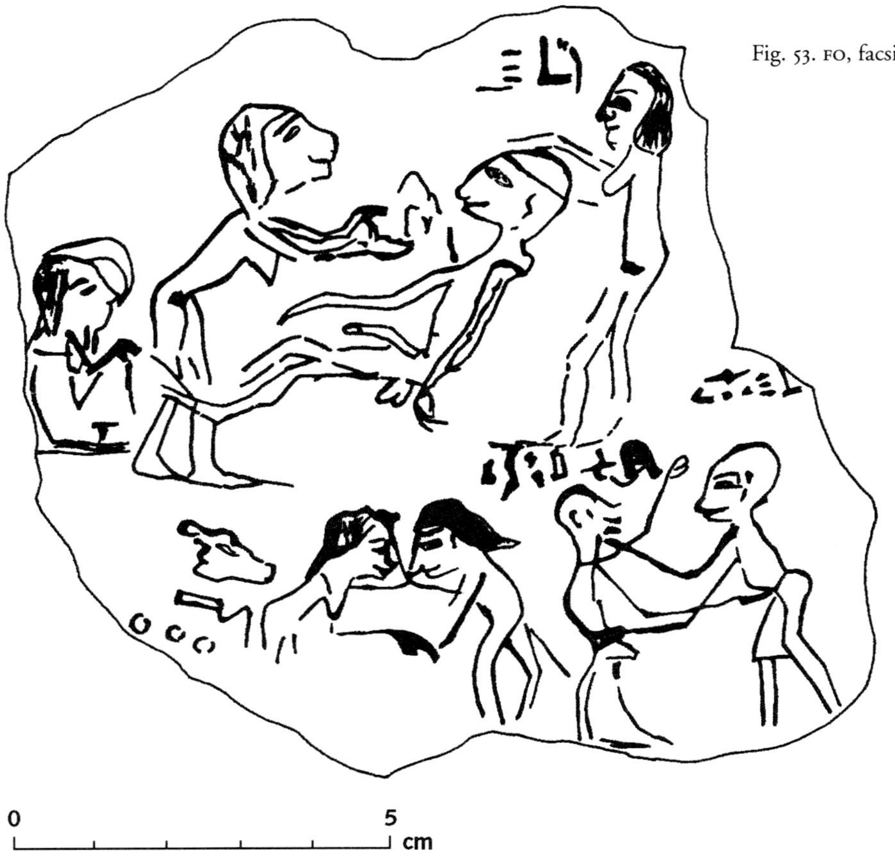

Fig. 53. FO, facsimile drawing

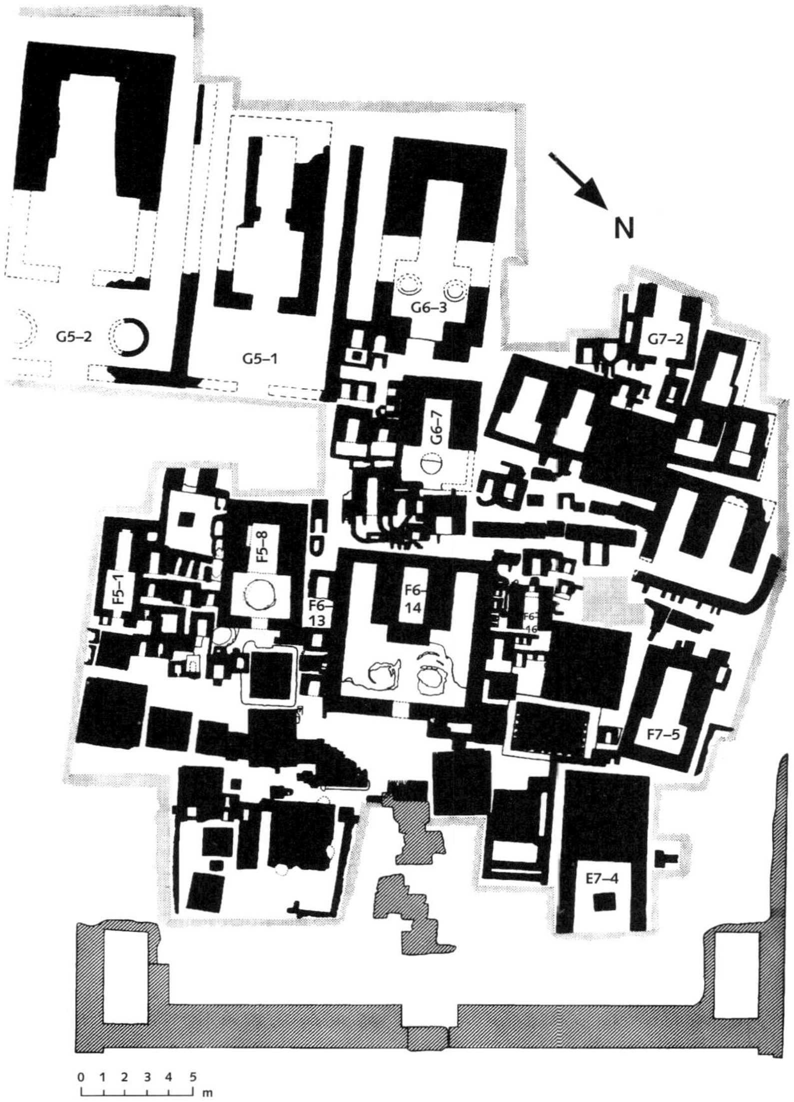

Fig. 54. Detail plan of the Middle Kingdom cenotaphs

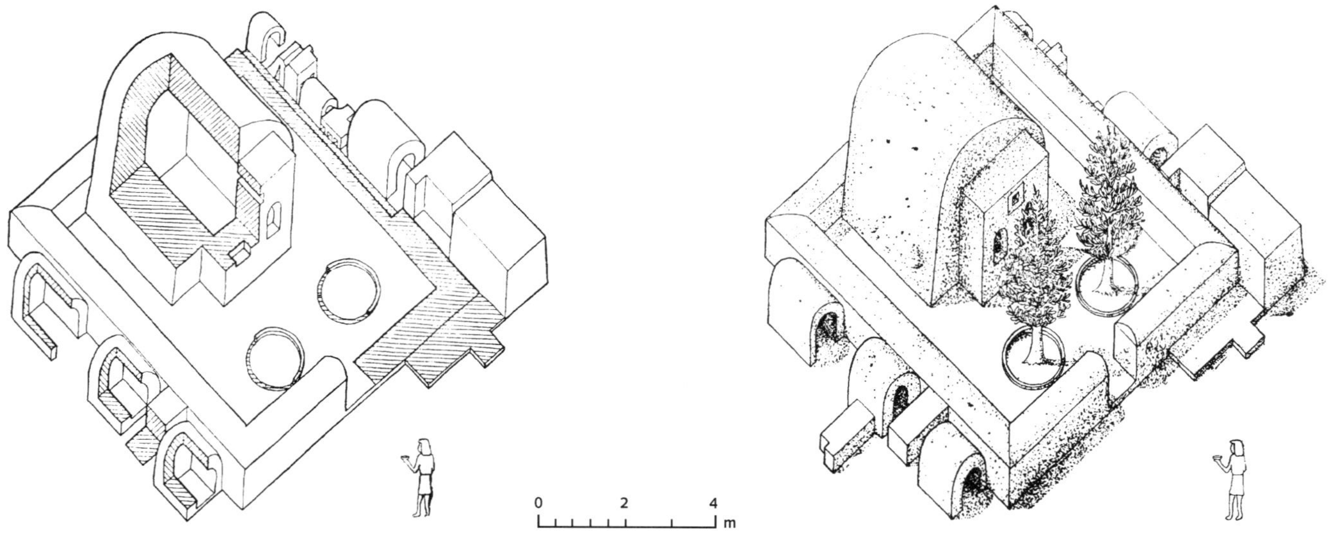

Fig. 55. External and section reconstruction views of cenotaph F 6–14

Middle Kingdom Objects from the Memorial Chapel Area

The Ramesses Temple was built over part of the vast area of large and small memorial chapels. The appearance of these chapels has been discussed in detail by O'Connor, based on his excavations ("The 'Cenotaphs' of the Middle Kingdom at Abydos," in *Mélanges Gamal eddin Mokhtar,* BdE 97/2 [Cairo, 1985], pp. 161–77). A large number of stelae, statuary, and offering tables had been essentially "quarried" from the site by the agents of Mariette and others (references in Simpson, *The Terrace of the Great God at Abydos* [New Haven and Philadelphia, 1974]). It is possible that some of the stelae, etc., had been removed during the New Kingdom and Ramesside construction and placed along the outer wall of the Kom el Sultan. Several relatively small stelae inscribed in hieratic were discovered during the Pennsylvania–Yale excavations in disturbed fill not connected with specific chapels. A few were found *in situ,* and a larger stela was found *in situ* on a limestone base (C 5, below).

C 1 (figs. 56–57, pl. 5b)

Cairo JdE 91253
Expedition 67.234 A, B
RP 6 E (W) 63
Limestone, in two pieces
46.5 x 26 x 5 cm

Nineteen lines of text in hieratic, black ink. Facsimile by Barry J. Kemp, transcription by Simpson autographed by Mark Stone. Aside from filiation citations, some thirty-two individuals are listed, including three *swnw,* "physicians," a chief physician, three treasury scribes, and a copyist of the local court. Cited by O'Connor in *Mélanges Gamal eddin Mokhtar,* p. 175.

(1) *Ḥtp dꞽ nsw (n) Gb, Ptḥ Skr Wsꞽr-ḫntyw* (sic)*-ꞽmntyw*
(2) *psḏt ꜥꜣt psḏt nḏst dꞽ.sn pr(t)-ḫrw <kꜣw ꜣpdw tꜣ ḥnqt> m ḫꜣ tꜣ ḥnqt snṯr*
(3) *mrḥt mnḫt ḫꜣ m ḫt nbt nfrt wꜥbt ꜥnḫt nṯrw ꞽm n*
(4) *kꜣ n Wsꞽr swnw Ꞽꞽ-snb ꞽr n ꜥnḫ-t(ꞽ)-sꞽ mꜣꜥt-ḫrw n kꜣ n Wsꞽr*
(5) *swnw Rn.f-snb ꞽr n Sꜣt-Ꞽp mꜣꜥt-ḫrw n kꜣ n Wsꞽr ꜥnḫ-t(ꞽ)-sꞽ [mꜣꜥt-ḫrw] n*
(6) *kꜣ n sꜣt.s Sꜣt-Ꞽp ꞽrt n ꜥnḫt(ꞽ).s(ꞽ) mꜣꜥt-ḫrw n kꜣ n sꜣ.s Ꞽmny-snb*
(7) *ꞽr.n ꜥnḫ.t(ꞽ)sꞽ mꜣꜥt-ḫrw n kꜣ n sꜣ.s Ḫnty-ẖty-m-sꜣ.f*
(8) *ꞽr.n ꜥnḫt(ꞽ)sꞽ mꜣꜥt-ḫrw n kꜣ n Sꜣt-Ꞽp mꜣꜥt-ḫrw n kꜣ n Gbw*
(9) *...... n kꜣ n Pny(?)-šry(?) n kꜣ n Ꞽꜣꜣy mꜣꜥ-ḫrw n kꜣ n Sn-Mwt ...*
(10) *... n kꜣ (n) wr swnw Sn-wsrt(?)-Ꞽꞽ-snb mꜣꜥ-ḫrw n kꜣ n sš pr-ḥḏ*
(11) *Sn ...... w mꜣꜥ-ḫrw n kꜣ n [sš] pr-ḥḏ Ḥqꜣ(?)-snb.n.f n kꜣ n sš pr-ḥḏ Snb*
(12) *n kꜣ n Snbtꞽfꞽ ꞽr (n) Sššt n kꜣ n Snbtꞽfꞽ-šrꞽ mꜣꜥ-ḫrw*
(13) *n kꜣ <n> Gbw ꞽr n Sššt n kꜣ n swnw Mnw-ḥtp*
(14) *[n kꜣ n] ... sꜣ-nb ... n kꜣ n sš spẖrw n(?) qnbt*
(15) *[Sꜣ]-ꜣst(?) mꜣꜥ-ḫrw n kꜣ n sš ... -snb n kꜣ n Ḫnt-snb.f*
(16) *n kꜣ n Tmꜣy ...... n kꜣ n Ꞽw-snb ꞽrt.n mwt.s*
(17) *n kꜣ <n> Sꜣt-Ḥḏ(t) mꜣꜥt-ḫrw n kꜣ n ḥry pr Snnw(?)-šry n kꜣ n Sw*
(18) *ḏt .... n kꜣ n Ḥddꞽ-Sꜣt-Ꞽp n kꜣ n Ꞽ..ꞽw(?)*
(19) *n kꜣ n Nfrw ...... n kꜣ n ḫtmty(?) (?) Mṯnt*
Ḥtp dꞽ nswt n kꜣ(w).s(n)

(1) An offering which the king gives <to> Geb, Ptah, Sokar, Osiris-foremost-of-the Westerners, (2) the great Ennead, the lesser Ennead, that they may grant an invocation offering <cattle, fowl, beer, cakes> consisting of a thousand breads, beer, incense, (3) oil, cloth, a thousand of every fine, pure thing whereon the gods live to (4) the ka of the Osiris, the physician, Iey-seneb, born of Ankhtysy (fem.) the vindicated, to the ka of the Osiris, (5) the physician Renef-seneb, born of Sat-Ip (fem.), the vindicated, to the ka of the Osiris Ankhtysy (fem.), [vindicated] to (6) the ka of her daughter Sat-Ip, vindicated, born of Ankhtysy (fem.) the vindicated, to the ka of her son Ameny-seneb, (7) born of Ankhtysy (fem.), the vindicated, to the ka of her son, Khenty-khety-em-saf, (8) born of Ankhtysy (fem.) the vindicated, to the ka of Sat-Ip (fem.), the vindicated, to the ka of Gebu, (9) ...... to the ka of Peny(?)-the younger, to the ka of Iaay, the vindicated, to the ka of Sen-Mut ... (10) ... to the ka (of) the chief physician, Senwosret(?)-Iey-seneb, the vindicated, to the ka of the treasury scribe (11) Sen ...... u, the vindicated, to the ka of the treasury-[scribe] Heqa(?)-senebenef, to the ka of the treasury scribe Seneb, (12) to the ka of Senebtyfy, born of Sesheshet (fem.), to the ka of Senebtyfy the younger, vindicated, (13) to the ka (of) Gebu, born of Sesheshet (fem.), to the ka of the physician Min-hetep, (14) [to the ka of] .... , to the ka of the copyist of the local court (15) Si(?)-Ese, the vindicated, to the ka of the scribe ...-seneb, to the ka of Khent-senebef(?), (16) to the ka of Temay ...... to the ka of Iu-seneb, born of his mother, (17) to the ka <of> Sat-Hedjet (fem.), the vindicated, to the ka of the majordomo Senenu(?) the younger, to the ka of Su- (18) djet(?) .... to the ka of Hededi-Sat-Ip, to the ka of Ijiu(?), (19) to the ka of Neferu ...... to the ka of the sealer(?) Metjenet(?). An offering which the king gives to their kas.

For an invocation to several persons, cf. the phrase, *n kꜣ n nty nb rn.f ḥr wḏ pn,* H. Frankfort, *JEA* 14 (1928), pl. 21.1, from Abydos. When I saw it in February, 1994, the text was badly faded and the lower part illegible.

For a list of physicians represented in the Middle Kingdom, see P. Ghalioungui, *The Physicians of Pharaonic Egypt* (Mainz am Rhein, 1983), pp. 23–26, where a total of twenty (three without names), are cited. Compare also F. Jonckheere, *CdE* 52 (1951), pp. 237–68. A chief

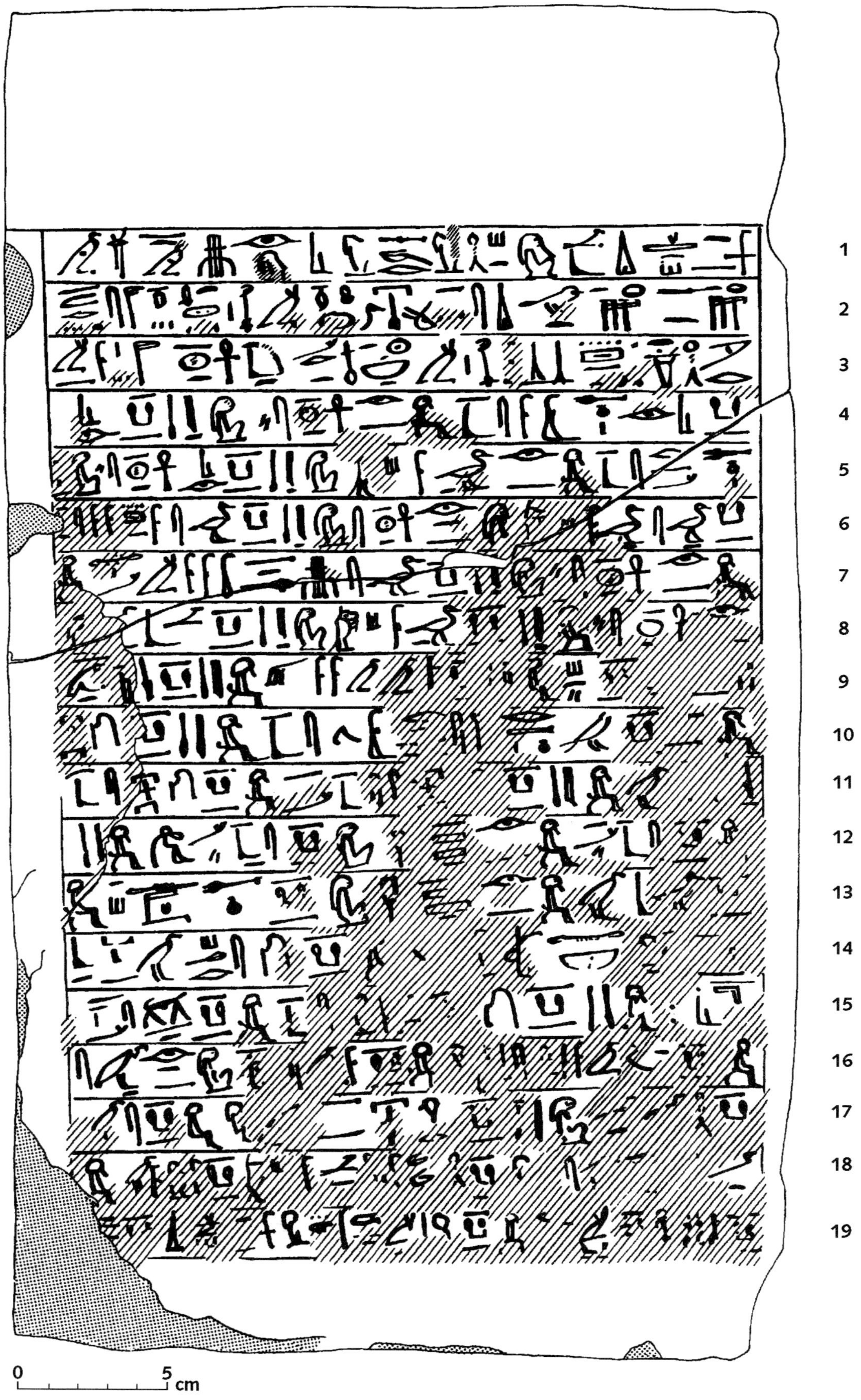

Fig. 56. c 1, facsimile drawing

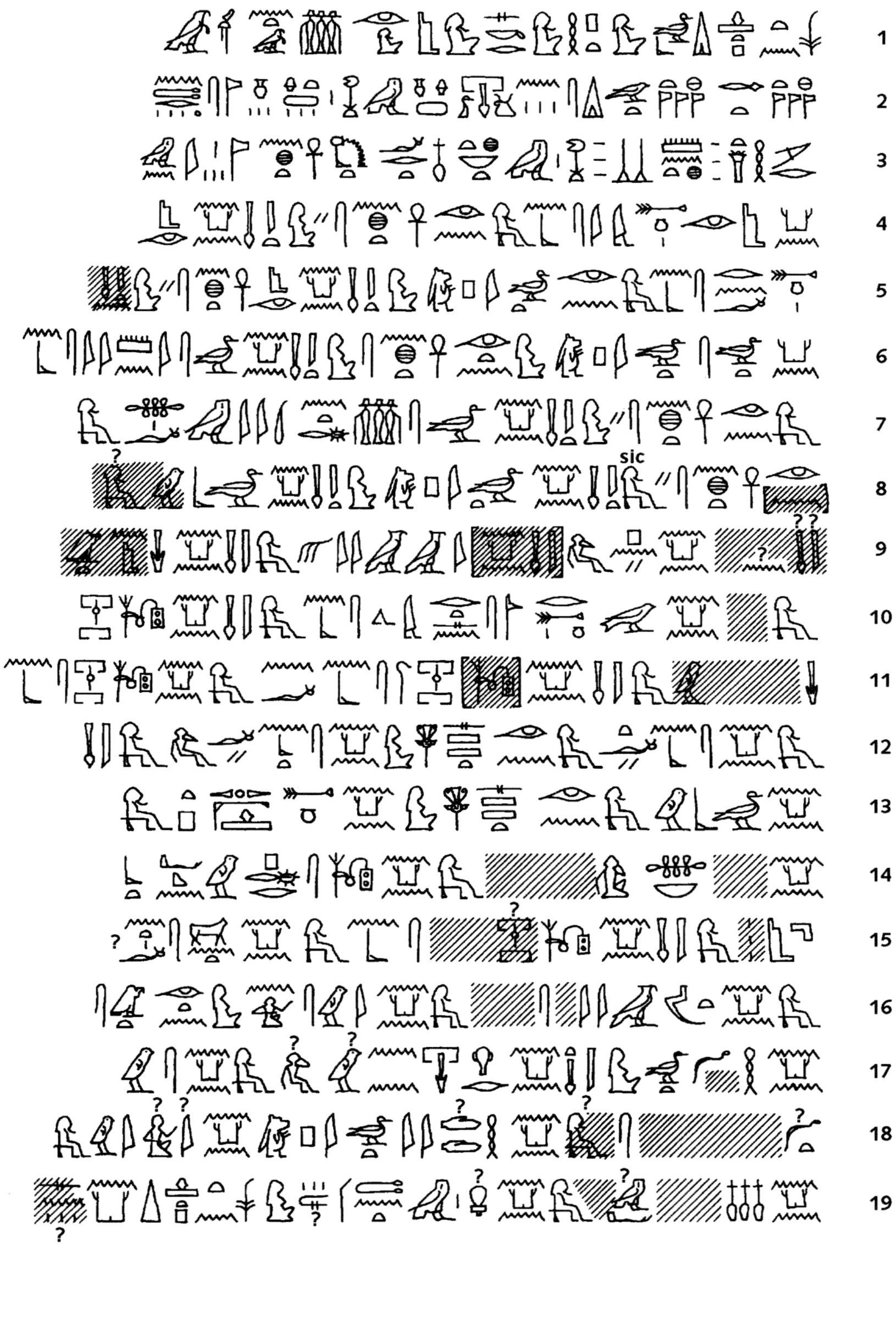

Fig. 57. C 1, transcription

physician Renef-seneb is known from Sinai (Jonkheere no. 56, Ghalioungui no. 63), but the name is common enough to make an identification with the man of line 5 doubtful. A general bibliography on the subject is provided by Ghalioungui, *The Physicians*, pp. 103–110. The three physicians and the chief physician listed on our stela thus increase the number known from the Middle Kingdom substantially, and double those known from Abydos.

C 2 (FIG. 58)

Cairo JdE 91245. Expedition 69.212
RP
Block/Stela
Limestone
34 x 26 x 9 cm
One column and seven lines of hieratic in black ink with brush.

(1) *ḫꜣ m tꜣ ḫꜣ m ḥnqt ḫꜣ m kꜣw ꜣpdw ḫꜣ m ḫt nb ꜥnḫt nṯr im rꜥ nb*
(2) *ḥtp di nsw Wsir nb ꜣbḏw n kꜣ n*
(3) *Sꜣt-Ỉmny-Š.f-Wꜣḥ-mnw ir.n Mkt nb(t) imꜣḫ*
(4) *n kꜣ n Mkt irt n Sꜣt-Ỉꜥḥ mꜣꜥ nb(t) imꜣḫ*
(5) *Sꜣ š.f sꜣ Ỉꜥḥ irt n Mkt*
(6) *n kꜣ n Šfti mꜣꜥ nb(t) imꜣḫ*
(7) *Wꜣḥ-mnw mꜣꜥ nb imꜣḫ ir n*
(8) *Gr nb(t) imꜣḫ*

(1) A thousand bread, a thousand beer, a thousand cattle, fowl, a thousand of everything on which a god lives every day.
(2) An offering which the king gives (to) Osiris, lord of Abydos for the ka of
(3) Ameny-Sit-Shef-Wah-menu, born of Meket, possessor of honor,
(4) for the ka of Meket, born of Sit-Iah, vindi<cated>, possessor of honor,
(5) Si-Shef Si-Iah, born to Meket,
(6) for the ka of Shefti, vindi<cated>, possessor of honor,
(7) Wah-menu, vindi<cated>, possessor of honor, born to
(8) Ger, possessor of honor.

It is unclear whether some of these names represent compound names (cf. P. Vernus, *Le surnom au Moyen Empire* (Rome, 1986), or bipartite or tripartite filiation. On some of the names, cf. *Sꜣ-šftw, PN* I, p. 284.21; *Sꜣt-Ỉꜥḥ, PN* I, p. 285.16; *Mkt, PN* I, p. 166.19; *Wꜣḥ-mnw, PN* I, p. 73.17. *Gr,* which is clear, is not represented in *PN.* Note the anomaly of *mꜣꜥ-ḫrw* written simply as *mꜣꜥ* without *ḫrw.*

C 3 (FIG. 59, PL. 6A)

UM 69–29–131. Expedition 69.208
RP exterior east corner of chapel F 6 12
Limestone
7 x 13 x 2 cm
Top line in lunate of stela with cartouche of Amenemhet II: *n nsw bity Nwb-kꜣw-Rꜥ, di ꜥnḫ,* "for (of) the king of the southland and northland, Nubkaure, given life ...." Cited by O'Connor, *Expedition* 12, no. 1 (1969), p. 33.
UM storage photograph 22–6.

C 4 (FIG. 60)

Cairo JdE 91283 (included with other ostraca). Expedition 69.86
RP J 6 (N)
Limestone, black ink
11 x 9 x 4 cm
Small stela with six lines of text in hieratic. Illustrated by O'Connor, *Expedition* 12, no. 1 (1969), p. 33, lower right. In this most simple of stelae, a man records his name and the names of his mother, his wife, his wife's mother, his son, and his brother (or his son's brother).

(1) *Ḥr-nḫt*	Hor-nakht
(2) *ir n Ttw*	born of Tetu
(3) *ḥmt.f Rn.s-ꜥnḫ*	his wife Renes-ankh
(4) *irt n Nbt-Ỉwnt*	born of Nebet-Iunet
(5) *sꜣ.f Ḥr-nḫt*	his son Hor-nakht
(6) *sn.f Ddw*	his brother Dedu

C 5 (FIG. 61, PLS. 6B–7)

Cairo JdE 91243. Expedition 69.207
RP set into interior face of NW wall of the forecourt of memorial chapel E 7–4 (see fig. 54)
Limestone
52 x 33 x 13 cm. Set in limestone base 56 x 32 x 11 cm with recessed rectangle in center 5 cm deep
Illustrated *in situ* in O'Connor, *Expedition* 12, no. 1 (1969), p. 33 top left. Round top stela of Me<k>et-ankhu. A notation indicates that there is one faint line of hieratic on the left side, apparently not traced and now illegible (1994). Cited by O'Connor in *Mélanges Gamal eddin Mokhtar,* p. 175.

On the left a standing male figure with short wig, broad collar, short kilt, facing right, holds a staff at a diagonal in the left hand and a horizontal *kherep* staff in the right hand. Seven columns of text in the same direction serve as the formula with titles and name.

(1) *Ḥtp di nsw (n) Ws-ir nb ꜣbḏw di.f pr(t) ḫrw tꜣ ḥnqt* (2) *snṯr ḫt nb nfr(t) wꜥbt ꜥnḫ nṯr (i)m m ḥꜣbw nw*(?) (3) *nṯr pn nb ꜣbḏw n kꜣ n imꜣḫ* (4) *ḫtmty bity smr wꜥty n mrwt rdi.n* (5) *nb tꜣwy ꜣw ib.f ḫft sp.f ḫr irw.f* (6) *imy-r pr wr M<k>t*(?)*-ꜥnḫw* (7) *ms n Sꜣt-Ppy-Ỉdi*(?) *nb(t) imꜣḫ*

(1) An offering which the king gives to Osiris, lord of Abydos, that he may give an invocation offering of bread and beer, (2) incense, and all things good and pure on which a god lives, on festivals of(?) (3) this god, lord of Abydos, for the ka of the honored one, (4) the royal seal bearer, sole companion of love, whom the (5) lord of the two lands has caused to rejoice according to his deed for his actions, (6) the chief steward Me<k>et(?)-ankhu (7) born to Sit-Pepy-Idy(?), possessor of an honored state.

The title "chief steward" has both the *wr*-bird and old man with staff, where regularly one or the other is represented but "never" both. The suggested reading of the name Sit-Pepy-Idy(?) I owe to Detlef Franke.

The first part of the owner's name, "*Mꜥt,*" is curious. I have considered the possibility that it is a title, but this has not been productive; a logical reading is *Mkt-ꜥnḫw,* a name attested in Fakhry, *The Monuments of Sneferu at Dahshur,* vol. 2: *The Valley Temple,* part 2:

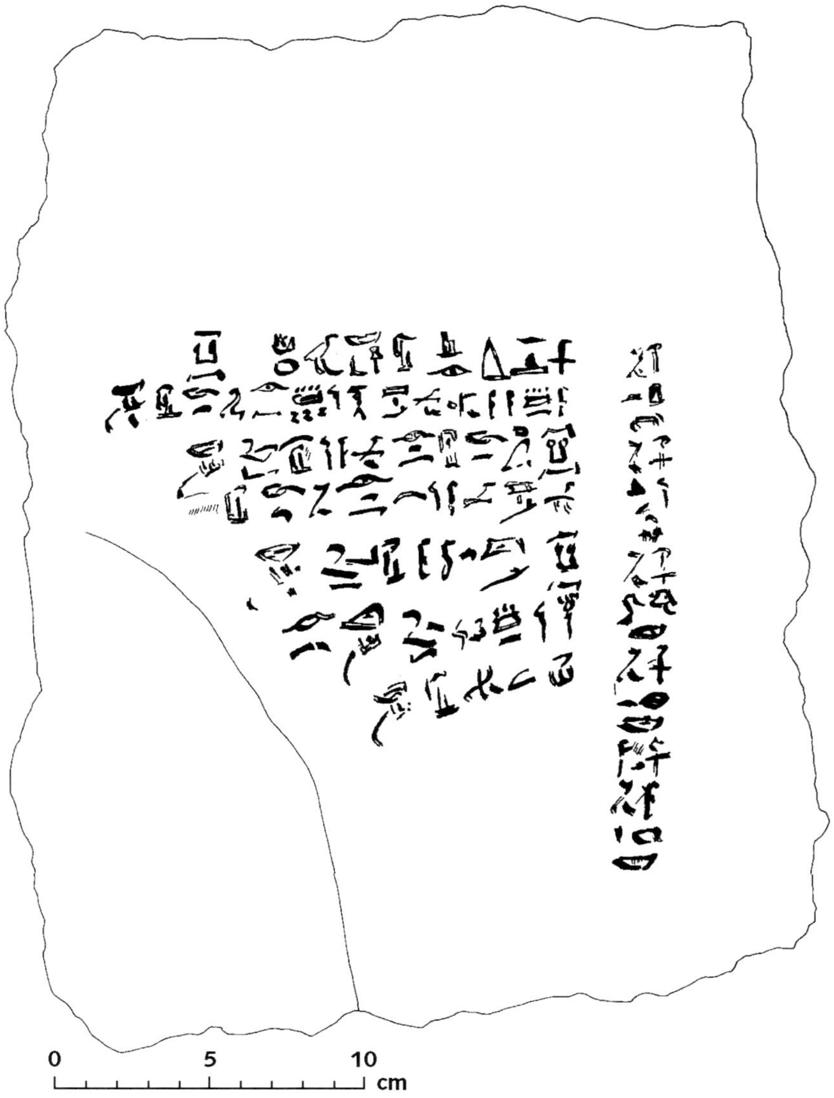

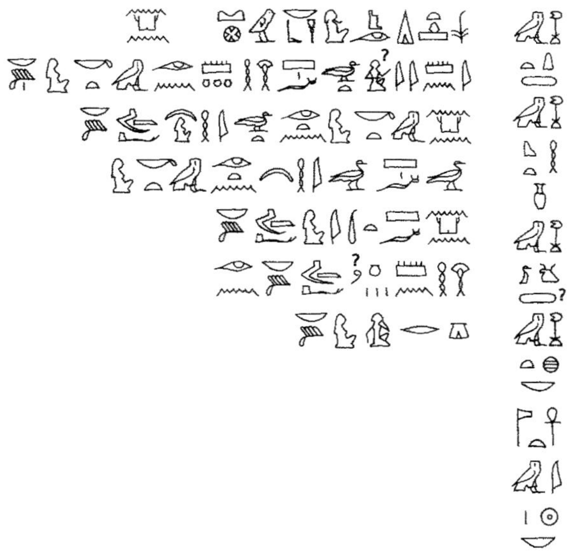

Fig. 58. c 2, facsimile drawing and transcription

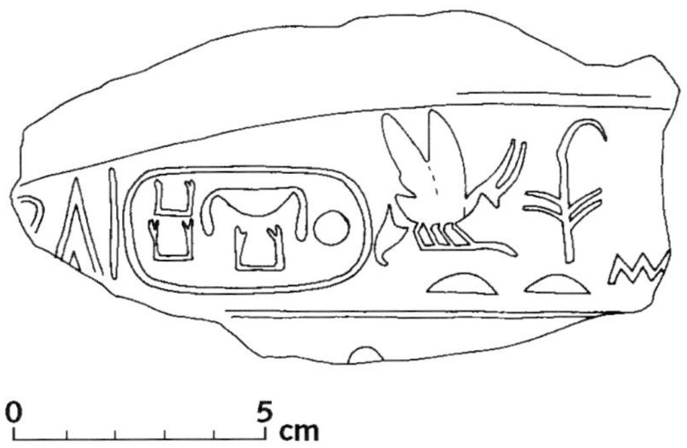

Fig. 59. c 3, facsimile drawing

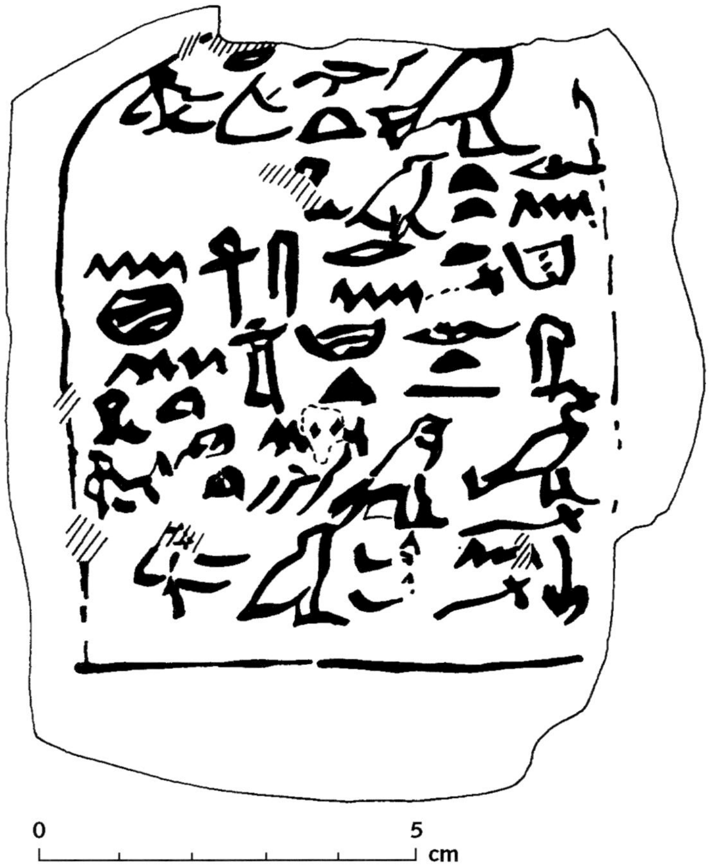

Fig. 60. c 4, facsimile drawing

Fig. 61. C 5, facsimile drawing

The Finds (Cairo, 1961), p. 21, no. 9, excavation no. 120 = Chevereau, *RdE* 43 (1992), no. 393 = D. Jones, *A Glossary of Ancient Egyptian Nautical Titles and Terms* (London, 1988), 93, no. 190 = W.A. Ward, *Index of Egyptian administrative and religious titles of the Middle Kingdom* (Beirut, 1982), 1411. D. Franke, *GM* 134 (1993), p. 40 read the name as *Rdit*(?)-*ꜥnḫw* with reference to a graffito of this man at Aswan dated in Year 4 of Amenemhet III, with the cartouche miscopied (see fig. 62; W.M.F. Petrie, *A Season in Egypt* [London, 1888], p. 81, pl. 3, no. 81).

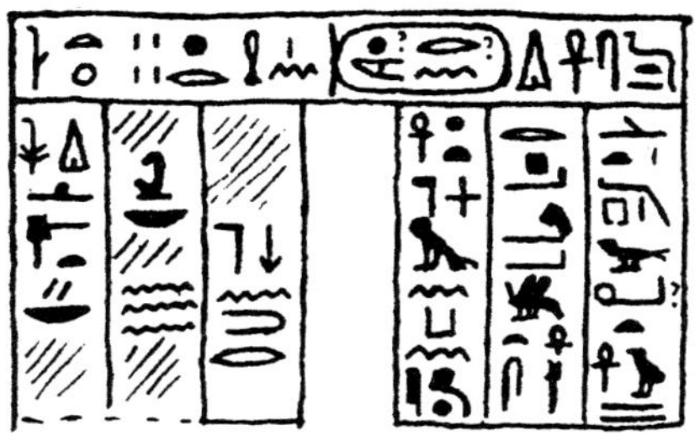
Fig. 62. Aswan graffito of Meket-ankhu

Franke is certainly correct in noting that the individual is the same man. In the Aswan graffito the first element is written with one of the arm signs (Sign List D 36–44). The writing of C 5 now with initial *m* excludes Franke's tentative reading as *Rdit*(?), but the matter is not completely solved. At least C 5 can be dated to the reign of Amenemhet III and not considerably later, as suggested by the poor quality of the stela. On the right, a standing male figure with neck-length wig, broad collar, garment to knees, and hands at the side, faces left with three columns of text:

> (1) *sꜣ.f mry n st ib.f iry-pꜥt ḥꜣty-ꜥ sm ḫrp šndyt nb* (2) *rḫ st rd.f hr nmtt mḏd wꜣwt n(t) smn-*(3)*-ḫ sw Kꜣ-iwnw-m-sꜣ.f ms n Sꜣ-nḫt*
>
> (1) His beloved son of the place of his heart, the count and hereditary prince, *sem*-priest, controller of every kilt, (2) who knows the place of his foot, serene of steps, who adheres to the paths of the one who has advanced (3) him, Ka-iunu-em-saf, born of Si-Nakht(?).

For reading of the name I am again indebted to Detlef Franke.

C 6 (FIG. 63, PL. 8A)

UM 69–29–135. Expedition 69.214
RP South Wall
Limestone
Top part 10 x 6 x 3.5 cm; lower part 14 x 14 x 3.5 cm
"Window Stela." Illustrated and translated by O'Connor, *Expedition* 21, no. 2 (1979), p. 49.
Texts: right side: "Ukh-hotep, vindicated." Center: "For the ka of Senefer-Ptah." Left column in two parts: (1) "...... for Osiris by; (2) [viewing] the beauties of Wepwawet [on the] first [procession] by (1/2) the honored Ukh-hotep born of Hetepe(t)."
For the names, see Ranke, *PN* 1, pp. 315.14; 84.9. Since the name Ukh-hotep is associated with Meir, one can assume that this *ex-voto* from a memorial chapel was dedicated and built by a resident of Upper Egyptian Nome XIV.
UM storage photograph 16–26.

C 7 (FIG. 64, PL. 8B)

UM 69–29–147. Expedition 69.216
RP
Limestone
16 x 10 x 8
Basin or statuette niche 2 cm deep, with rounded end. Text is lightly incised with hieroglyphs painted blue:

> An offering which the king gives (to) Osiris, lord of Abydos, that he may grant an invocation offering of bread and beer, cattle, and fowl to the ka of the butler (*wbꜣ*), Ukh-hotep, born of Jt, the vindicated.

This is also likely an *ex-voto* from a citizen of Upper Egyptian Nome XIV.
UM storage photograph 16–22.

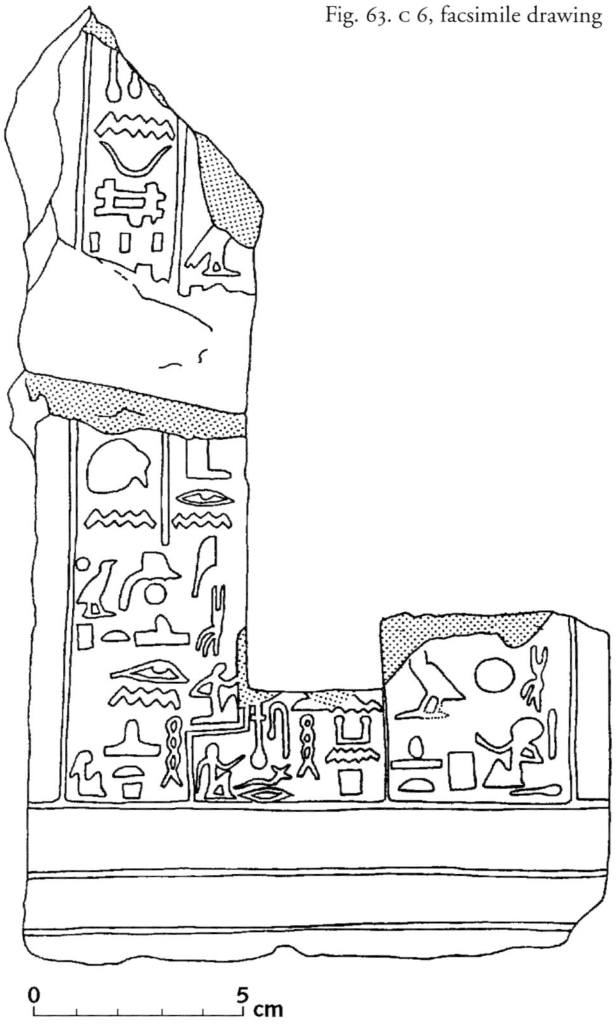

Fig. 63. C 6, facsimile drawing

Fig. 64. c 7, facsimile drawing

c 8 (fig. 65, pl. 8c)

UM 69–29–122. Expedition 69.150
Close to north side, T 12 in loose, sandy soil ca. 60 cm below surviving top of G 6 E
Limestone
18 x 12 x 5 cm
Seated dedicant with three lines of text above:

> (1) The honored Inyotef, (2) his mother Sit-Neb (or Sit-Ka), (3) his beloved friend (*ḫnms*) Meket(?).

On the left, six lines of text:

> (1) His father (2) Henu, (3) his brother Senwosret, (4) his brother Ameny, (5) his beloved wife *Ỉtꜣ* the vindicated.

UM storage photograph 16–22.

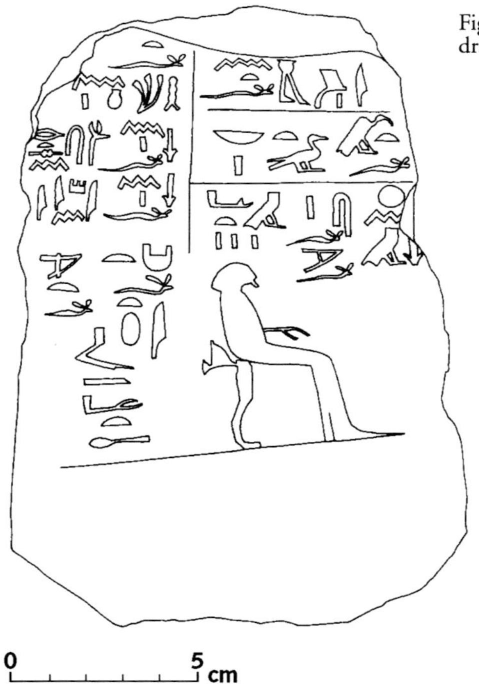

Fig. 65. c 8, facsimile drawing

c 9 (fig. 66)

Cairo JdE 91244. Expedition 69.211
RP
Limestone
20 x 15 x 5 cm
Small, crude stela with incised scene and cursive text. In lunate, standing figure of man facing right, holding lotus to his face with his left hand. To the right, two columns of text, my reading very uncertain: *Ỉtf-ꜥꜣ ir.n Ḥsw,* "Yotef-aa, engendered by Hesu." To the left, two columns of text: "Nakhti, the vindicated, possessor of an honored state." Below, four lines of text, right to left:

> An offering which the king gives (to) Osiris, lord of Djedu, the great god, lord of Abydos, may Anubis, he who is upon his mountain, grant an offering, that he may give an invocation offering of bread, beer, cattle fowl, … for the ka of the honored one *Ỉtf-ꜥꜣ*(?), the vindicated.

For the name, see *PN* 1, p. 50.16.

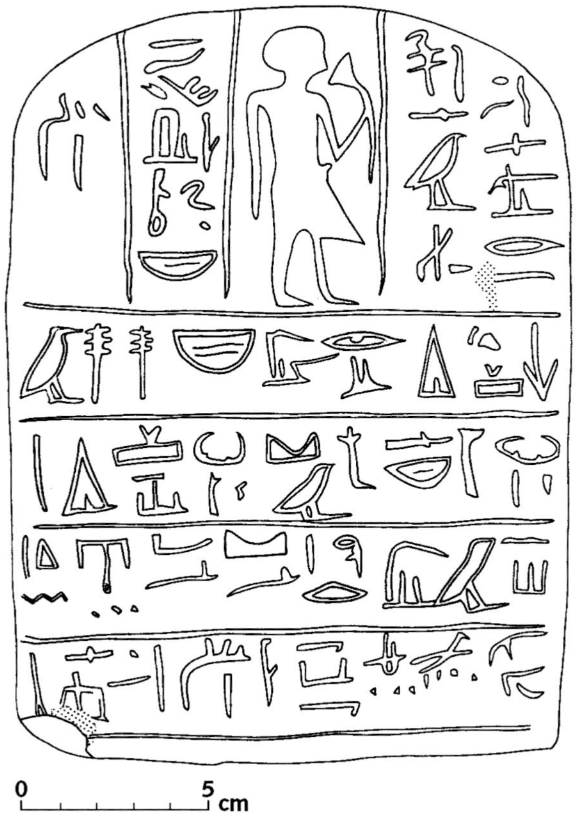

Fig. 66. c 9, facsimile drawing

c 10 (fig. 67, pl. 8d)

UM 69–29–56. Expedition 69.203
RP, fill over area between memorial chapels F 6–14 and F 5–11
Limestone
43 x 24 x 14 cm
Lower section of stela. In the upper register, partly preserved, three standing men in short kilts ending above the knees face left toward

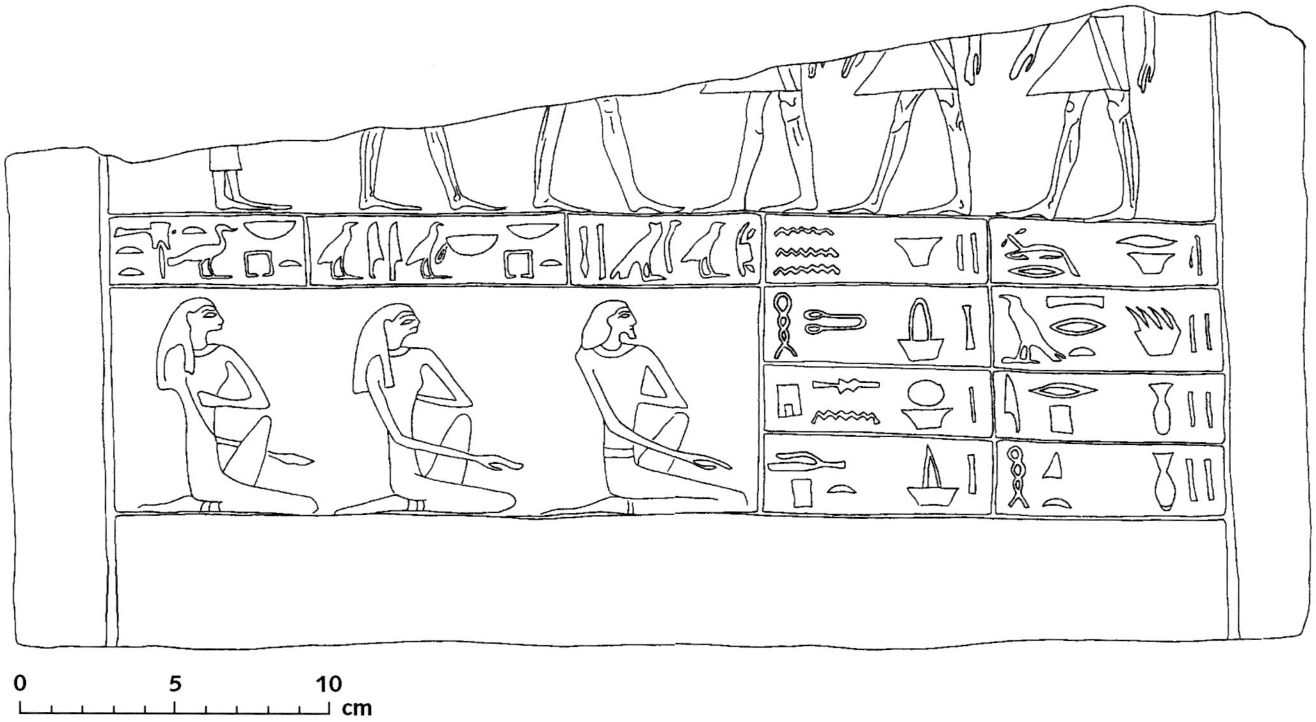

Fig. 67. C 10, facsimile drawing

two standing men followed by a woman, all facing right. Where preserved, the hands are at the sides. The leg musculature is prominently indicated. In the register below, three seated figures, a man and two women, face to the right toward an offering list. The man has a neck-length wig, broad collar, and beard; the women have tripartite wigs and broad collars. All three sit with right leg below the hip and left knee raised, right hand extended. The three are labeled:

(1) The henchman Aam (*šmsw ꜥꜣm*), the vindicated, (2) the lady Kuyu (*Kwyw*), (3) the lady Sit-Satet.

The offering list, in two columns of four items each, reads:

(1) Water, 2 bowls, (2) *ḥṯ* bread, 1 basket, (3) *psn* cake, 1 basket, (4) a taste (*dpt*), 1 unit, (5) a meal (*ỉwꜥ-rꜣ*), 1 unit, (6) a roast (*ꜣšrt*), 2 units, (7) wine (*ỉrp*), 2 jars, (8) beer (*ḥnqt*), 2 jars.

UM storage photograph 22–35.

C 11 (FIG. 68)

Cairo JdE 91283 (misc.). Expedition 69.191
RP
Limestone, smoothed surface
12 x 12 x 4.5 cm
Horizontal line and three vertical columns in black ink with texts:

šmsw Mnw-nḫt-m-ḥꜣt, Ỉṯtt (fem.), *Ms* (fem.), *Sꜣt-Ḥwt-Ḥr* (fem.), *nbt ỉmꜣḫ*

C 12 (FIG. 69)

Cairo JdE 91249. Expedition 69.151 <945>
Ca. 75 cm local west of T 14, loose spoil 1 m below top of temple
Limestone
22 x 15 x 5.5 cm
Small stela, cursive hieroglyphs in black ink, in two pieces.
A. Lunate with standing male facing right and column of text continuing with horizontal line retrograde: *Ḫmnw-nḫt ỉr.n Sꜣt-kꜣ.*

B. Nine lines of text:

(1) *Ḫnmw-ḥtp ỉr.n Rn.f ꜥnḫ*
(2) *Rn.f ꜥnḫ* (fem.) *ỉrt.n Ỉp* (fem.) *mꜣꜥ-ḫrw*
(3) *. . . t* (fem.) *ỉr. . . .*
(4) *Sꜣt-kꜣ* (fem.) *ỉrt.n Rn.f-ꜥnḫ* (fem.) *mꜣꜥ-ḫrw*
(5) *Nḫt-ꜥnḫ* (m.) *ỉrt*(?)*.n Tti* (fem.) *mꜣꜥ-ḫrw*
(6) *Ỉt-ꜥꜣ* (m.) *ỉr.n Ỉd* (fem.) *mꜣꜥ-ḫrw*
(7) *Ḫmnw-nḫt* (m.) *ỉr.n Ỉdw* (fem.) *mꜣꜥ-ḫrw*
(8) *Ḫmnw-nḫt* (m.) *ỉr n Ṯtỉ* (fem.) *mꜣꜥ-ḫrw*
(9) *Ḥr-ḥtp* (m.) *ỉr.n Ỉnỉ* (fem.) *mꜣꜥ-ḫrw*

C. Vertical column on left continued by shorter vertical column:

(1) *Ḥtp dỉ nsw Ws-ỉr nb Ḏdw nṯr ꜥꜣ nb ꜣbḏw dỉ.f pr(t)-ḫrw (tꜣ ḥnqt . . .) ỉmꜣḫ Ḫnmw-nḫt* (m.) (2) *ỉr.n Sꜣt-kꜣ* (fem.) *mꜣꜥ-ḫrw*

Fig. 68. C 11, facsimile drawing

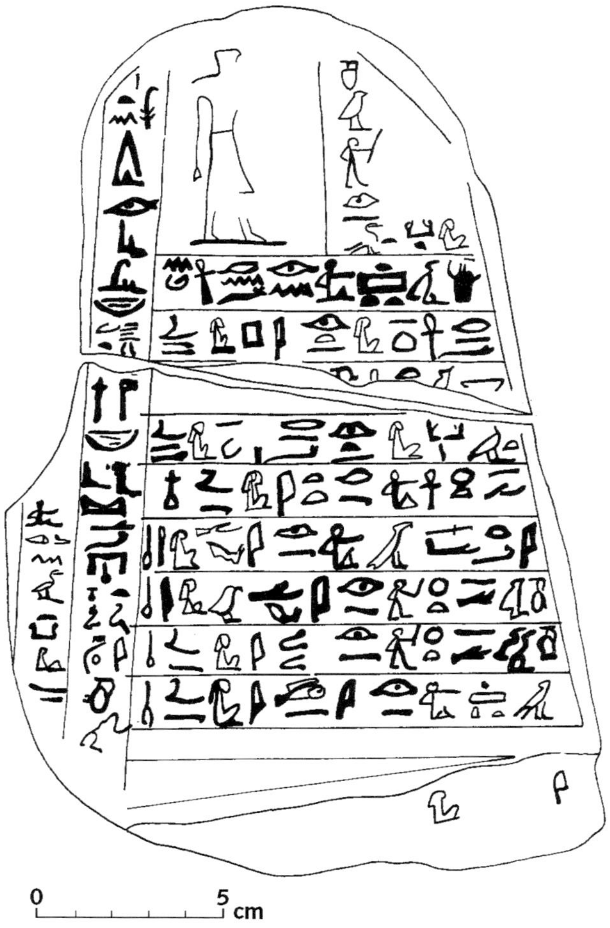

Fig. 69. C 12, facsimile drawing

C 13 (FIG. 70)

Cairo or Abydos storeroom

Janet Richards Survey 1988, Square 725/940

Found *in situ* in a small mud brick chapel next to a pair of tomb shafts, hence probably part of a tomb rather than a memorial chapel.

Limestone

19.5 x 21 x ? (not recorded) cm

Miniature stela with round top, beveled edge on bottom and left side of enclosed area. Four lines of text continued by four columns, scene, and a line continuing text below scene. The text of the first line is written in a cartouche with the ruler's prenomen in a vertical cartouche within the horizontal cartouche. Incised hieroglyphs, some with traces of black paint. Copied by Stephen Harvey, inked by Mark Stone.

> (1) *ʿnḫ Ḥr ʿnḫ mswt ʿnḫ nsw bity Ḫpr-kꜣ-Rʿ ʿnḫ ḏt*
> (2) *di nsw* (sic) *Gb Ws-ir nb Ddw*
> (3) *Ḫnty-imntyw nb ꜣbḏw Wp-wꜣwt Tꜣ-ḏsr di.f*
> (4) *prt-ḫrw tꜣ ḥnqt ḫꜣ.k kꜣ ꜣpdw ḫꜣ.k šš mnḫt m snṯr qbḥw*
> (5) *ḥsy n nb* (6) *.f mꜣʿ irr ḥs* (7) *sst.f m ḫrt-hrw rʿ nb* (8) *imꜣḫ Ddw*
> (9) *ms n Rn.s ʿnḫ*

(1) (Long) live the Horus Ankh-mesut, (long) live the king of the southland and northland, Kheperkare (Sesostris I), living forever. (2) <An offering> which the king gives to Geb, Osiris, lord of Djedu, (3) Khenty-amentiu, lord of Abydos, Wepwawet <lord of> the necropolis, that he (sic) may grant (4) a voice offering of bread and beer, your thousand cattle and fowl, your thousand alabaster and linen comprising incense and libations, (5) one truly praised of his (6) lord, who performs what he (7) praises throughout the course of every day, (8) the honored Dedu (9) born to Renesankh.

On the left, a seated figure faces right to an offering table heaped with offerings.

The text is incised with several orthographical errors. No title or profession is cited for the donor. Assuming the stela dates from the reign of Sesostris I, the orthographical details are of interest.

C 14 (FIG. 71)

Cairo JdE 91248. Expedition 69.219 <1013>

RP

Limestone

29.5 x 21 x 6 cm

Round-top stela with incised(?) hieroglyphs, four lines of text and three registers below with figures.

A.

> (1) *Ḥtp di nsw Ws-ir* (2) *Ḫnty-imntyw, nb ꜣbḏw,* (3) *di.f pr(t)-ḫrw tꜣ ḥnqt kꜣw ꜣpdw šš mnḫt snṯr* (4) *n kꜣ n imꜣḫ ʿnḫw nb imꜣḫ Sꜣt-Ḥmnw mꜣʿ-ḫrw*

B. Bearded male seated on chair at left facing an offering table and three women seated on ground facing left toward him. The three women are captioned:

> (1) *snt.f Ḏw mꜣʿt-ḫrw* (2) *snt.f Qdmy mꜣʿt-ḫrw* (3) *snt.f Itꜣ mꜣʿt-ḫrw*

Fig. 70. c 13, facsimile drawing

C. Four women seated on ground, facing right, right hand on lap, left hand crossed over breast, captioned:

(1) *Bbwt* (2) *snt.f Sḏmy* (3) *sn[t.f . . .] mꜣꜥ[t]-ḫrw* (4) *snt.f Ḥnwt*

D. Four figures seated on ground with same arm positions, facing right, a male followed by a female and two males, captioned:

(1) *imy-rꜣ pr Sꜣ-Ip* (2) *snt.f Wꜣḏt* (3) *sn.f Imny* (4) *sn.f Sḥtp-ib-Rꜥ*

The reading of the first name seems to be thus, although alternatively one might read *imy-rꜣ pr wr Ip*, and the second name *Ḥḏt*.

C 15 (fig. 72)

Cairo JdE 91220. Expedition 69.205 <999>
RP
Limestone
65 x 49 x 22 cm

Offering table with offering foods and containers in raised relief, channel for liquid, and incised hieroglyphs along the border. Reading from left to right, down side, and continuing right to left below:

Ḥtp di nsw Inpw tpy ḏw.f imy wt nb tꜣ ḏsr di.f mw ḥnqt sntr mrḥt ddt pt qmꜣ tꜣ n imꜣḫ ḫr nṯr ꜥꜣ nb pt imy-rꜣ tꜣ mḥw Nḫti ir(?) *n Ḫntt-bꜣw*

May the king give an offering to Anubis, he who is on his mountain, who is in the place of bandaging, lord of the necropolis, that he may grant water, beer, incense, oil, that which the sky gives and the earth creates, to the one honored before the great god, lord of the sky, the overseer of the northland Nakhti born(?) of Khentet-bau.

Reading from right to left, down side, and continuing to right:

Ḥtp di nsw Wsir nb Ḏdw Ḫnty-imntyw nb ꜣbḏw Wp-wꜣwt nb ꜣbḏw di.f prt-ḫrw tꜣ ḥnqt kꜣw ꜣpdw šs mnḫt ḫt nb nfrt wꜥbt ꜥnḫt nṯr im n kꜣ n imꜣḫ imy-rꜣ tꜣ mḥw Nḫt nb imꜣḫ

Fig. 71. c 14, facsimile drawing

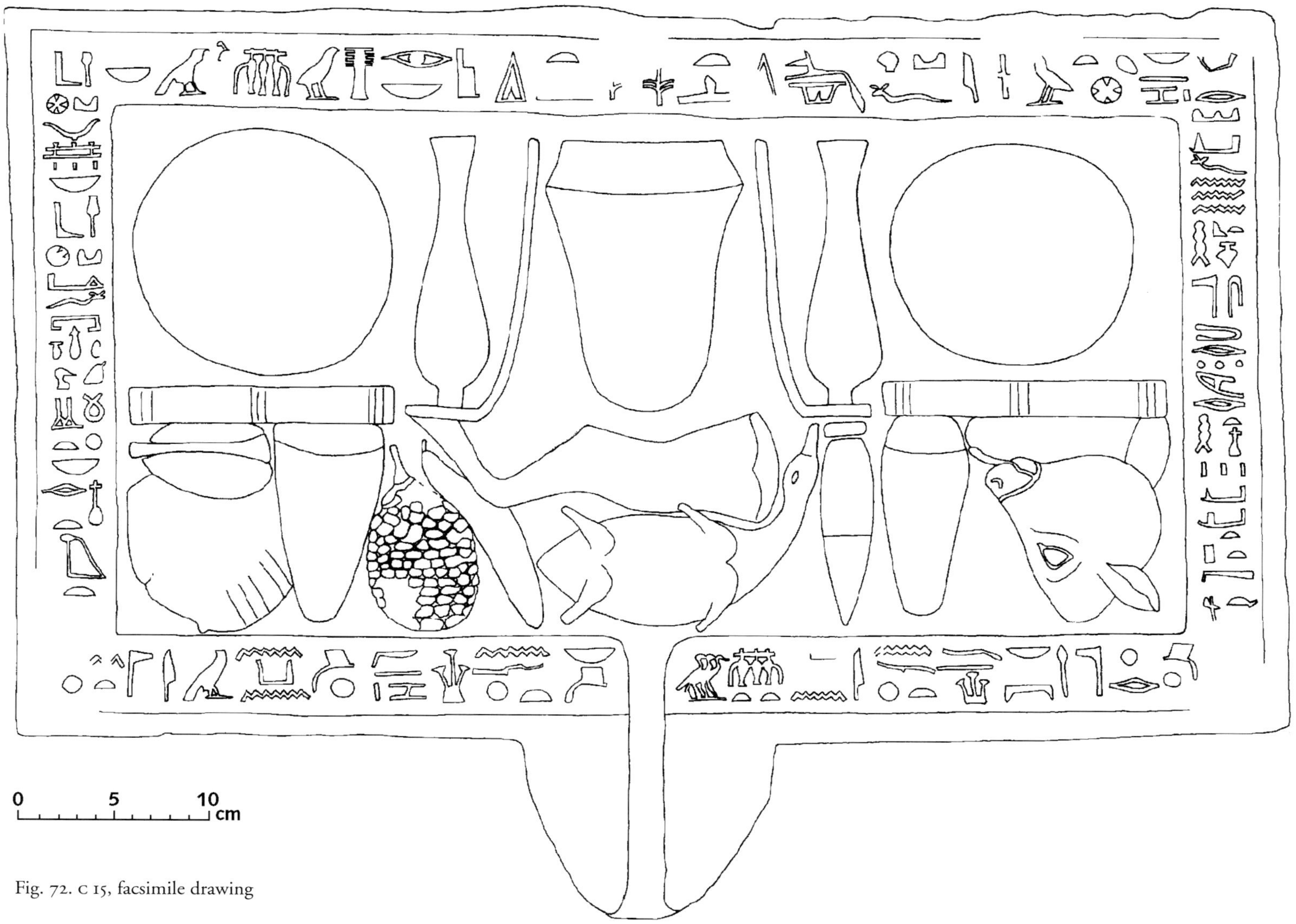

Fig. 72. C 15, facsimile drawing

> May the king give an offering to Osiris, foremost of the westerners, lord of Abydos, and Wepwawet, lord of Abydos, that he may grant a voice invocation of bread, beer, cattle, fowl, alabaster and linen, and every good and pure thing on which the god lives, to the ka of the honored one, the overseer of the northland Nakht, possessor of honor.

The title *ỉmy-rȝ tȝ mḥw* is frequent at the Abydos North necropolis/memorial chapel district: cf. CCG 20090, 20135, 20562, 20592 (owner), and 20723. It does not seem to be one of major importance. The name *Ḫntt-bȝw* is attested in *PN* 2, p. 310.22 (cf. *PN* 1, p. 292.23) and in *Sȝt-Ḫntt-bȝw* in CCG 20734.

C 16 (FIG. 73)

Cairo JdE 91242. Expedition 69.218 <1012>
RP
Limestone
22 x 16 x 5 cm

Stela with incised scene and hieroglyphs with additions (or outlines) of both in ink, very crude workmanship. Round-top stela with winged sun disk in lunate. Below this a line of hieroglyphs:

> *Ḥtp dỉ nsw Ỉnpw tpy ḏw.f ỉmy wt ỉmȝḫw Np*(??)
>
> An offering which the king gives and Anubis, he who is on his mound (to) the honored Nep(??).

The last name is more than doubtful. Below this line of text is a crudely carved scene. On the left a woman stands facing right holding a flower in her left hand, dressed in a close-fitting garment extending just above her ankles, with the caption: *ỉmȝḫ Ddt-Sbk,* "the honored one, Dedet-Sobek." Facing her is a male in a garment reaching just above his knees, seated on a chair with low backrest cushion and floral terminal; his right hand is crossed over his chest and the left extended above his lap. Between the two figures is a table of offering breads and various offerings, including an ox head and haunch of meat, as well as several objects just in front and above the male figure, among them a jar and a trussed duck. To the rear of the seated male is the vertical label, curiously facing right: *Wn ỉr.n Ddt,* "Wen, born of Dedet." Below this register is another with figures and hieroglyphs, some of the latter in ink. All figures face left. The first, a male with kilt holding a staff, the second probably similar the third not well represented, the fourth probably a male on a lower level, possibly a child, and the last a woman in a long dress holding her right hand up. The first is captioned in ink as *imꜣḫ Nḫt*(?), "the honored one, Nakht(?)." To the rear of this figure is female name *Ddt* written vertically in ink facing right. The caption above the larger scale figure of a woman on the extreme right reads *imꜣḫ Ddt,* "the honored one Dedet." The child(?) in front of her has the caption *imꜣḫ Ỉpi*(?). The other ink signs in the register cannot be made out satisfactorily. At the base of this small stela are three figures in the center seated on the ground facing left toward an offering table of loaves with a few of the traditional offerings to the right and left, including a haunch, an ox head, and a trussed duck. Above the offering table is the ink text *imꜣḫ* .... Beneath the feet of the woman and child and to the right of the three seated figures are several incised hieroglyphs facing right: *rtw* or *ỉr tw,* and a group in ink.

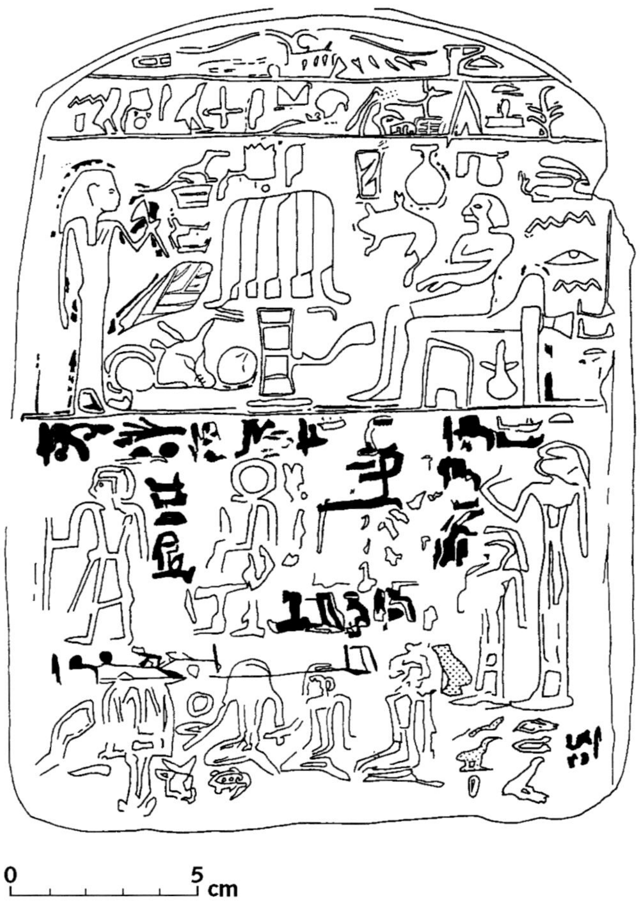

Fig. 73. C 16, facsimile drawing

C 17 (FIG. 74)

Cairo JdE (included with 91283). Expedition 69.193
RP in chapel of F 6–23
Limestone
12 x 9 x 2.5 cm
Small stela with five lines of text in hieratic, the first: *n kꜣ n imꜣḫyt,* the following four only partly decipherable.

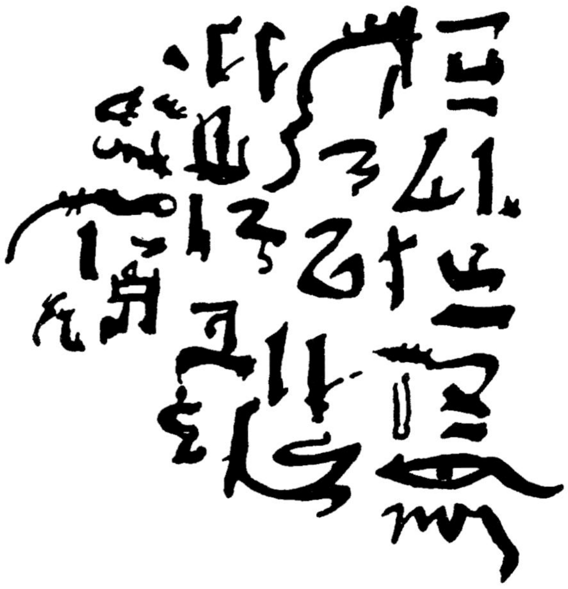

Fig. 74. C 17, facsimile drawing

C 18 (FIG. 75)

Cairo JdE 91247. Expedition 69.196 <990>
East corner of court of T. 14
Limestone
19 x 14 x 6 cm
Stela with incised figures and hieroglyphs with traces of color: line of text at top in blue on yellow ground; male figures, including child and text in top register red; child in middle register red; last figure in lower register red. The top has been slightly rounded and the sides have a pattern of rectangles, some painted red. The horizontal line in the lunate reads right to left:

> *Ḥtp di nsw Ws-ỉr nb imntt nfr(t) di.f pr(t) ḫrw tꜣ ḥnqt kꜣ n imꜣḫ Ỉmn-ḥꜣt*
>
> An offering which the king gives (to) Osiris, lord of the beautiful west, that he may grant an invocation offering of bread, beer, and oxen to the honored one, Amenhat.

Beneath the lunate are three registers:

A) A man and woman on the left face right. He wears a short kilt, short shoulder-length wig, broad collar, and carries a staff in his left hand vertically and a scepter in his right hand horizontally. His wife follows him. She wears a long fitting dress with shoulder strap, tripartite wig, and clasps her husband with her left hand. He is captioned: *imꜣḫ Ỉmn-m-ḥꜣt,* she *ḥmt.f Sꜣt-?,* "the honored one Amenemhat and his wife, Sit-?." Facing them on the right is a male figure presenting fowl. He wears a short kilt, broad collar necklace, and short hair. At his feet facing him to the right is a small boy, left hand to mouth, seated on the ground. The figures are respectively captioned: *sꜣ.f mr Ỉmn-ḥtp and sꜣ.f Ỉmn-ḥꜣt,* "his beloved son Amenhotep" and "his son Amenhat."

B) Four similarly clad standing women face to the right. Each wears a long tight-fitting garment, a tripartite wig, and the first two show indications of shoulder straps. All have arms at the sides, with a small boy held by the hand by the first woman and touched on the shoulder by the second woman. The four women are respectively captioned:

> (1) *nbt pr Sꜣt-Ḥwt-Ḥr mꜣꜥt-ḫrw* (2) *sꜣt.f*(?) (3) *sꜣt.f Ỉmnwt*(?) *mꜣꜥt ḫrw* (4) *sꜣt.f Ḥtpi-ꜥnḫ mꜣꜥt ḫrw* (5) *sꜣ.f Dd-?*
>
> (1) The lady Sit-Hathor, vindicated, (2) his daughter(?) ..., (3) his daughter Amenut(?), vindicated, (4) his daughter Hetepi-ankh, vindicated, (5) his son Ded, vindicated(?).

C) The third register consists of six standing figures, somewhat smaller, facing right, wearing the long tight-fitting dress (except perhaps for the first, third, and sixth), The last is perhaps a male. Traces of hieroglyphs occur with all, but the only certain readings are the designation *sꜣt.f,* "his daughter," for the third, fourth, and fifth figures.

C 19 (FIG. 76)

UM 69–29–128. Expedition 69.195
RP T. 28, found *in situ*
Limestone
24 x 15 x 7 cm

Small round top stela in black ink, very faded. Four lines of text with offering formula, the second line ending in *nṯr ꜥꜣ nb ꜣbḏw,* the third line ending in *n kꜣ n ỉmꜣḫ,* and the fourth line with hieroglyphs of which it is difficult to make sense, possibly a name with the elements *qꜣ* and *sbk* (there is also the crocodile god *ỉq*). The scene below has a brown painted background and consists of a standing man to the left facing right with the body painted a dark red, the kilt white; his left arm is crossed over his chest. He is faced by another male figure painted light red with a white kilt, on a smaller scale. Between these figures is a smaller ink figure or determinative of a woman. The smaller male is captioned *sn.f Nb-bḥw nb ỉmꜣḫ,* "his brother Neb-behu, possessor of an honored state," although the name might be read as *Kbḥw.* Neither name is attested in *PN.* Above the female is an ink text difficult to read, and possibly the label for the main figure, although his name probably occurred in the fourth horizontal line above.
UM storage photograph 17–4.

Fig. 75. C 18, facsimile drawing

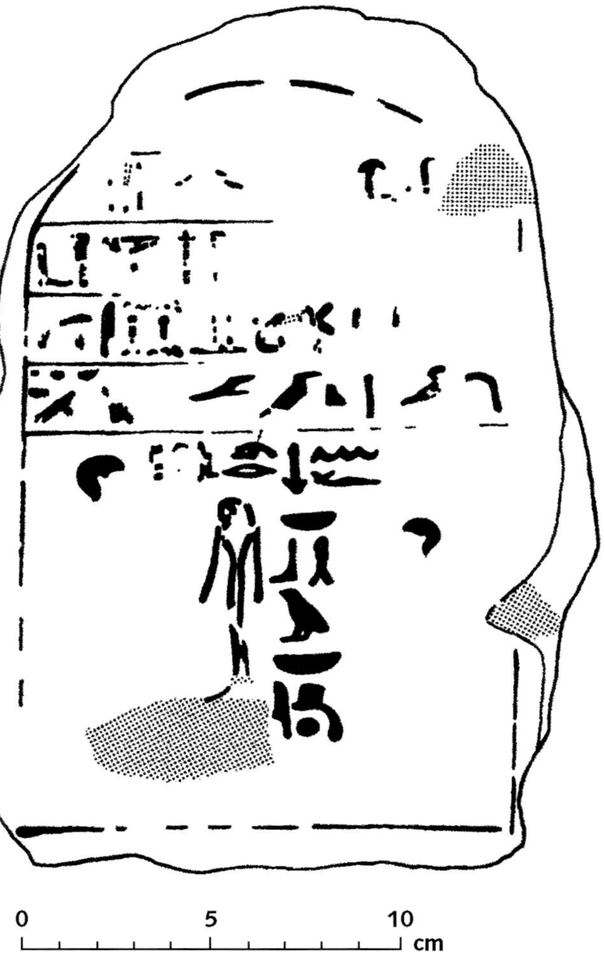

Fig. 76. C 19, facsimile drawing

C 20 (FIG. 77)
UM 69–29–215. Expedition 69.103
RP H 7 (N)
Limestone
28 x 19 x 9 cm
Three columns of text in ink, cursive hieroglyphs.

(1) *ỉrt.n sꜣ.f Sꜣ-Sꜣtt*(?) (2) *ḥmt.f-Ỉꜥw* (3) *wnm*(?) …*-ḥtp*

UM storage photograph 19–24.

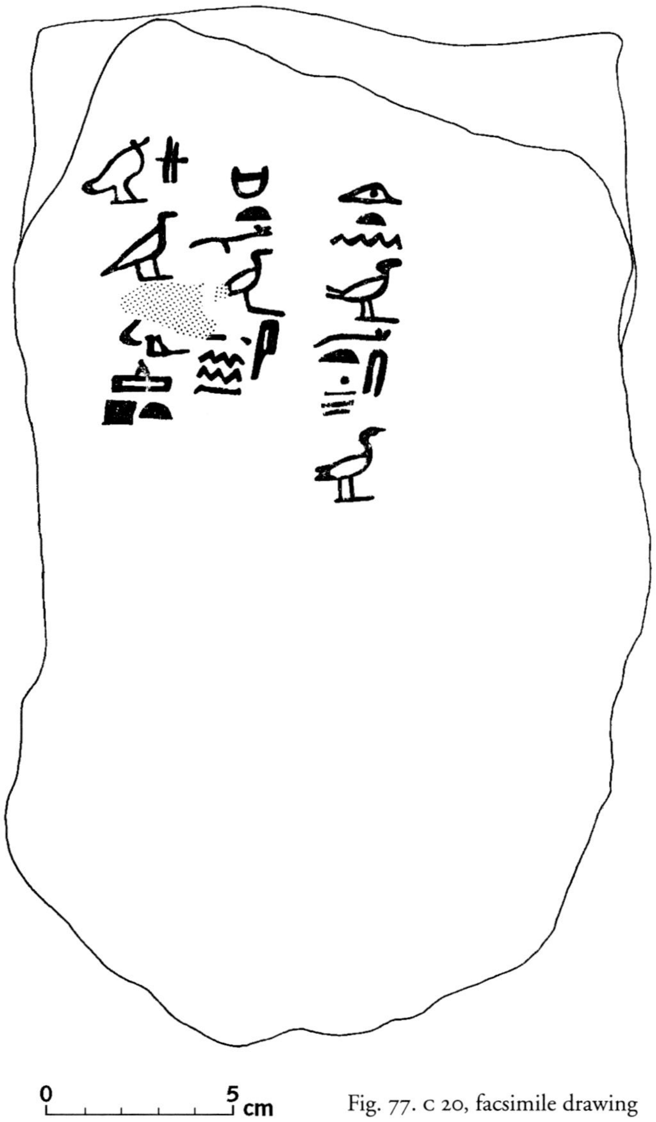

Fig. 77. C 20, facsimile drawing

C 21 (FIG. 78, PL. 9A)
UM 69–29–180. Expedition 69.169
RP rear
Limestone
9 x 5.5 x 5 cm
Fragment of stela with three lines of text, including the cartouche, incised:

(1) … *bity Sḫm-Rꜥ*-… (2) … *nsw* … (3) ….

The sign following *Sḫm* is a vertical difficult to identify. Perhaps this is Sekhem-Re-Wadj-khau, Sekhem-Re-Wah-Khau, or Sekhem-Re-semen-tawy of Dynasty 17 (see J. von Beckerath, *Handbuch der ägyptischen Königsnamen,* MÄS 20 [Berlin, 1984]).
UM storage photograph 17–15.

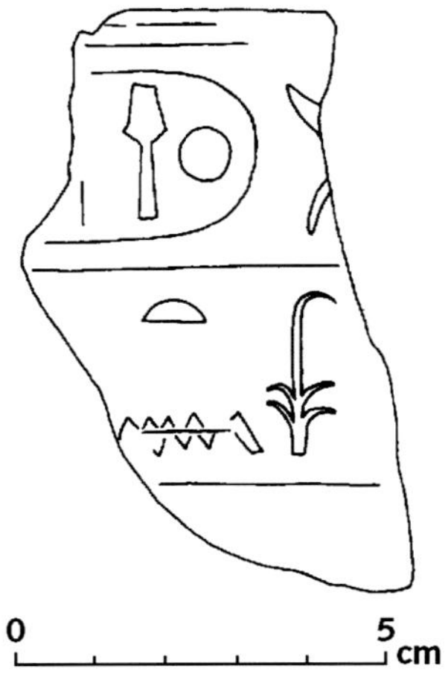

Fig. 78. C 21, facsimile drawing

C 22 (FIG. 79)
Cairo JdE 91279. Expedition 67.268
RP 6 F(E) 31
Limestone
15 x 12 x 4 cm
Trial piece, double sided, incised. One side with *nb* sign and *nṯr*(?) sign in field and two columns of text in part:

(1) *sš qdt Nḫt* … (2) *sꜣ sš qd(t)* ….

(1) The outline scribe Nakht … (2) son of the outline scribe ….

The second side bears a very finely carved head and shoulders of a figure with two "gold of honor" strands, earring, but face missing (not drawn or photographed). Perhaps drawn and carved by the outline scribe Nakht cited on the other side.
Field photograph A '67 OP 70

C 23 (FIG. 80)
Cairo JdE 91279. Expedition 68.76
RP 4 E (W)
Limestone
13.5 x 15 x 3.5 cm
Small, crude fragment of stela in two registers, the man in the upper register left painted red, the two women on the right in the lower register painted yellow, the incised text green, wigs black.
Upper register: Two seated figures face each other with an offering tray and offerings between them, the figure on the left with kilt male, the figure on the right with long garment female.
Lower register: On the right two women face each other holding lotus flowers. The one on the right standing(?) and the one on the left seated on the ground, a small offering tray and offerings between them. Each holds a lotus flower. Following the woman seated on the ground is another seated on the ground holding a lotus flower, also with a small offering tray and offerings in front of her. The line of

text above the figures reads: *nbt pr Ỉki mꜣꜥt ḫrw, nbt r s ......* , and a painted text by the third figure reads *sꜣt.s Ḏd.*

Fig. 79. c 22, facsimile drawing

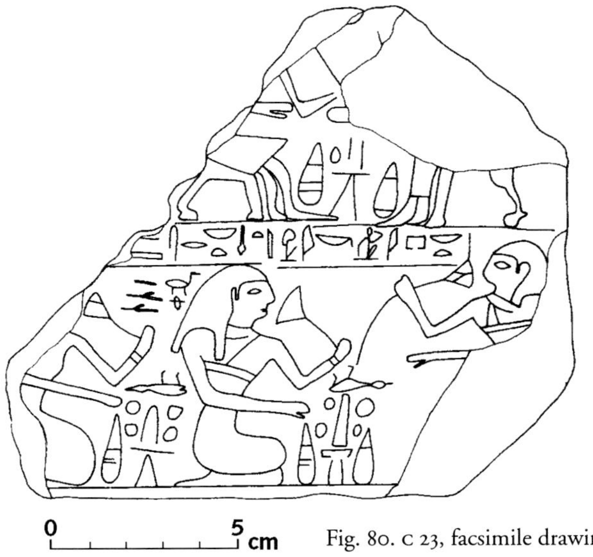

Fig. 80. c 23, facsimile drawing

C 24 (fig. 81, pl. 9b)

UM 69–29–149. Expedition 67.3
RP 4 C(W) 3
Fragment of red granite
13 x 9 x 3.5 cm
Cartouche of *Sn[ws]rt.*
UM storage photograph 16–17.

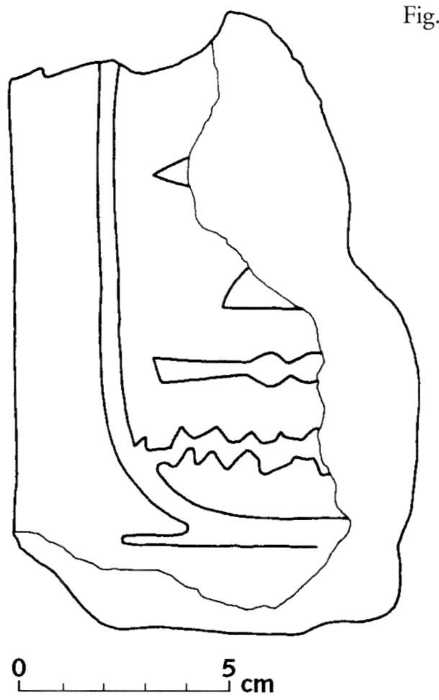

Fig. 81. c 24, facsimile drawing

C 25 (fig. 82, pl. 9c)

UM 69–29–141. Expedition 67.535
RP 7 F(E) 65
Limestone
15 x 17 x 4.5 cm
Fragment of crude offering table with basins and channel. On the right the text: *[i]n snt.f sꜥnḫ rn.f Sꜣt-Ttrt*(?). On the left the text: ... *.f sꜥnḫ rn.f Sꜣt-Ttrt*(?).
UM storage photograph 16–30.

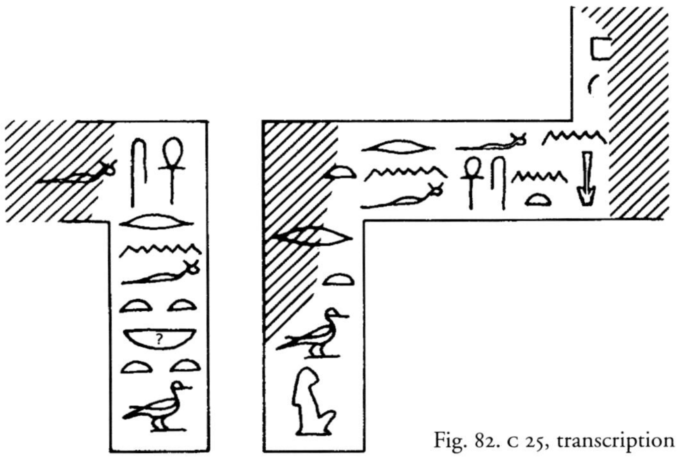

Fig. 82. c 25, transcription

C 26 (fig. 83, pl. 9d)

UM 69–29–166. Expedition 67.549
RP 7 G(E) 3
Limestone
12.5 x 18 x 6.5 cm
Crude stela fragment with two standing figures facing right, a man(?) on the left and a woman on the right. Both have left hands crossed

over the chest. A vertical text in front of the first figure provides the end(?) of her name … *ḥki, mꜣʿt ḫrw,* with traces of a column of text to the right facing left. In front of the second figure is the text: *snt.f nbt pr Kki, mꜣʿt ḫrw.*
UM storage photograph 17–26.

C 27 (FIG. 84, PL. 9E)

UM 69–29–114. Expedition 69.24
RP H 7 (W)
Limestone
15 x 7.5 x 4.5 cm
Fragment of stela with two lines of text incised. Middle Kingdom?

(1) … *nfr-ḥtp* (2) …*-snb mꜣʿ-ḫrw*

UM storage photograph 16–7.

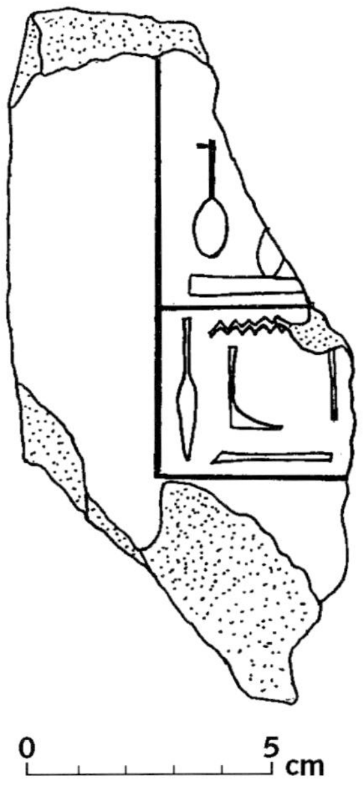

Fig. 84. C 27, facsimile drawing

C 28 (FIG. 85, PL. 9F)

UM 69–29–172. Expedition 68.11
RP 7C (S)
Limestone
10 x 7 x 2.7 cm
Fragment of text in three lines with incised signs.

(1) … *tꜣ* … (2) … *rḫty S[ḥtp?]* … (3) … *.f rn* (or *ỉr n*) ….

UM storage photograph 17–16.

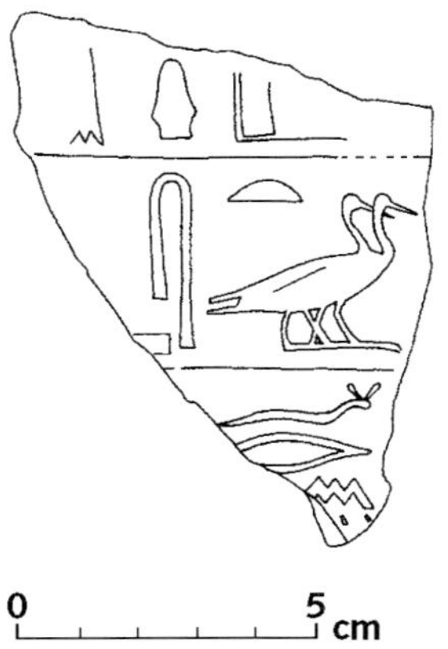

Fig. 85. C 28, facsimile drawing

C 29 (FIG. 86, PLS. 10A–C)

UM 69–29–397. Expedition 69.88
RP H 7(S)
Limestone
10.5 x 8 x 7 cm
Offering table fragment with text on top and side. Top: on right of channel: … *wt ỉr n mwt.f,* "… ut, born of his mother;" left of channel: … *wʿb Ỉti ỉr n Nnt*(?). Front:

(1) *ḥm*(?) *Swkt*(?), (2) *sꜣ.s Ỉrrw,* (3) *sꜣt.s Ỉṯṯ*

UM storage photograph 14–23, 24, 25.

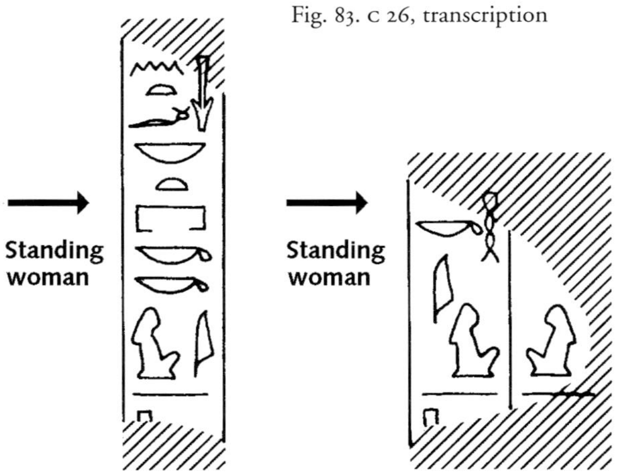

Fig. 83. C 26, transcription

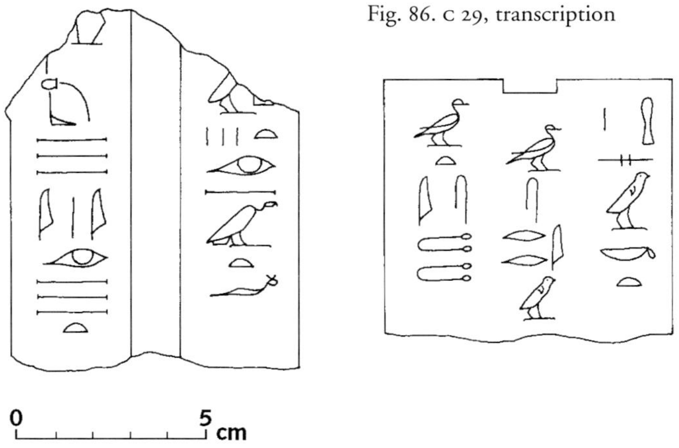

Fig. 86. C 29, transcription

C 30 (FIG. 87, PL. 10D)
UM 69–29–92. Expedition 67.540
RP 7 F(E)
Limestone
17 x 24.5 x 11 cm
Cited in Hölzl, 1990, pp. 156, 158. Fragment of painted stela, male bodies painted red. In upper register a seated pair on a chair with black-and-white markings, facing right, the man with a beard and shoulder-length wig, the woman beside him with her left hand reaching behind his shoulder. He is captioned *Nb.sn,* and she is captioned *ḥmt.f ꜥnḫ.* They sit in front of an offering table with offerings. A smaller figure sits on the ground facing them with right hand extended to the offering stand. He has the caption *Mnw-ḥtpw.* In the register below, four figures face right toward a smaller male figure on the right facing left. The ink text on the right reads: *Ḫw-ꜥnḫ Sbk-ḥtp.* This may apply to the male or perhaps the first element to the first woman and the second to the male. Between the heads of the first and second right facing figures is the caption *Ddt-nht,* and there are traces of names in front of the third and fourth right facing figures.
UM storage photograph 15–30, 31.

C 31 (FIG. 88, PL. 10E)
UM 69–29–138. Expedition 67.90
RP 5 E(W) 21
Limestone
13.5 x 10 x 6 cm
Channel from an offering tray. On the left of the channel the title *ỉmy-rꜣ pr …* with the vertical text to the right: *ms n Sꜣt-Ỉmn.* On the right of the channel the vertical text ending in *Sꜣt …,* perhaps the same name.
UM storage photograph 16–19.

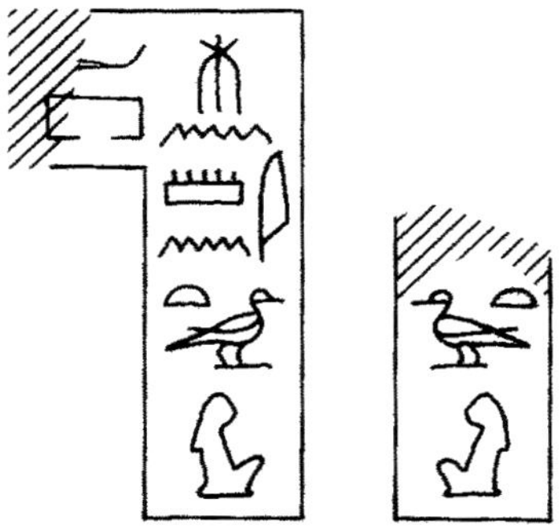
Fig. 88. C 31, transcription

Fig. 87. C 30, facsimile drawing

C 32 (FIG. 89, PL. 11A)

UM 69–29–117. Expedition 69.40
RP Kom Sultan Tr 1A
Limestone
28 x 20.5 x 7.5 cm
Stela fragment, late Middle Kingdom/Second Intermediate Period. Upper register: seated man facing right toward table of offerings with offerings above, short pleated kilt, necklace, short wig, right hand extended toward offering table, left crossed over chest holding napkin. Lower register: similarly seated man facing right toward offering table and offerings above. On the right, two columns of text facing right.

(1) … *[ḫnty(?)] imntyw(?) nb [ꜣ]b[ḏw]*, … *it.*(?)*.f ḥry qnbt Snb*(?) ….

UM storage photograph 17–7.

Fig. 89. C 32, facsimile drawing

C 33 (FIG. 90, PL. 11B)

UM 69–29–103. Expedition 67.676
RP 7 E (N+S)
Limestone
9 x 12 x 4.5 cm
Lower right corner of offering table with text facing right vertically continuing horizontally (?) *Rwḏ-ꜣbḏw*(?) *ir.n* …. The vertical portion is difficult to understand, the horizontal section provides a name for which the suggested reading is *Rwḏ-ꜣbḏw,* not otherwise attested.
UM storage photograph 16–11.

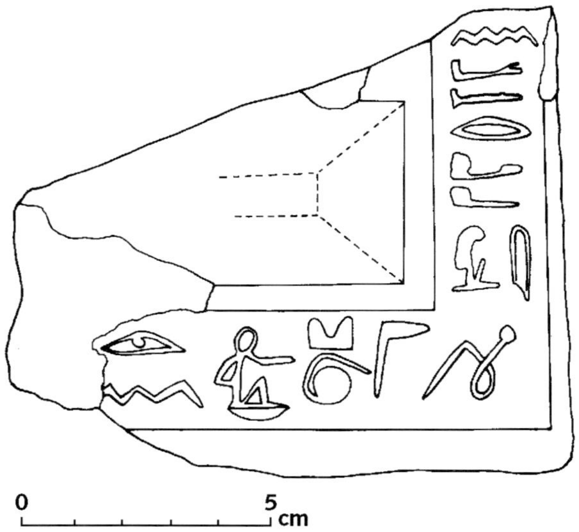

Fig. 90. C 33, facsimile drawing

C 34 (FIG. 91)

Not catalogued, in Abydos storehouse
RP
Limestone stela(?)
ca. 12.5 x 13.9 cm
Recorded by Prof. Silverman in 1985. Traced from photograph slide.

(1) …
(2) boat hieroglyph followed by cartouche
Ḫꜥ-ḫpr-Rꜥ (Sesostris II) right to left
(3) *sꜣt.f Nb-it,* left to right.
(4) …

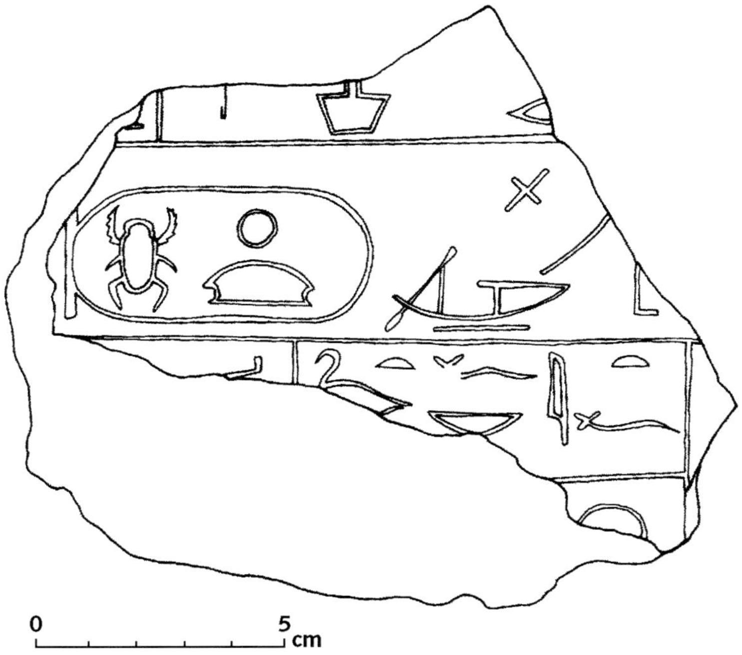

Fig. 91. c 34, facsimile drawing

New Kingdom and Later Objects

In this section inscribed objects that can be assigned to the New Kingdom or later are included. It is difficult to date stelae, etc., to specific dynasties, and some of the objects in this section may well belong to the Third Intermediate Period or later.

NK 1 (figs. 92–94, pls. 11c–12b)

Cairo JdE 91221. Expedition 67.291
RP 7 C (W) 17. Found in dump
Black granite
Height 26 cm; width 19 cm; depth 11 cm
Lower part of seated statue of the adjutant of the entire army Iamu, temp. Amenhotep II. Right arm and hand rests on right thigh; no trace of left arm, so presumably on chest. Inscriptions on both sides and back of seat as well as on lap in roughly pecked out hieroglyphs. Possibly the middle of the back of the seat continued upward into a back support so that the two central columns of text were longer than the others; in this case it might be possible to identify the upper part of the statue in a museum collection. The official is not otherwise known. Elements of the laudatory phraseology are well represented in other texts. The place name *Ỉntsꜣw* is not otherwise attested.

Back of seat:

(1) *Ḥtp di nsw Ỉmn it nṯrw Ḥr nb Ḥr-dw ......*
(2) *šms nsw n rpꜥt ḥꜣty-ꜥ irty nsw ḏrw pḏt psḏt ....*
(3) *... n tn hꜣy m rmṯ ...*
(4) *Ḥr nb Ḥr-dw m Tintsꜣw ......*
(5) *nsw bity ꜥꜣ-ḫprw-Rꜥ di ꜥnḫ r nty ir sp nfr n ....*
(6) *... ḥnꜥ wꜣḥ n.i ḫt(?) ṯni ....*

(1) An offering which the king gives (to) Amun, father of the gods, and Horus, lord of Hor-du .... (2) the follow(ing) of the king, for the hereditary prince and count, the eyes of the king (at) the limits of the nine bows .... (3) ...... kindred among men .... (4) Horus, lord of Hor-du in Tinetsau ... (5) the king of the southland and northland, Aakheperure (Amenhotep II), given life, to the effect: as for a good occasion of .... (6) (town?) together with dedicating property(?) for me every ....

Right side of seat:

(1) *Ḥtp di nsw Ptḥ rsy inb.f nfr ḥr ḥry ...... [Ws-ir]*
(2) *ḫnty imntyw Wnn-nfr nb tꜣ ḏsr nb(?) ......*
(3) *ꜣḫ wsr m ẖryt-nṯr pr ......*
(4) *n kꜣ n rpꜥt ḥꜣty-ꜥ stp n nsw ḫnt tꜣwy ḏ ꜥ(?) ...... [idnw n]*
(5) *mšꜥ mi ḳd.f st rs(?)-tp mꜣꜥ iwty mhwy ......*
(6) *mty n nb.f ir ḥsst n nb tꜣwy tḫ iwsw ......*

(1) An offering which the king gives (to) Ptah-South-of-his-Wall, goodly of countenance, chief of ...... [Osiris] (2) foremost of the westerners, Wenen-nefer, lord of the sacred land, lord(?) of ...... (that they may grant) (3) spirithood and might in the necropolis and that which comes forth .... (4) for the ka of the hereditary prince and count, whom the king chose from out of the two lands, who seeks out (?) ...... [adjutant of] (5) the army in its entirety, truly watchful(?), without negligence ...... (6) who is precise for his master, performing what is praised by the lord of the two lands, plummet of the balance ....

Left side of seat:

(1) *ꜥq ḥsw pr mrw ....*
(2) *n nsw idnw n mšꜥ mi qd[.f] ......*
(3) *Ỉꜣmw mꜣꜥ-ḫrw ms n nbt pr ......*
(4) *iꜣw(?) m pr nsw iw m(?) .... [n]*
(5) *gm.tw wn.i n sp(?) ....*
(6) *r st.i ḥr nmtt(?) nb(.i) ....*

(1) One who enters praised and comes forth loved .... (2) of the king, adjutant of the army in [its] entirety .... (3) Iamu, the vindicated, born to the house mistress .... (4) (who reached?) old age(?) in the king's house .... (5) fault on my account was [not] found; never .... (6) at my station in the journeys(?) of (my) lord(?) ....

Lap:

prr ....
which comes forth ....

Notes on phraseology: For the frequent *pḥ iꜣw,* "to reach old age," see *Urk.* 4, pp. 34.11, 905.5, etc., although the sign read here as *iꜣw* might alternatively read *smsw. Ỉrty nsw,* "the eyes of the king," is a frequent epithet of military men, cf. *Urk.* 4, pp. 968.8, 1015.15; G.T. Martin, *The Memphite Tomb of Horemheb*, (London, 1989), p. 172, but without this specification (*ḏrw pḏt psḏt*). For *stp n nsw ḫnty tꜣwy,* see, ibid., p. 174. For an interesting parallel to *ꜥq ḥsw pr mrw,* see *ꜥq ẖr nfrwt pr ẖr ḥswt ḥr irt sḫrw nw tꜣ pn m wꜥꜥwt,* I.E.S. Edwards, *Hieroglyphic Texts in the British Museum* 8 (London, 1939), pl. 5, ll. 7–8. *Tintsꜣ(w),* not otherwise attested to my knowledge, may be in the Levant or Nubia. Significant, if properly understood, is the existence of a cult of Horus there. For the proposed reading *Ḥr-dw,* suggested by my student, Jennifer Houser, see H. Gauthier, *Dictionnaire géographique des noms contenus dans les textes hiéroglyphiques* 4 (Cairo, 1927), p. 40. The location is Hardi, in Upper Egyptian Nome XVI or XVII. The sign with the *bik* falcon  is attested in this geographical designation, and one expects the term *ḥm-nṯr* to follow, "priest of Horus of Hordu in Tinetsau." A priesthood of this Horus of a foreign land seems somewhat curious. Since this adjutant of the

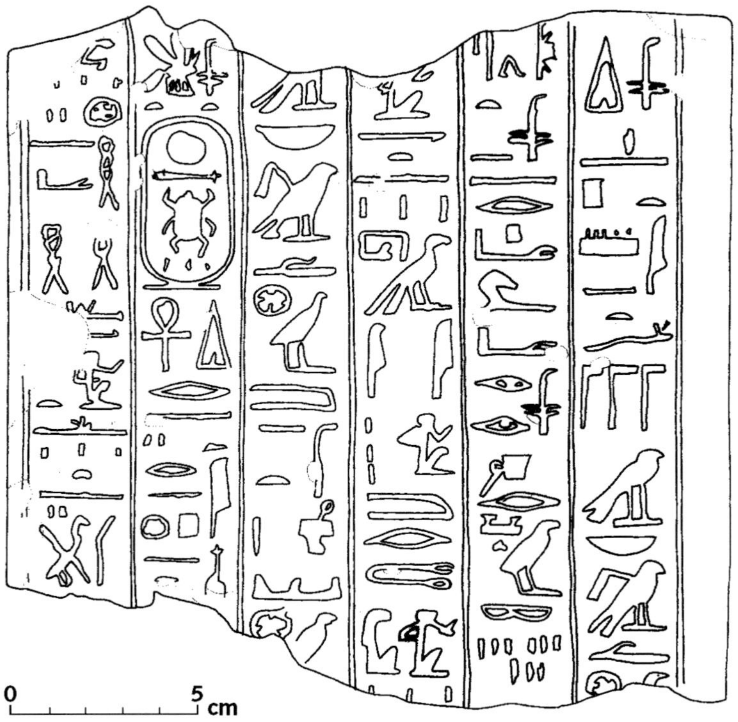

Fig. 92. NK 1 back of seat, facsimile drawing

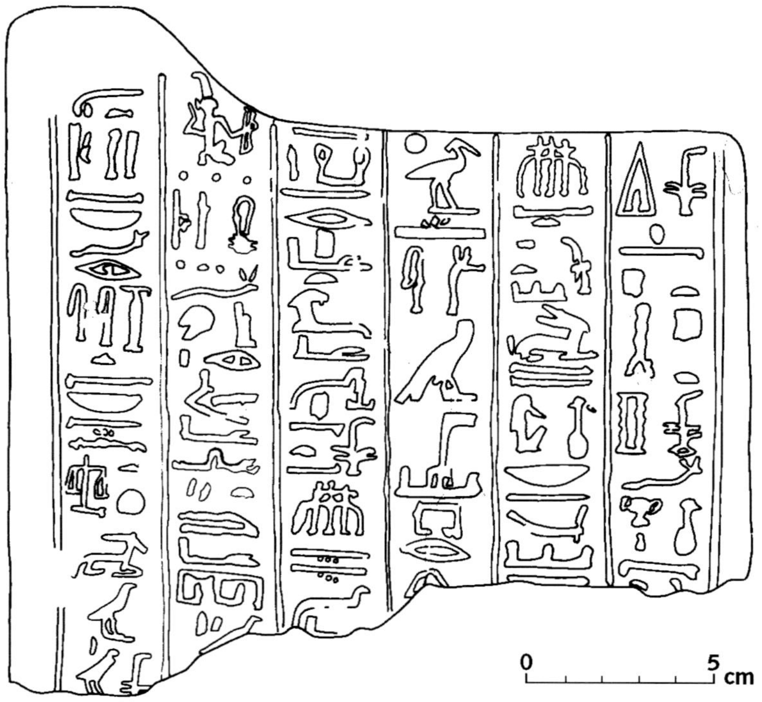

Fig. 93. NK 1 right side of seat, facsimile drawing

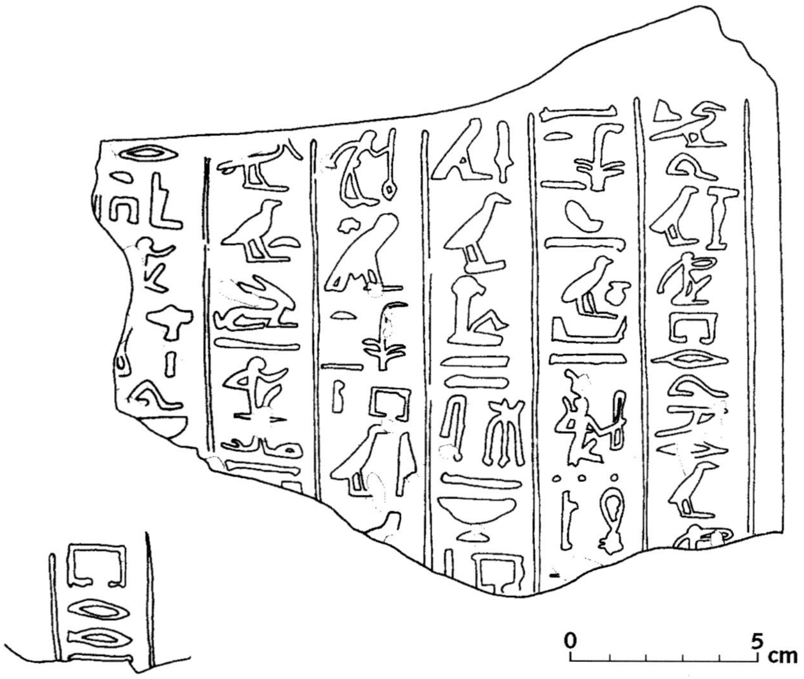

Fig. 94. NK 1 left side of seat and lap text, facsimile drawing

army is apparently not otherwise known, Iamu extends the list of the three or four of these officials of Dynasty 18 recorded by Schulman, *Military Rank ...,* pp. 133–34. Another adjutant of the army of this reign, Amenemheb called Mahu, is listed by P. Der Manuelian, *Studies in the Reign of Amenhotep II* (Hildesheim, 1987), pp. 120–21. Expedition photographs.

NK 2 (fig. 95, pl. 13)

Cairo JdE 91252. Expedition 67.237
Limestone. RP 6 E (S) 66. Dynasty 18(?)
41.3 x 28 x 2.8 cm

Round-top stela of the king's scribe Si-Mut and family. Hieroglyphs roughly incised with the figures and offerings in relief in slightly sunk panels. In the lunate of the stela a sun disk with a single wing on the left is balanced by a wedjat eye on the right, a well represented type. In the first register the bearded Osiris is represented seated on the left, with *atef* crown and crossed scepter and flail facing right toward a table with vegetable, bread, and other offerings. Facing him is the stela owner with upraised arms, face and arms painted red, wearing a long garment over the kilt, followed by his daughter(!), her hands hanging down at the side and wearing a long tight-fitting garment with a shoulder strap shown, and a lotus fillet in her hair. A single column of text before the god, facing right and seven columns over the offering table and the owner and his relation, facing left, read:

> (1) *Ws-ỉr nb ꜣbḏw* (2) *r(dỉt) ỉꜣw* (3) *n Ws-ỉr sn tꜣ* (4) *n nb nḥḥ ỉn* (5) *sš nsw Sꜣ-*(6)*-Mwt* (7) *sꜣt.f Wr-*(8)*-l*
>
> (1) Osiris, lord of Abydos. (2) Giving praise (3) to Osiris, kissing the ground (4) for the lord of eternity by the (5) king's scribe Si-(6)-Mut, (7) (and) his daughter Wer-(8)-el.

In the second register a man and woman are seated together facing right on a high backed chair, the front leg of the chair seemingly slanted to rest on (behind) the lady's feet. He wears a long garment, holds a *kherep* scepter in his left hand and a napkin in his right. She wears a long garment, with a shoulder strap showing, and clasps her companion's left shoulder with her left hand and his upper right arm with her right hand. They are captioned respectively: *sꜣ.s Ḥwy* and *nbt pr Bỉꜣt,* "her son Huy and the lady Biat." Facing them toward the left are three standing men in kilts, the first pouring a libation into a high stand with his right hand and holding a napkin in the left, the second and third holding the belt sash(?) with right hand and a napkin in the left. They are respectively identified by texts facing left as: *sꜣ.s Ḥr-Mnw, sꜣ.s sš Sny,* and *sꜣ.s Ḥwrwy,* "her son Hor-Min, her son the scribe Seny, her son Huruy."

In the lowest register of the stela are three lines of text:

> (1) *Ḥtp dỉ nsw Ws-ỉr ḥqꜣ ḏt nṯr ꜥꜣ nb ꜣbḏw dỉ.f pr(t) ḫrw tꜣ ḥnqt kꜣ ꜣpdw ḫt nbt wꜥbt ꜥnḫ nṯr* (2) *ỉm.s n kꜣ n ẖry ḥꜣb ḥry-tp ỉmy pr-mḏꜣt sš ꜥnn nsw n ḫft-ḥr Sꜣ-Mwt* (3) *snt.f nbt pr šmꜥyt n Ỉmn Bỉꜣt sꜣ.f Ḥwy*
>
> (1) An offering which the king gives to Osiris, Heqa-djet, the great god, lord of Abydos, that he may grant an invocation offering consisting of bread, beer, cattle, fowl, and every good thing upon which the god lives (2) to the ka of the chief lector priest who is in the library, the scribe of the royal tablet of the court Si-Mut (3) his companion, the house mistress, the chantress of Amun Biat, her son Huy.

Notes: The seated male and the three standing males in the second register, all with traces of red paint, are described as *sꜣ.s,* "her son," but not as his son. For the title, "scribe of the royal tablet of the court," see W.A. Ward, *Index of Egyptian administrative and religious titles of the Middle Kingdom* (Beirut, 1982), no. 1361. For an early study of stelae with the winged disk with one wing and the wedjat eye, see L. Bull, "Two Egyptian Stelae of the XVIII Dynasty," in *Metropolitan Museum Studies* 2, part 1 (1929), pp. 76–84. For a more recent discussion of the monopteral disk, see D.M. Mostafa, "A propos d'une particularité dans la décoration des tympans des stèles cintrées du Nouvel Empire," *GM* 133 (1993), pp. 85–96, wherein Mostafa notes that the wing is always over the divinity, the wedjat eye over the dedicant, the best dated examples ranging from Amenhotep I to Amenhotep III, and that the majority of the stelae come from Abydos. The subject is also addressed by R. Hölzl, "Round-Topped Stelae from the Middle Kingdom to the Late Period. Some Remarks on the Decoration of the Lunettes," in *Sesto Congresso Internationale di Egittologia, Atti,* vol. 1 (Turin, 1992), pp. 285–89. The name Si-Mut is frequent in the New Kingdom (*PN* 1, p. 282.3; I. Hoffmann, *Indices zu Materialien zur Wirtschaftsgeschichte des Neuen Reiches* [Wiesbaden, 1970], p. 88 = 1110). For *ḥry tp n pr-mḏꜣt,* see G.T. Martin, *The Memphite Tomb of Horemheb* (London, 1989), p. 172. In our occurrence, perhaps read instead: *ẖry ḥꜣb ḥry-tp ꜥꜣ m pr-mḏꜣt,* reading ꜥꜣ instead of *ỉmy.*
Egyptian Museum photograph.

NK 3 (fig. 96, pl. 14a)

Cairo JdE 91260. Expedition 67.472
RP 7 F (N) 2
Limestone, with scene in shallow sunk relief, hieroglyphs incised, originally painted blue, register lines red.
19 x 14 x 5 cm

Stela fragment of Nebpehtyre-mose. Lower left corner. 1st register: legs from seated(?) figure of god(?). Five registers of text, right to left:

> (1) *nṯr ꜥꜣ nb ꜣbḏw ḥmt.f nb(t) pr Mwt*(?) (2) ....(?) *wꜥbt* (3) .... *Nb-pḥty-Rꜥ-ms* (4) .... *mꜣꜥ-ḫrw m ẖryt-nṯr* (5) ....

Note: The name is not represented in *PN* 1.
Expedition photograph.

NK 4 (fig. 97)

Cairo JdE 91274. Expedition 67.4
RP 4 C (N+W) 4
Limestone
23 x 17 x (not recorded) cm

Illustrated in O'Connor, *Expedition* 12, no. 1 (fall, 1969), p. 32, upper left. Anthony Leahy (personal communication) dates the stela to the Third Intermediate Period. Upper right section of round top stela, with seated and standing deities and text captions. A seated deity or king wearing the double crown facing right is followed by a seated

Fig. 95. NK 2, facsimile drawing

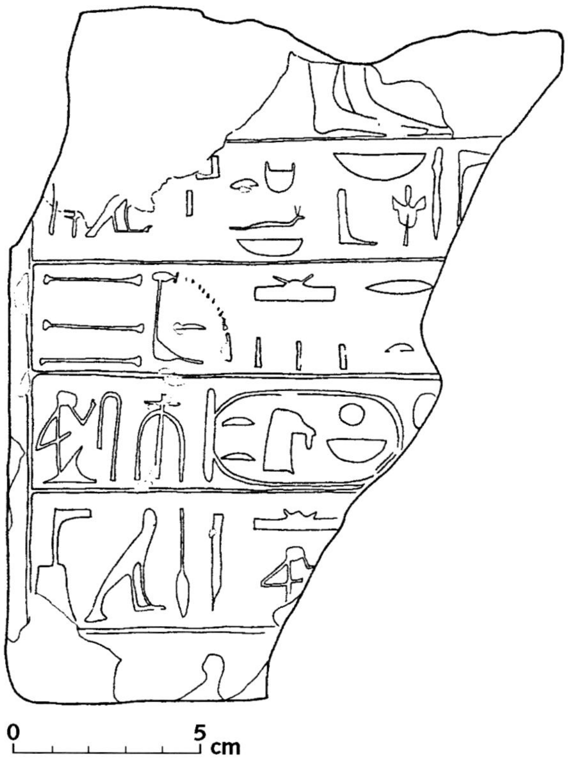

Fig. 96. NK 3, facsimile drawing

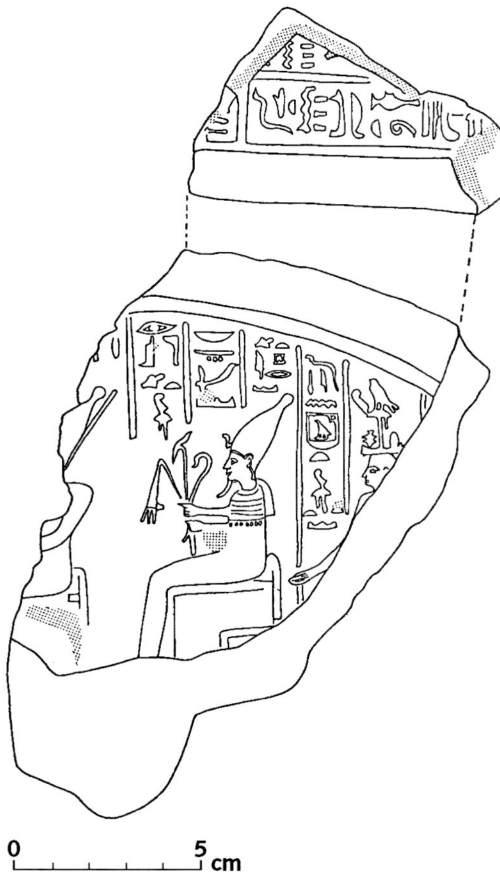

Fig. 97. NK 4, facsimile drawing

figure of Osiris with white crown with uraeus, beard, and holding the flail, crook, and *wꜣs* scepter in his hands, followed by a standing figure of Hathor with the standard of the west on her head. Five columns of text from left to right, facing left read:

> (1) ... (2) *Ws-ir ḫnt imntyw* (3) *nb tꜣ ḏsr* (4) *ḫnt igr(t)* (5) *ḏd mdw in Ḥwt-Ḥr nbt imntt.*

On the reverse in perpendicular direction are parts of two columns of text reading:

> (1) ...(?) (2) *ḏd.tn di.k ḥswt* (?).......

NK 5 (FIG. 98, PL. 14B)

Cairo JdE 91254 or 91247. Expedition 69.153 <947>
RP 6 E S, near pavement, *in situ*(?)
Limestone, some red color preserved on lower left corner of Amen-Re's throne, Mut's dress, and dedicant's face and dress
25 x 28 x 9 cm
Left section of inscribed rectangular stela or lintel of Khay in two registers. Illustrated in O'Connor, *Expedition* 12, no. 1 (fall 1969), p. 32, top right.

In the upper register on the left, Khay and his wife (*snt*, companion), facing left, kneel before the Theban triad of Amen-Re, Mut, and Khonsu, facing right. Amen-Re is seated on a throne placed on a pedestal, wears the tall plumes and a beard, and holds a *wꜣs*-scepter in his left hand and extends the ankh in his right hand. He is followed by a standing figure of Mut, who clasps him with her left arm and holds the right arm vertically, holding the ankh; she wears the double crown, a vulture headdress and a long, tightly fitting garment. Her feet are placed on the ground and not on the pedestal. She is followed by Khonsu, standing on a pedestal, wearing the lunate crown, a uraeus on his brow, a side lock, and holding with both hands a combination of a *wꜣs* scepter, *djed* pillar, ankh, and flail. The triad is captioned in three vertical columns as: "Amen-Re, lord of the thrones of the two lands, lord of the sky; Mut the great, lady of Ishru, and Khonsu in Thebes." Facing them are the kneeling dedicants: Khay with hands upraised in praise, wearing a long wig, broad collar and full-length garment; followed by Kaia, wearing a full wig with incense cone, and a long garment, her hands raised in praise with the right hand bearing a sistrum. Five columns of text above them read in the same direction toward the deities: "Praising Amen-Re, Mut, and Khonsu, that they may grant life, prosperity, and health to the ka of the Osiris Khay and his companion (*snt*), the lady, the chantress of Amen, Kaia." In the fragmentary right end of the upper register a standing representation of Osiris with crook and flail faces left to a similar kneeling dedicant with hands upraised in praise facing right. Three columns of text facing right read: "Praising Osiris Wenennefer, that he may grant the sweet breath [of life?] in the necropolis and bread, beer, cattle, and fowl to the ka of the Osiris Khay."

In the lower register are two boats, the one on the left complete with papyriform prow and stern and with a steering oar. The boat is in sail and has the caption: "Sailing southward to the western side of Thebes, in the following of Amen." In the rear of the boat the dedicant and his wife are seated on separate chairs, facing front (left), he bearing a scepter and she a sistrum or other object. Facing the pair is

Fig. 98. NK 5, facsimile drawing

a standing figure offering incense(?). The pair have the vertical captions: "Khay and the lady (?)," and the standing figure the caption: "his son Reia (*Rꜥỉ*)." On the other side of the mast, facing the pair are three seated women each identified as "her daughter." The first is Hathor, the second Weret(?), and the third Baket the Elder (*wrt?*) or Baket-Mut. To the right are the remains of the stern of the second boat, facing right in the opposite direction, as indicated by the steering oar. Above are two lines of text:

> (1) .... all the gods of *Ta-djeser* in the (boat) festival in Abydos; (2) .... Kaia (*Kꜣỉ*), the vindicated.

The boat journeys evidently represent the traditional voyage of an Abydene couple to Thebes (left boat under sail) and a return to Abydos (right boat probably without sail, using the northward current). Egyptian Museum photograph.

NK 6 (FIG. 99, PL. 15A)

UM 69–29–116. Expedition 69.39
RP H 7 (E)
Limestone stela, upper portion
17 x 18.5 x 3 cm
Raised relief with red paint for men and border and yellow for women. In lunate a *shen* sign flanked by *wedjat* eyes. No trace of text below lunate and above figures. On left, facing right, seated man in close-fitting wig with beard and broad collar necklace, lotus held in left hand before face, napkin in right hand. Behind him, clasping him, his wife with tripartite wig, broad collar, and shoulder strap; back of chair indicated. In front of the pair in the center offerings on table. On right side, facing the seated pair a standing man with close-fitting wig, broad collar, beard, and waist-high garment extends a

hes-vessel with water libation to the seated pair and is followed by his wife, who wears a short wig and shoulder strap. The lower part of the stela, along with any inscription, is missing.
UM storage photograph 16–35.

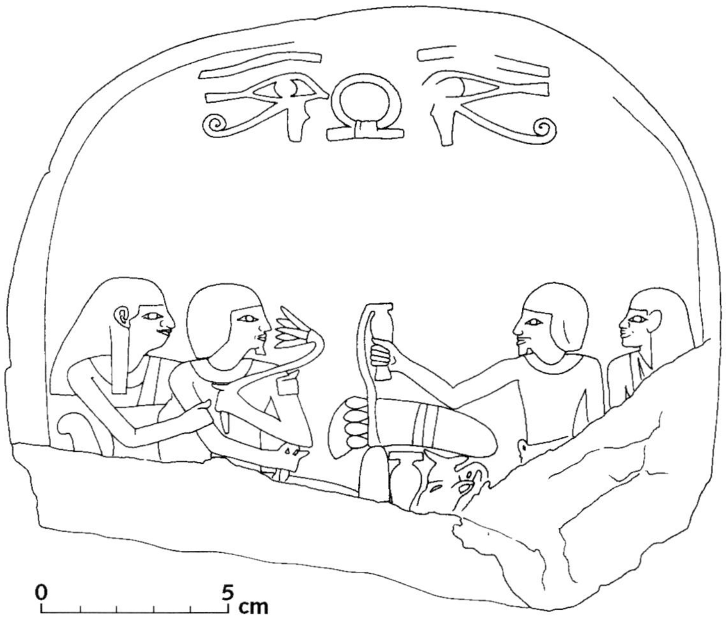

Fig. 99. NK 6, facsimile drawing

NK 7 (FIG. 100, PL. 15B)

UM 69–29–60. Expedition 67.25
RP 5 C (S+E) 1, in dump
Limestone stela, upper left section
48 x 36 x 11 cm
New Kingdom or later. In the lunate on the left is a bull standing in front of a sunshade. In the register below two seated figures face to the right before offerings on a mat. The first with shoulder-length wig holds a *kherep* scepter in his left hand and extends his closed right hand in front of him; he wears a waist-high garment. He is followed by his wife, seated(?), with an incense cone on her head. Six columns of text, of which the first is fragmentary, read: "... Re, the vindicated, (and) the lady, chantress of Amen, Tutuia (*Twtwiꜣ*)." The last name is not represented thus in *PN* 1, 2. In an additional register below, on the right facing right, are the heads of two figures, the second with a cone on her head, the first with name missing but with male determinative followed by "the vindicated," and the second "her daughter Bak[et]-Amen."
UM storage photograph 18–6.

NK 8 (FIG. 101, PL. 15C)

Cairo JdE 91280. Expedition 69.154
RP F 6 W, Tomb 7
Limestone
22 x 34 x 8 cm
Stela fragment, two adjoining pieces of lower half. Yellowish limestone with traces of red paint, crude workmanship. Of the upper register the legs of two men, facing left, followed by two seated women facing in the same direction, remain. The lower register is complete. On the left a seated pair of man and wife on a low platform, facing right, the man in front, the woman clasping her husband. The man holds a lotus with his left hand in front of his face; both figures have incense cones; he faces a low table with offerings. Four columns of text above:

> *ỉn (?)-ty n Wsỉr Bꜣk, ḥmt.f nb(t) pr ...*
> By the(?) of Osiris Bak; his wife the lady (?)

Facing left toward the seated pair a dedicant extends a *hes* libation vessel with his right hand. Two columns of text identify him as *sꜣ Nb-wꜥ(w)*? Following him another son extends a bouquet with his left hand. He is identified as "his son Amen-mose ...." Following this figure is a shorter male, right arm on chest, left hanging, identified by the column of text as "his son *Pty*(?)." Two additional columns of text read: "his son *Ỉr...*(?)" and "his daughter *.iw*." In the lower right corner of the stela are two seated figures, and perhaps these texts refer to them, although the first appears to be a female; both have incense cones. Above these are a seated pair of husband and wife on a high-backed chair, the man with incense cone and lotus held before him. The traces of his name are similar to those of the name of the first of the sons who extends the *hes* vessel: *Nb-wꜥ*. The caption above the woman reads: "his wife Sedjemy." Although the stela is relatively clear in the original and photographs, the readings are problematic, and repeated collation has proved of little avail.
Egyptian Museum photograph.

NK 9 (FIG. 102)

Uncatalogued 69.5
RP
Limestone
22 x 10.5 x ? cm
Fragment of temple relief. Bearded figure (royal?) presenting a shrine with right hand. Figure red, shrine yellow with cartouche of "Horemheb, beloved of Amen."
No photograph.

NK 10 (FIG. 103, PL. 16A)

UM 69–29–54. Expedition 69.201
RP T 19
Limestone
21.5 x 34 x 9 cm
Illustrated in O'Connor, *Expedition* 12, no. 1, (fall, 1969), p. 36. Left half of a lintel. On the right is a seated Osiris on a podium in a shrine facing left, with white crown with plumes, bearded, holding a *wꜣs* scepter and flail and the caption: "Osiris, Lord of Abydos, the great god." Facing him toward the right, a man and two women with upraised arms in praise, each with broad collar, the man with short kilt and short wig, the women with shoulder-length wigs and tight-fitting garments above ankles. Six columns of text:

> (1) Giving praise to Osiris, kissing the ground for the Lord of Ta-djeser, by the deputy (*ỉdnw*) (2) of the detachment of ʿAten

is resplendent (*Ꞽtn-ṯḥnw*),' (3) Karoya (*Kꜣryiꜣ*); (4) his mother *Ḏḥwty*, and (5) his wife the lady (6) *Ꞽtf-rsw*.

For the dedicant, see *PN* 1, p. 346.27 (ref. to *ASAE* 10 [1910], p. 109), and for the name of the wife, see *PN* 1, p. 51.14. At the right edge of the block are the traces of a seated Osiris facing the opposite direction with the same headdress, hence the block was approximately twice the length and served as a small lintel. The same individual with this title along with his wife and mother, as well as several other members of his family, his father, two sons, three daughters, and three brothers, is represented by a stela from Abydos (CCG 34061; Mariette, *Cat. Gen. des Mon. d'Abydos*, p. 385, no. 1062; J. Lieblein, *Dictionnaire des noms hiéroglyphiques en ordre généalogique et alphabetique, Supplément* (Leipzig, 1892), p. 756, no. 1942). There is also a jamb from the same monument from Abydos, reused as a support for a coffin in Cemetery G, in which Osiris-Heqa-Djet is included in the offering formula and the title is expanded to *idnw n pꜣ sꜣ ꜥꜣ n Ꞽtn-tḥnw* (C. Ayrton and A.P. Weigall with A.H. Gardiner, *Abydos* 3 (London, 1904), pp. 50–51, pl. 19.4). The designation *Ꞽtn-tḥnw* is used for the

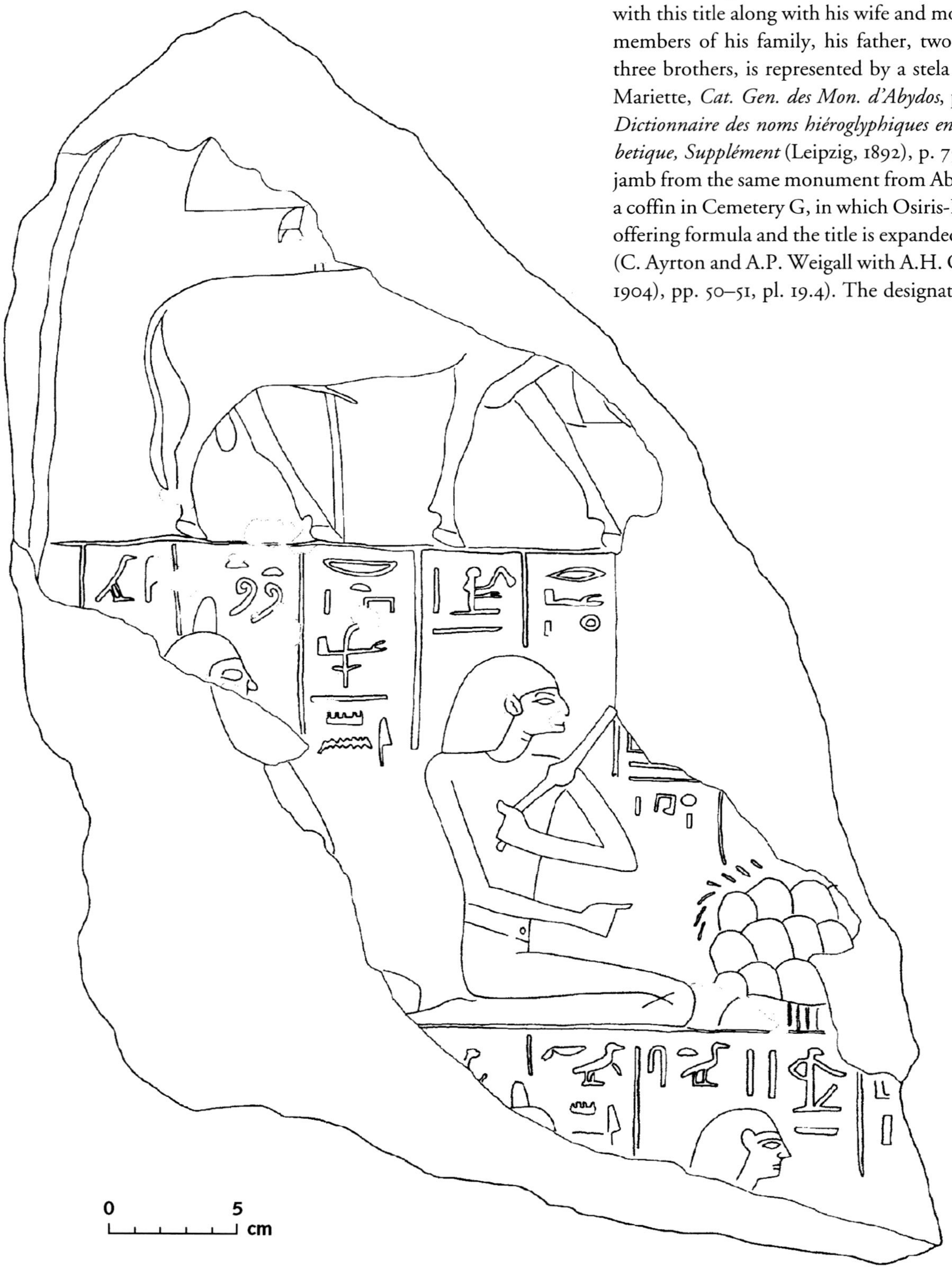

Fig. 100. NK 7, facsimile drawing

Fig. 101. NK 8, facsimile drawing

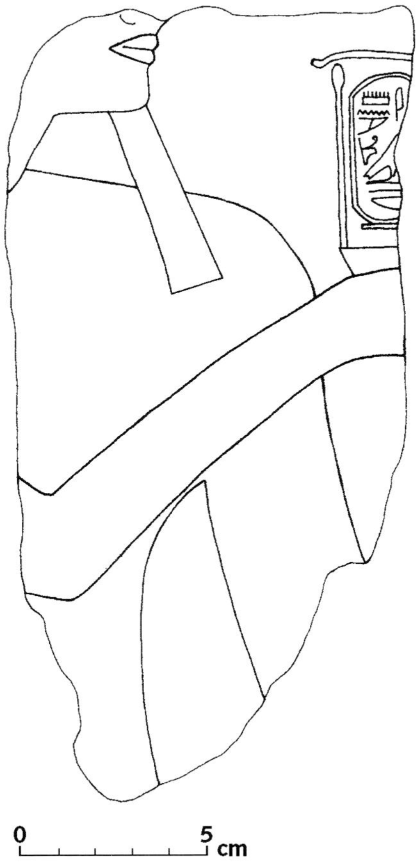

Fig. 102. NK 9, facsimile drawing

Fig. 103. NK 10, facsimile drawing

ship of Amenhotep III, and this may be the present context. The references to the ship name have been collected by D. Jones: *A Glossary of Ancient Egyptian Nautical Titles and Terms* (London, 1988), p. 231, no. 4. For a similar title, see *wꜥw n pꜣ sꜣ n Ỉmn* (A. Mariette, *Catalogue général des monuments d'Abydos* (Paris, 1880), p. 1063). The title of Karoya is cited in *Wb.* 3, *Belegstellen*, p. 119, under 413.20. Other references to this individual's monuments: G. Legrain, *Répertoire généologique et onomastique du Musée du Caire* (Geneva, 1908), p. 153, no. 266, with filiation and family table; A.R. Schulman, *Military Rank, Title and Organization in the Egyptian New Kingdom,* MÄS 6, (Berlin, 1964), p. 135, no. 317; and R. Hari, *Répertoire onomastique amarnien*, Aegyptiaca Helvetica 4 (Geneva, 1976), no. 290.

Blocks from the Amarna period were recorded from the debris of the "Ramesses II portal temple" (D. Silverman, in *Akten des vierten internationalen Ägyptologen-Kongresses, München,* Band 2 [Hamburg, 1985], pp. 273–75). O'Connor and Silverman regard them as indications of an early structure of Akhenaten there. I have always doubted that they originally came from Abydos. B.J. Kemp in *LÄ* 1 (1975), col. 32, does not rule out an original Abydene provenance. In any case, the worship of Osiris by the (former or prospective?) Atenist Karoya is noteworthy. Probable date of the stela and related elements is the reign of Amenhotep III. A similar lintel from Abydos, perhaps by the same sculptor, is illustrated by H. Frankfort, *JEA* 14 (1924), p. 243, pl. 23, no. 2.
UM storage photograph 22–32, 34.

Fig. 104. NK 11, facsimile drawing

NK 11 (FIG. 104, PL. 16B)

UM 69–29–127. Expedition 69.172
RP G 6 N
Limestone
16 x 12 x 3.5 cm
Small, irregular offering stela, text within lunate in black ink, scene incised. On right facing left is a representation of Osiris on a pedestal with crook and flail, *atef* crown with plumes, uraeus on brow, before high table with offerings and flame(?). Facing Osiris is a man in long garment, shaved head, with arms raised in praise. Text above: *"Weeb*-priest Wenen-nefer."
UM storage photograph 16–20.

Fig. 105. NK 12, facsimile drawing

NK 12 (FIG. 105, PL. 16C)

Cairo JdE 91263. Expedition 67.684 <702>
RP 4 (E)
Limestone
23 x 14 x 5.3 cm
Upper left section of round-top stela. Late New Kingdom or Late Period. In lunate: wing of winged sun disk. Below on left remains of five columns of text, blue paint in dividing lines, above standing figure of falcon-headed god with sun disk encircled by uraeus, holding combined *wꜣs* scepter, flail, and crook, facing right toward table with offerings. Traces of red paint.

> (1) ...... (2) great god, lord of Abydos, (3) ruler of eternity, (4) may he give a good (5) burial in ....

Expedition photograph.

NK 13 (fig. 106, pl. 17a)
UM 69–29–80. Expedition 67.382
RP 7 E(N) 1
Limestone
26.5 x 15.5 x 5.5 cm
Lower right portion of a stela, with figures and signs in very rough sunk relief. In the register above, the dedicant on the right facing left raises his hands before an offering table and a seated god on a podium, facing right. The man wears a mid-calf garment. In the register below, three women face to the left, the first with only the back of her wig preserved, the second and third each raise one hand. The name of the second is unreadable(?), and the name of the third is possibly to be read as *Sꜣt-ꜣst.*
UM storage photograph 15–25.

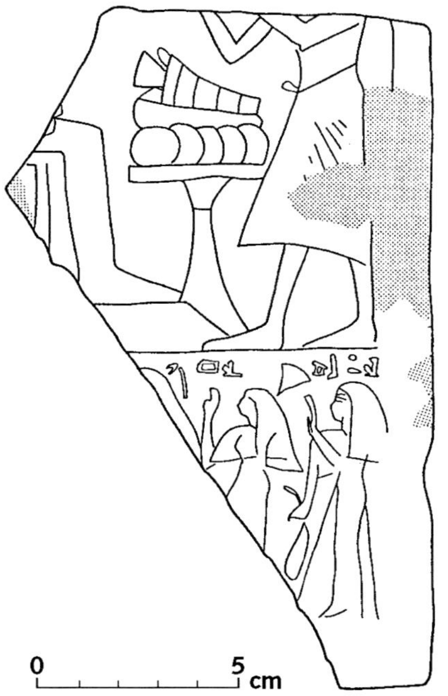

Fig. 106. NK 13, facsimile drawing

NK 14 (fig. 107, pl. 17b)
UM 69–29–79. Expedition 67.357
RP 7 D (W)
Limestone
17 x 9.5 x 6.5 cm
Left portion of a stela with seated falcon-headed god facing right, holding an ankh in his right hand and a *wꜣs* scepter in his left hand, only the end of it preserved. Above the god the end of a text: *Ro-Setau.* The figure is in rough shallow sunk relief, the hieroglyphs roughly incised.
UM storage photograph 15–10.

NK 15 (figs. 108–109)
Cairo JdE 91290. Expedition 69.152
RP G 6 (N) in loose spoil near T 13, local north side ca. 30 cm below top of T
Limestone with scene and text on both sides in ink
17.5 x 17 x 3 cm
Recto: Standing figure of dedicant on left facing right with pleated kilt to just below knees. He offers a libation vessel in his right hand and a bouquet in his left hand above an offering stand toward a seated figure of Osiris, the latter holding crook and flail, wearing the *atef* crown, with the throne on a podium. A column of text with the figure of the god reads Osiris. Above the dedicant is the text: *n r*(?) *sḏm Ḥwy,* "(?), the servitor Huy."
Verso: A seated man facing left holding a long staff at a diagonal. He wears a long garment. The chair has a high back, lion's feet terminals, and shows fretwork on the side. Above is a column of text with the man's name: *Rnpw*(?).

Fig. 107. NK 14, facsimile drawing

NK 16 (fig. 110, pls. 17c–d)
UM 69–29–38. Expedition 69.200
RP T. 17, immediately SW of T. 17, level of surviving top of T. 17
Indurated polished limestone
15 x 11 x 10 cm
Fragment of engaged statuette of a man with the right hand of his wife on his proper right shoulder, the cartouche Nebmaatre on his right breast and the beginning of the cartouche Amen-[hotep] on his right upper arm. He wears a two-strand necklace with the ties clearly painted red. On the back pillar are the remains of two lines and seven columns of text. In the top line is a large *wedjat* eye. In the line below is the offering formula reading to the right: *Ḥtp di nsw Ỉ[m]n* .... Beneath the *hetep* sign are the tops of three columns on the left facing right and four columns on the right facing left.

Fig. 108. NK 15 recto, facsimile drawing

Fig. 109. NK 15 verso, facsimile drawing

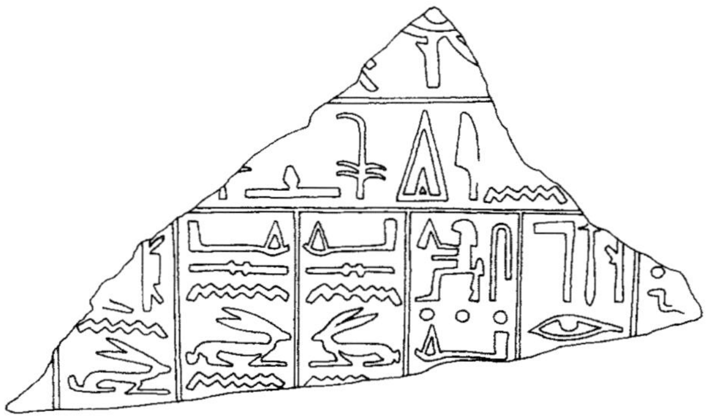

Fig. 110. NK 16, facsimile drawing

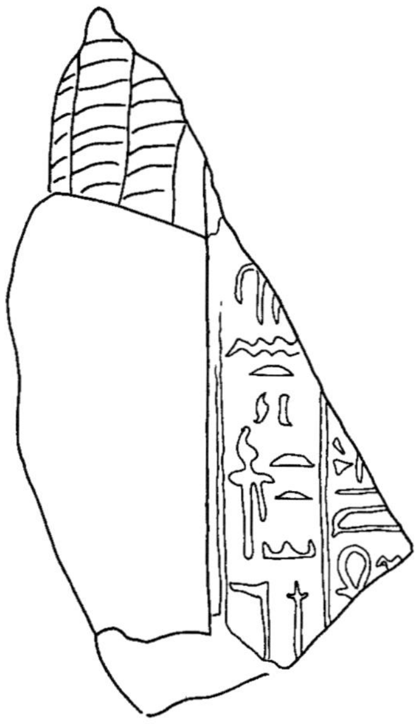

Fig. 111. NK 17, facsimile drawing

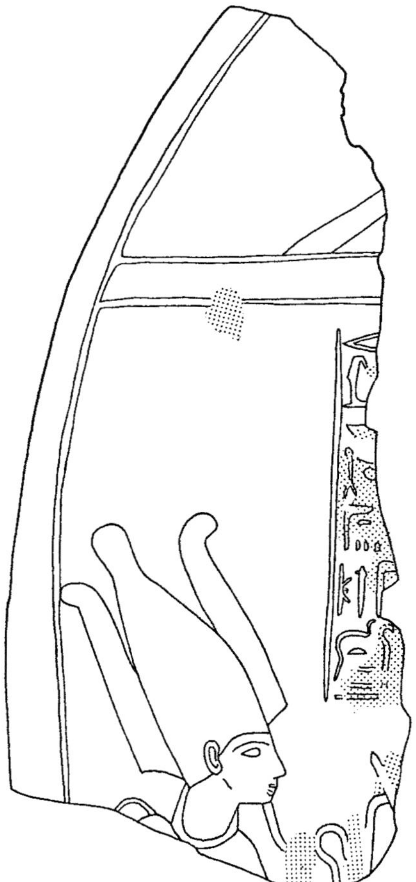

Fig. 112. NK 18, facsimile drawing

Left:

(1) *di.sn wn* ...... (2) *šmsw n wn* ...... (3) ....

(1) May they grant that ... be ...... (2) the following(?) of Wen-[nefer](?).

Right:

(1) *di.sn wn* ...... (2) *špsw di* ...... (3) *nṯr ꜥꜣ ir*(?) (4) ....

(1) May they grant that ... be ...... (2) gifts. Give ...... (3) the great god, Osiris(?) ...."

UM storage photographs 22–14, 15.

NK 17 (FIG. 111, PLS. 17E–F)

UM 69–29–8. Expedition 67.118
RP 5 F (S+W) 21
Limestone
16 x 8 x 9 cm

Fragment of statuette with braided wig and two-strand necklace. On back support part of two columns of text facing left:

(1) ...*ḫnty-imntt nṯr ꜥꜣ* ... (2) ...... *bꜣ*(?) *m ꜥnḫ* ... .

(1) ... foremost of the west, great god ... (2) ... ba(?) in life ....

UM storage photographs 22–8, 9.

NK 18 (FIG. 112, PL. 18A)

UM 69–29–69. Expedition 67.173
RP 6 E(N+E)
Limestone
27 x 10.5 x 7 cm

Left edge of a round-top stela. In lunate part of a *wedjat* eye(?). On left, head of Osiris with *atef* crown and beard, holding crook and *wꜣs* scepter. Column of text facing right: "Osiris, lord of eternity, [king] of the gods, great god, ruler of eternity."
UM storage photograph 15–22.

NK 19 (FIG. 113, PL. 18B)

Two fragments of same stela, not joining
Left: UM 69–29–62. Expedition 67.31
RP 5 D (E+S) 1
Limestone
14 x 19.5 x 4.5 cm

Right: UM 69–29–84. Expedition 67.463
RP 7 E (E) 82
Limestone
16.5 x 18.5 x 6 cm

Left section: On left, a figure of Osiris with beard and crossed hands in three dimensions. To the right of the figure, a column of text indented:

... *nṯr nb ꜣbḏw di.f šms kꜣ.f m* ... *ḥꜥꜥw*

... the god, lord of Abydos, may he grant the following of his ka in rejoicing(?) ....

Indented again, part of a scene with two lines of text below, reading right to left. In the scene on the left an offering table, to the right of which is a standing figure of a god on a podium holding a *wꜣs* scepter, facing left, followed by a standing figure with a staff and a name beginning with *sꜣ*. The end of the first line of text reads: *nṯrw nbw ꜣbḏw,*

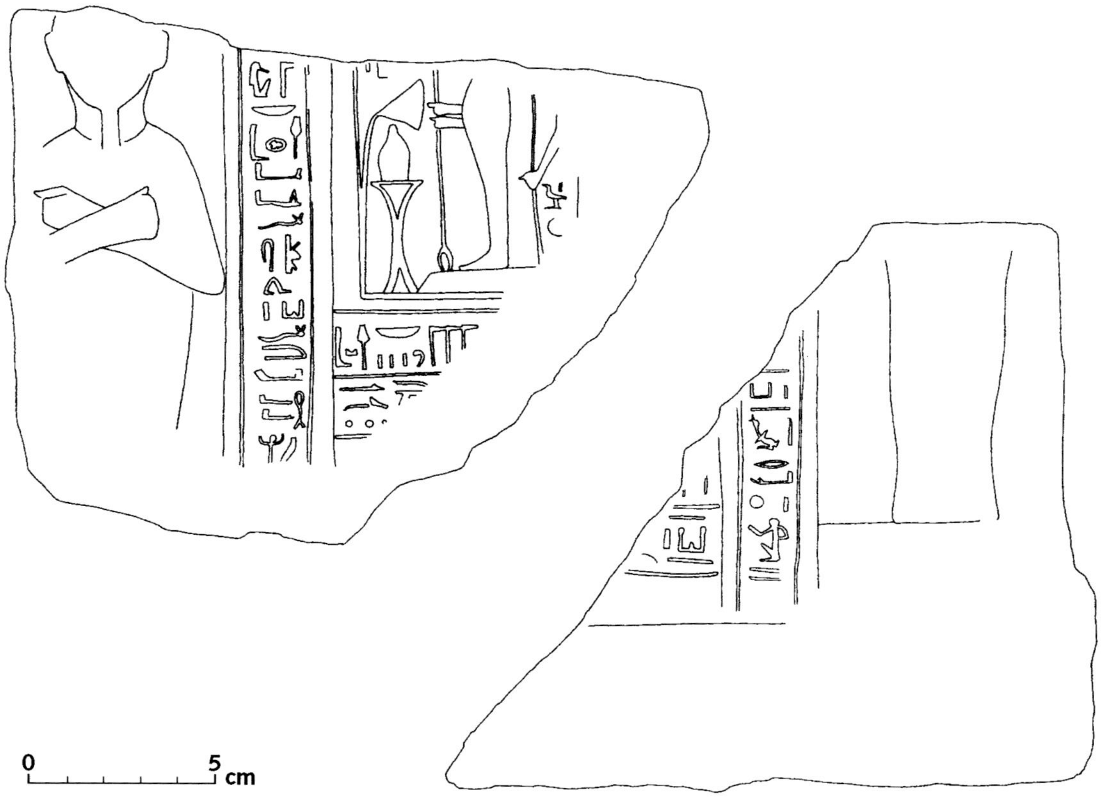

Fig. 113. NK 19, facsimile drawing

"all the gods of Abydos." The text of the second line appears unreadable(?).

Right section: On the right a similar figure in three dimensions (Osiris?). An indented column of text, facing left, ending with: ... *n kꜣ n Ṯꜣi-Rꜥ mꜣꜥ-ḫrw,* "for the ka of Tjay-Re, vindicated." To the left, two lines of text, facing right, the first reading: *n kꜣ n Ṯꜣi-...,* "for the ka of Tjay-......." The second line is unreadable. The name formation *ṯꜣi* + deity + *imw,* "may God N seize them," is attested from the late New Kingdom on (*PN* I, pp. 387.12–388.6).
UM storage photographs 15–17, 18.

NK 20 (FIG. 114, PL. 18C)

UM 69–29–74. Expedition 67.238
RP 6 F (N)
Limestone
19.5 x 16.5 x 6 cm
Fragment of upper left section of round-top stela. New Kingdom or later. Figures very roughly cut, partly incised, partly in sunk relief; hieroglyphs very roughly incised. In lunate a winged sun disk (disk missing) with *wesekh* vessel below in center and *wedjat* eye on left. The scene consists of three standing deities, facing right toward an offering table with a duck. The first is a falcon-headed god with sun disk with uraeus; he holds a *wꜣs* scepter with both hands. The second is a falcon-headed deity with sun disk with uraeus; the left hand is raised and the right holds an ankh. The third is a woman with disk between horns and vulture headdress; she has her left hand upraised and holds an ankh in her right hand. They are captioned respectively as follows:

> *ḏd mdw in Wsir ḏd mdw in Ḥr ḏd mdw in ꜣst wr(t) mwt nṯr*
>
> Recitation by Osiris, recitation by Horus, recitation by Isis the great, mother of the god.

Expedition photograph OP 102 B/W 9 (27).

NK 21 (FIG. 115)

Cairo JdE 91269. Expedition 67.384
RP 7 E (N+W) 3
Limestone. 14.5 x 18 x ? cm
Lower left corner of stela. Hieroglyphs roughly incised and originally filled with blue pigment; register lines filled with red pigment. Scene at top in rough sunk relief. Remainder of scene: legs of man facing left with garment to just above ankles. Three lines of text from right to left:

> (1) ... *Ws-ir ḥqꜣ ḏt di.f* ... (2) ... *ḫnm nbw* (?) *n kꜣ n Ws-ir* ... (3) ... *[imy-rꜣ] šnwty [Ḥw?]y mꜥꜣ ḫrw, nbt pr Pwpꜣ* ....
>
> (1) ... Osiris-Heqa-Djet may he grant ... (2) ... all things united(?) for the ka of the Osiris ... (3) ... [overseer of the] double granary [Hu(?)]y, the vindicated, the lady Pupa ....

The last name is not recorded thus in *PN* I, 2.

NK 22 (FIG. 116, PL. 18D)

UM 69–29–95. Expedition 67.559
RP 8 C (S) 5
Limestone. 8 x 13.5 x 4.5 cm
Figure(s) in rough low relief, hieroglyphs incised. Fragment of upper left section of round-top stela. At top part of wing of the disk above a recumbent jackal. At left, facing right, is the head of Osiris with a vertical text in front in same orientation: *ḫnty imntt,* "foremost of the west(erners)."
UM storage photograph 16–12.

Fig. 114. NK 20, facsimile drawing

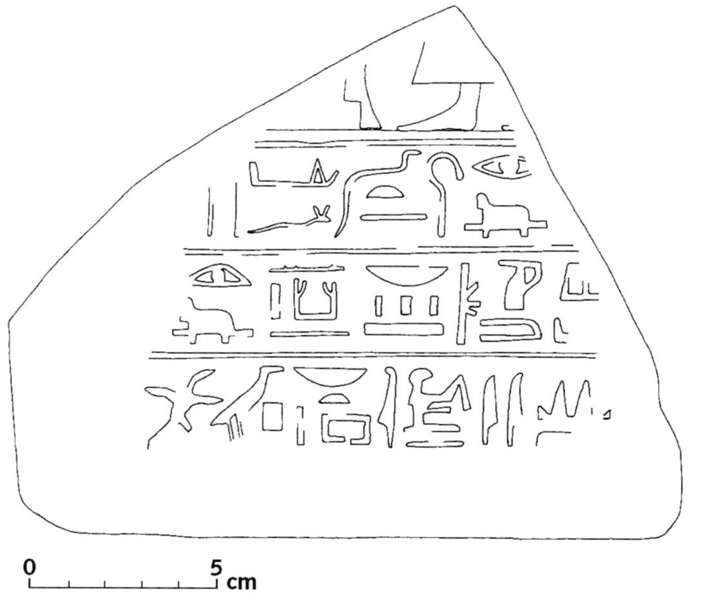

Fig. 115. NK 21, facsimile drawing

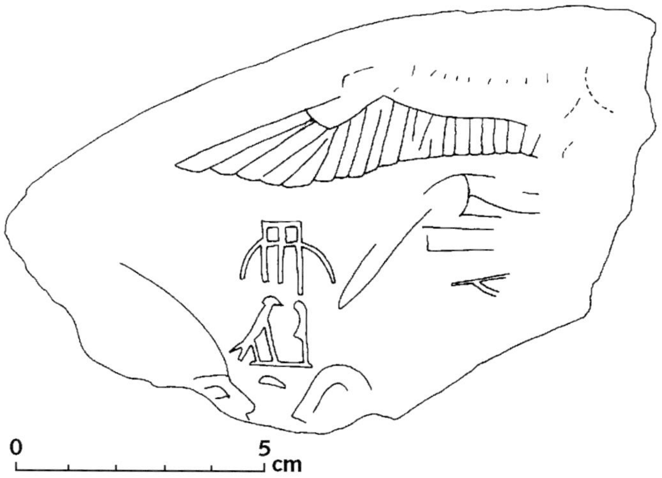

Fig. 116. NK 22, facsimile drawing

NK 23 (fig. 117, pl. 19a)

UM 69–29–113. Expedition 69.8
RP J 7 (N)
Limestone
22 x 17 x 8 cm
Fragment of upper section of stela. At left, facing right, the crown of Osiris with the vertical text in the same orientation: *Wsỉr ḫnty-ỉmn-tyw,* "Osiris, foremost of the westerners." To the right a vertical text in the opposite direction: *sš ḥwt-nṯr n ...,* "Scribe of the temple of ...."
UM storage photograph 16–33.

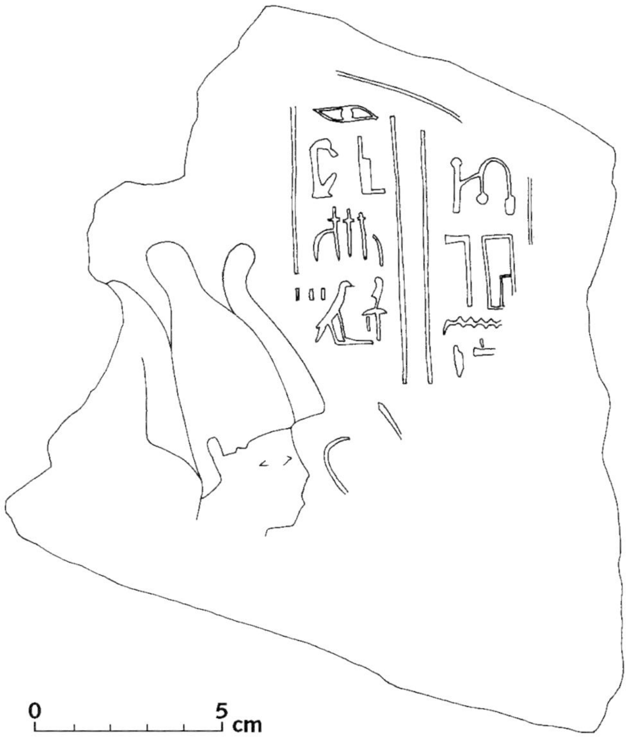

Fig. 117. NK 23, facsimile drawing

NK 24 (fig. 118, pl. 19b)

UM 69–29–148. Expedition 67.2
RP 4 C(W) 2
Red and gray granite with incised hieroglyphs with traces of red pigment
13.5 x 9.5 x 10 cm
Fragment of stela(?) with legs of two figures facing right and the lower part of a *wꜣs* scepter in the register above and part of two lines of text, right to left, below:

(1) ... *nṯr ꜥꜣ nb ꜣbḏw ꜣst* ... (2) *nb* ... *ꜣbḏw*(?)

(1) ... the great god, lord of Abydos (and) Isis ... (2) lord ... of Abydos(?).

NK 25 (fig. 119, pl. 19c)

UM 69–29–159. Expedition 67.264
RP 6 F(S+E)
Limestone(?)
10 x 12 x 10.5 cm
Fragment of naos(?) with remains of two lines of text on one side and two lines of text on under side(?):

(1) ... *mr.tn nṯrw.tn ḥs.tn nṯr pn špss*(?) ...
(2) ... *ỉꜣwt.tn n ẖrdw.tn* ... *ỉꜣw* ...

(1) ... as your gods love you and as this noble(?) god favors you ...
(2) ... [transmit] your offices to your children [after] growing old ....

Below:

(1) ... *(n) kꜣ n wbꜣ nsw* ... (2) ... *nmy*(?) *wbꜣ nsw* ....

(1) for the ka of the royal butler ... (2) ...(?) the royal butler ....

UM storage photograph 16–23.

NK 26 (fig. 120, pl. 19d)

UM 69–29–170. Expedition 67.687
RP 6 E (N+W)
Limestone
24 x 9 x 8 cm
Figures in sunk relief, hieroglyphs incised. Fragment of right side of a stela. In scene above remains of legs of two figures facing left. Below remains of a line of text:

Ḥtp dỉ nsw n Wsỉr ḫnt[y ỉmntyw] ....

May the king give an offering to Osiris, foremost [of the westerners] ....

UM storage photograph 17–33.

NK 27 (fig. 121)

UM 69–29–40. Expedition 67.636
RP 6 D
Limestone
36 x 31 x 14 cm

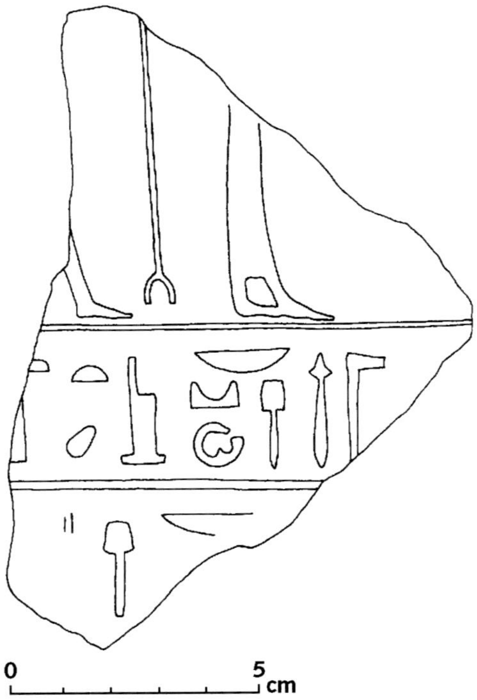

Fig. 118. NK 24, facsimile drawing

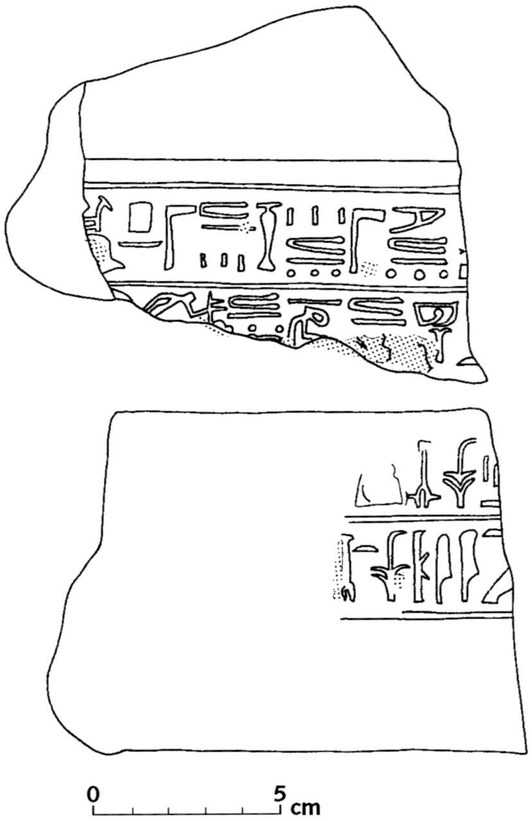

Fig. 119. NK 25, facsimile drawing

Fig. 120. NK 26, facsimile drawing

Fig. 121. NK 27, facsimile drawing

Fragment of upper part of stela. On left, standing figure of falcon-headed god with double crown, with *wꜣs* scepter in left hand and ankh in right hand, facing right toward offering table, and dedicant with brazier in right hand and left raised, kilt above knees. Above and on the left of the god is the vertical text:

(1) … *ḫft sꜣ* (2) *ꜣst bnr*(?) *mrr* (sic) *nṯr ꜥꜣ nb* (?) ….

On right, facing left, two columns of text:

(1) … *n kꜣ* (2) … *Ws-ỉr nṯr ꜥꜣ sḏm ꜥš* ….

NK 28 (fig. 122)

Location not identified. Uncatalogued
RP G 6 (N)
Limestone
41 x 15.5 x 20 cm
Stela/raised relief. Above striated wig of man facing left: three columns of text:

(1) … *n nb tꜣwy* … *ỉ*(?)
(2) *n nṯr nfr Sn-ḥtp mꜣꜥ-ḫrw*
(3) *ms n nb(t) pr Sw*(?) ….

The name *Sn(.ỉ)-ḥtp* is frequent in the New Kingdom (*PN* I, p. 309.16).

NK 29 (fig. 123, pl. 19e)

UM 69–29–65. Expedition 67.98
RP 5 F (W) 1
Limestone
16 x 15.5 x 4.5 cm
Small stela. Crude workmanship. On right, standing deity with tall plumes holding *wꜣs* scepter in right hand, nothing(?) in left, facing left. On left, facing right, a standing Toueris figure. Text vertical: *Ỉmn-Rꜥ ḫnt* ….
UM storage photograph 15–15.

NK 30 (fig. 124)

Cairo JdE 91266. Expedition 67.635
RP 5 E (S+W) 32
Limestone
16.5 x 22 x ? cm
Upper fragment of round-top stela with winged disk and six columns of text:

(1) … *Ḥr-ꜣḫty* (2) *dỉ.f* … *snṯr ḫt ḥr* (3) *sḏt mw nḏm ỉ*…*ty n kꜣ n* (4) *Ws-ỉr Ỉrt-r.w*(?) *sꜣ* (5) *ỉmy-rꜣ pr ḥḏ ỉmy-rꜣ* … (6) … *sꜣ* ….

The name *Ỉrt-r.w,* "The eye (of Horus, Amen) is against them," is frequent in the Late Period (*PN* I, p. 42.10); cf. the name *Ỉrt Ḥr r.w* at Abydos in Frankfort, *JEA* 14 (1928), p. 245.

NK 31 (fig. 125, pl. 20a)

Cairo JdE 91265. Expedition 67.608
RP 8 D (E) 32
Limestone
47 x 55 x 19 cm

Fig. 122. NK 28, facsimile drawing

Lower right section of stela with border pattern on right of spaces separated by four lines, some red preserved. At top, remains of a horizontal line of text: *ḏd wꜣs ḏt.* In center of preserved section a

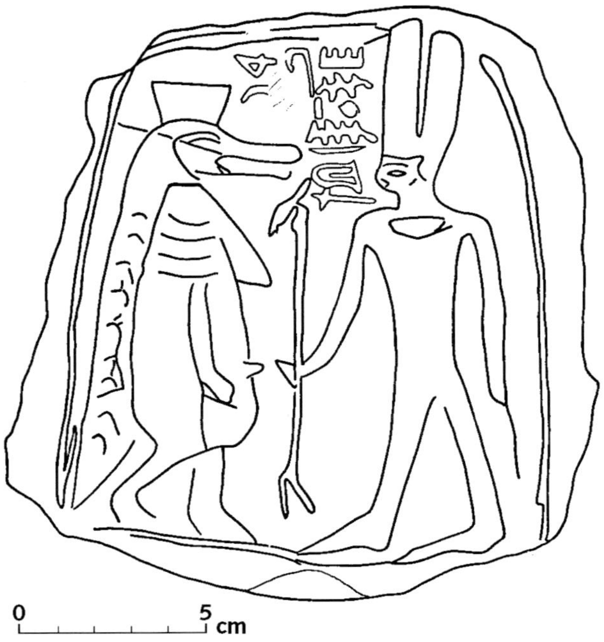

Fig. 123. NK 29, facsimile drawing

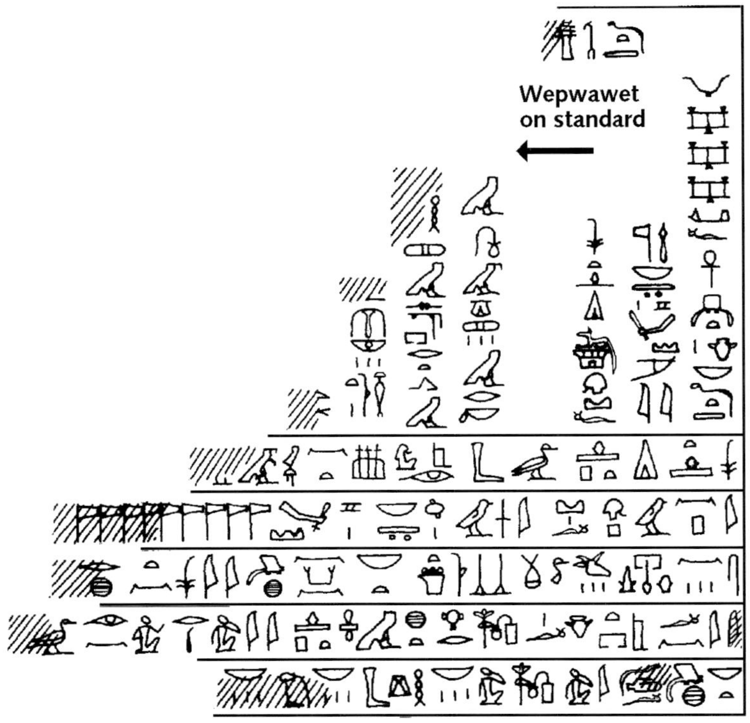

Fig. 125. NK 31, transcription

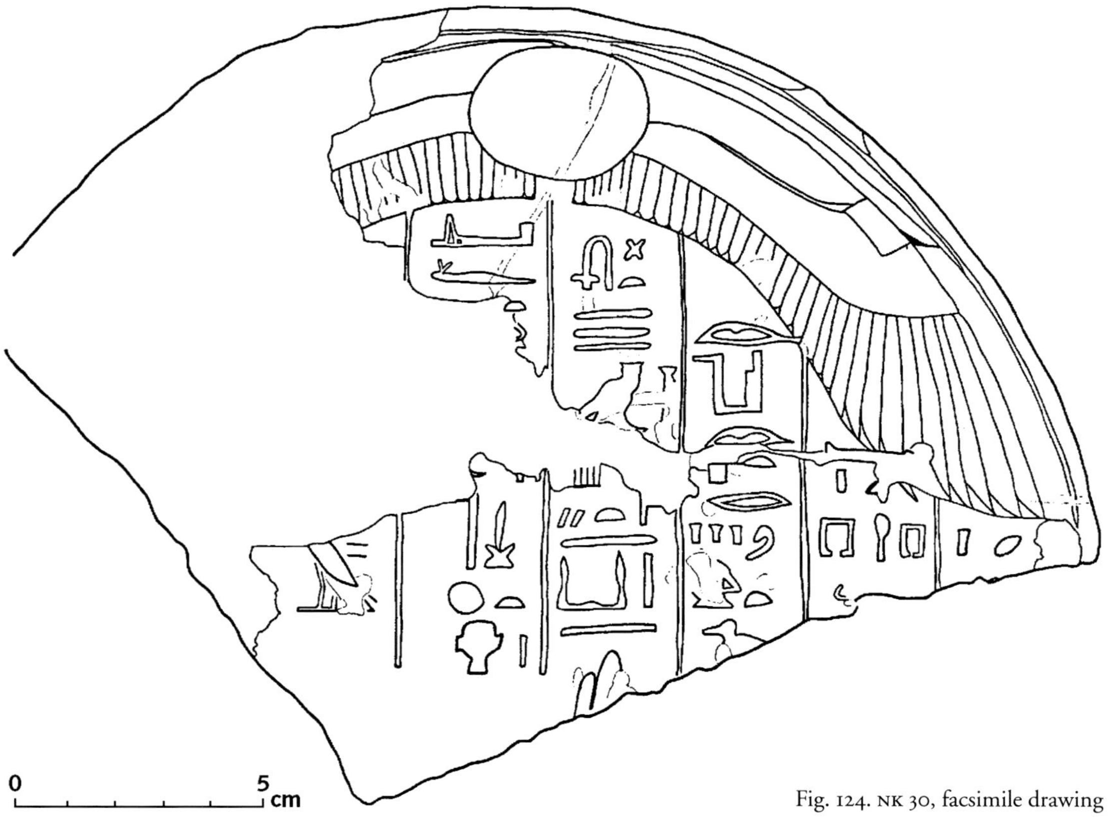

Fig. 124. NK 30, facsimile drawing

Wepwawet standard facing left. To the right of it, three columns of text with hieroglyphs facing left:

(1) *Ḥtp di nsw ỉnpw tpy ḏw.f* (2) *mry nṯr ꜥ3 nb t3 ḏsr* (3) *Wp-w3wt di.f ꜥnḫ 3wt-ib nb ḏt*

(1) An offering which the king gives (to) Anubis upon his hill, (2) beloved of the great god, lord of the necropolis, (3) Wepwawet, may he grant life and all joy forever.

To the left of the standard with hieroglyphs facing right three columns of text:

(1) *m w3g m rk-*(2)*-ḥ m prt Mnw m* (3) … *ḥbw tp rnpt*

(1) at the *Wag*-festival, at the burning (2) festival, at the procession of Min festival, at (3) … the festivals of the New Year.

Below this section are five lines of text from right to left:

(1) *Ḥtp di nsw ḥtp* (sic) *Gbw, Ws-ir ḫnty-imntyw* …… (2) *ỉnpw tpy ḏw.f imy wt nb t3 ḏsr psḏt* ………… *[di]* (3) *.sn prt ḫrw t3 ḥnqt k3w 3pdw sš mnḫt rnpwt nbt n k3 n im3ḫy rḫ*(?) *nsw* ………… *[mr]* (4) *y.f n st ib.f sš ḥry ḫtm Ḥtpi-irti*(?) *ir n S3(t)-*……… (5) *nbt im3ḫ ḏd.f ỉi sšw nbw ḫryw ḥb nbw wꜥbw nbw* ……….

(1) May the king grant an offering (to) Geb, Osiris-foremost-of-the-westerners …… (2) Anubis upon his hill, who is in the place of bandaging, lord of the necropolis, and the Ennead …… (3) that they may [grant] an invocation offering of bread and beer, cattle and fowl, alabaster and linen, for the honored one, king's acquaintance(?) …… (4) his [belov]ed of the place of his heart, the scribe responsible for the seal Hetepi-irti born of Sa- ……… (5) possessor (fem.) of an honored state. He says: O all scribes, all lector priests, all weeb priests ………."

The title *sš ḥry ḫtm,* with various following specifications, is well represented in W.A. Ward, *Index of Egyptian administrative and religious titles of the Middle Kingdom* (Beirut, 1982), nos. 1415–20, to which add G. Andreu, *BIFAO* 80 (1980), p. 144ff.

Egyptian Museum photograph. Transcription autographed by Mark Stone.

NK 32 (fig. 126, pl. 20b)

Cairo JdE 91250. Expedition 67. 278
RP 7 C (N)
Limestone
10 x 9.5 cm

Top part of a round-top stela. Under lunate with *shen* sign between two *wedjat* eyes, three lines of text from right to left:

(1) *Ḥtp di nsw Ptḥ-Skr* (2) *Ws-ir nṯr ꜥ3 nb 3bḏw* (3) *di.f prt ḫrw t3 ḥnqt k3w 3pdw šs mnḫt*

Expedition photograph A '67 OP.105 67 0111B.

NK 33 (fig. 127, pl. 21)

Cairo JdE 91276. Expedition 67.121
RP 5 F(S) 24
Limestone, 27 x 23 cm

Upper right corner of round-top stela with dedicant on right, facing left toward seated Osiris, with table piled with offerings between the figures. The dedicant wears a pleated garment and raises his hands in adoration. Osiris wears the customary white crown with uraeus and holds a *w3s* scepter. Remains of three columns of text over Osiris facing right:

(1) *[Ws]ir nb nḥḥ ḥq3* (2) *ḏt nṯr ꜥ3* (3) ….

Above and behind the dedicant are six columns of text facing left:

(1) *Rdit i3w n Ws-ir* (2) *sn t3 n Wnn-nfr di.f* (3) *qrs nfr m ḫt i3w ḫr* (4) *imntt wrt ḫft* (5) … *n k3 n* (6) *sšm ḥ3b n Ws-ir sš pr ḥḏ* …

Giving praise to Osiris, kissing the ground for Wennen-nefer that he may grant a goodly burial after old age in the great west according to … for the *ka* of the festival leader of Osiris, the scribe of the treasury ….

For the title, cf. H. Frankfort, *JEA* 14 (1928), p. 244, fig. 5.
Egyptian Museum photograph (1994).

NK 34 (fig. 128, pl. 22a)

UM 69–29–58. Expedition 67.15
RP 4 E (N+W) 1
Hard brown stone (a quartzite?)
18 x 14 x 5 cm

Stela with figures lightly incised and some hieroglyphs in sunk relief. In upper register a falcon-headed deity on left faces right and is identified as [Horus] son of Isis. Facing him is the dedicant pouring a libation over a table with bread(?) offerings with his right hand and holding aloft an incense container with his left hand. His head is damaged, as is the identifying text above the incense container. In the lower register a kneeling figure facing right with hands upraised in praise faces three lines of text, from right to left, of which the beginning is missing:

(1) … *[inḏ] ḥr.k nb.i* (2) … *iwt n.k tw* (3) … (?) *ir.n*(?) …*tf*

UM storage photographs 15–13, 14.

NK 35 (fig. 129, pl. 22b)

UM 69–29–67. Expedition 67.169
RP 6 B (N+W) 41
Limestone
13 x 17.5 x 4 cm

Upper part of stela. On left, seated deity with bracelets and armlets faces right, holding lotus with long stem in the left hand. The face appears to have been a cobra (Meret-seger?) altered in clumsy fashion by the addition of two beaks(?). The vertical caption reads: *Ḥtp di nsw Ḏḥwty nb*(?) *3bḏw*(?). In front of the deity is a stand heaped with offerings, on the other side of which a small male dedicant raises his hands in praise.
UM storage photograph 17.22.

NK 36 (fig. 130, pl. 22c)

UM 69–29–70. Expedition 67.175
RP 6 E (W)
Limestone
22 x 14 x 6 cm

Fig. 126. NK 32, facsimile drawing

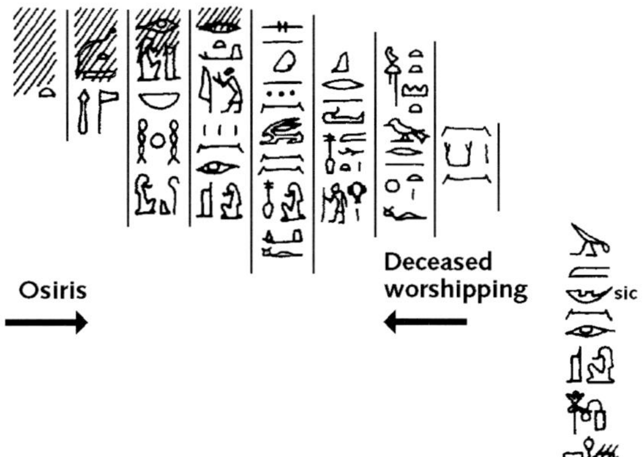

Fig. 127. NK 33, transcription

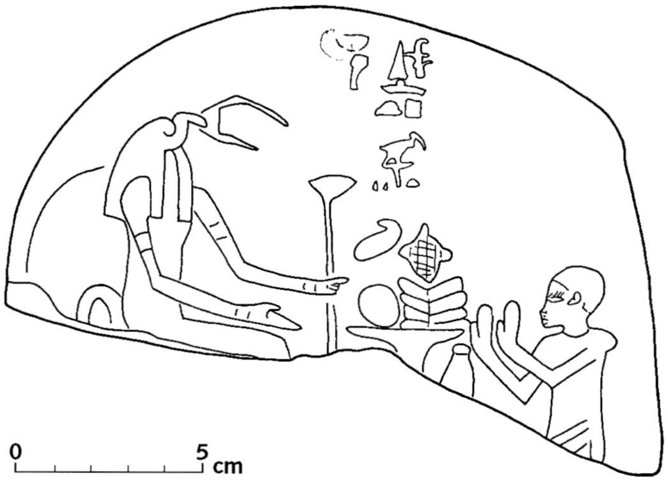

Fig. 129. NK 35, facsimile drawing

Fig. 128. NK 34, facsimile drawing

Fig. 130. NK 36, facsimile drawing

Five columns of text right to left, facing right:

> (1) ... *-ty Mn-mꜣꜥt-Rꜥ* <*n?*>*ḥḥ* (2) ... *rmṯ nb ꜥnḫ tp tꜣ nḥy* (3) ... *-y dwꜣ nṯr r (ir?) ḥr n* ... (4) ... *n.f wi ip.k(wi?)* (5) ...... *i*

UM storage photograph 15–23.

NK 37 (FIG. 131, PL. 22D)

UM 69–29–61. Expedition 67.26
RP 5 C (S+E) 2
Limestone
31 x 18.5 x ? cm
Lower right section of stela. Above: standing male figure walking to left, followed by standing female figure with cone on headdress, badly abraded scene. Below: beginning of text right to left in horizontal line: *ir.n iry ꜥt n Imn Sꜣ-*.... UM storage photograph 15–32.

Fig. 131. NK 37, facsimile drawing

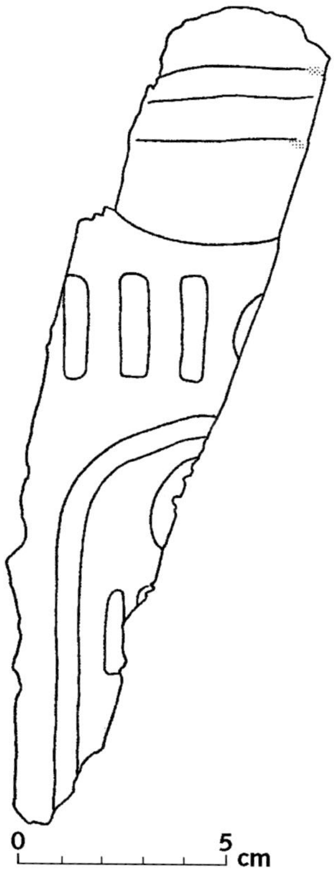

Fig. 132. NK 38, facsimile drawing

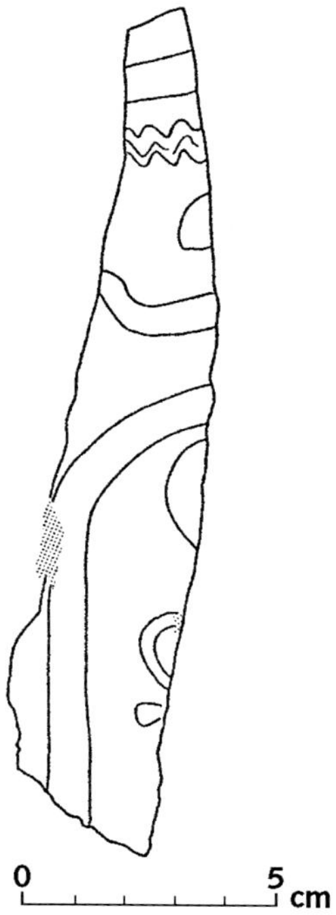

Fig. 133. NK 39, facsimile drawing

NK 38 (FIG. 132, PL. 23A)

UM 69–29–152. Expedition 67.87
RP 5 F (W) 18
Fine limestone
21 x 5 cm
Fragment of cartouche, vertical, facing right: *nb ḫꜥw Mn*(?)*-[mꜣꜥt?]-Rꜥ*. Seti I(?).
UM storage photograph 17.3.

NK 39 (FIG. 133, PL. 23B)

UM 69–29–153. Expedition 67.88
RP 5 E (W) 19
Fine limestone
18 x 3.5
Fragment of cartouche, vertical, facing left: *n it.*<*f*> *[Mn]-mꜣꜥt*(?)*-Rꜥ*. *S*eti I(?).
UM storage photograph 17–2.

NK 40 (FIG. 134)

Cairo JdE 91273. Expedition 67.84
RP 5 E (S) 15
Limestone
21 x 7 cm
Two incomplete columns of text facing right. Since the first (right) column is enclosed at the top by frame lines, perhaps the text is in retrograde, since it cannot begin with the right column.

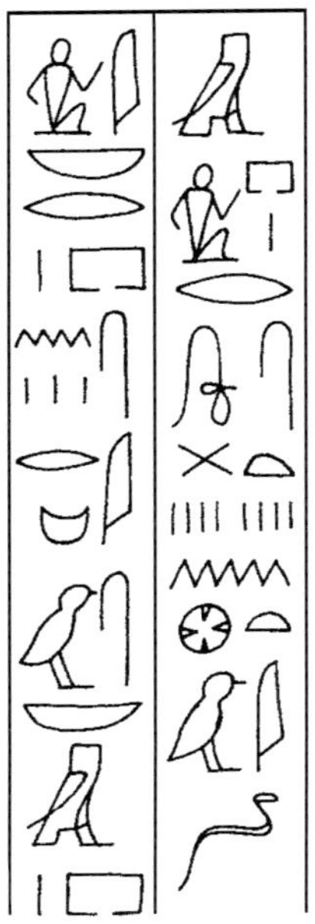

Fig. 134. NK 40, transcription

(1) *m pr.i r swꜣt Ḫmnt iw ḏd*(?) ... (2) *ii*(?) *nb r-pr.sn ir ḥmsw nb m pr* ....

(1) In my house in order to pass by Khemenet. Said(?) ... (2) O(?) lord of their temple. As for any resident in the house (temple) ....

BLOCKS OF THE AMARNA PERIOD

The significance of these blocks as indicative of a structure of Akhenaten at Abydos early in his reign has been discussed in some detail by Silverman ("The So-called Portal Temple of Ramesses II at Abydos," in *Akten des vierten internationalen Ägyptologen-Kongresses, München,* vol. 2 [Munich, 1985], pp. 271–77). There were twenty-six blocks, identifiable by style and type, of which seven were inscribed. Contrary to the earlier opinion of Kemp, Redford, and the writer, who considered the blocks as building material brought from Tell el Amarna, Silverman, following O'Connor, suggests that the Amarna blocks represent a small structure, a shrine or kiosk, built somewhere in the vicinity at Abydos. His main argument is the occurrence of the phrase *ḥry-ib qd.f ꜣḫt* ... as applied to the Aten, designating the Aten as residing in a location (temple, building) presumably outside Akhetaten. With the exception of a single relief noted below (NK 41), these blocks are not registered as expedition finds and are housed in the expedition storeroom at the site. The temple blocks, including the reused blocks, are scheduled to be published under the aegis of Prof. Silverman. An Amarna block with a ship found at Abydos is published by Petrie, *Abydos,* Part 2, pl. 39, upper left; additional references in Roeder, *Amarna-Reliefs aus Hermopolis* (Hildesheim, 1969), pp. 280 (J 2), 363.

NK 41 (FIG. 135, PL. 23C)

UM 69–29–179. Not catalogued
Limestone
14 x 13 cm

Three columns of text with dividers, reading from right to left, signs facing right:

(1) ... *Itn-ꜥnḫ wr imy ḥb sd nb* (2) *[šnnt] nbt I[t]n nb pt nb tꜣ ḥry-ib Rw[d-mnw?]* ... (3) ... *ꜥnḫ Itn m ꜣḫt It[n]* ....

The restoration was suggested to me by Donald Redford (personal communication).
UM storage photograph 17–29.

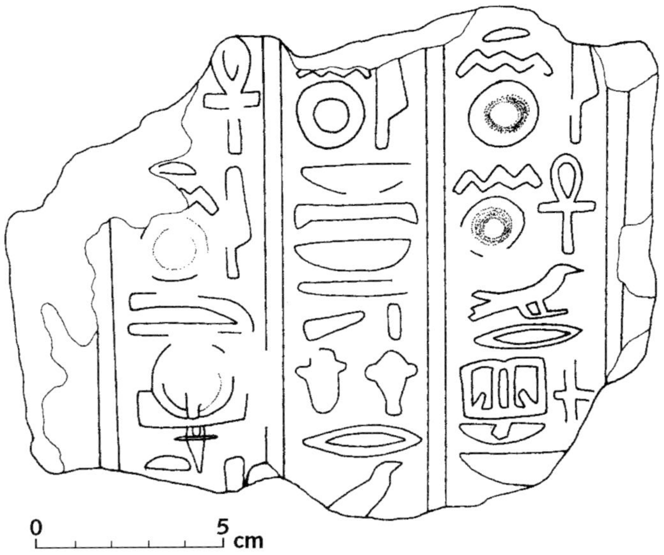

Fig. 135. NK 41, facsimile drawing

NK 42 (FIG. 136)

Not catalogued. Illustrated in Silverman, "The So-called Portal Temple of Ramesses II at Abydos," in *Akten des vierten internationalen Ägyptologen-Kongresses, München,* vol. 2 (Munich, 1985), pl. 34
Limestone
26 x 55 cm

Space on left uninscribed and undecorated, followed by the two vertical cartouches of the Aten above the horizontal epithet *di ꜥnḫ ḏt nḥḥ* and three partly preserved columns with dividers, signs facing left:

(1) ... *wr imy ḥb-sd nb šnnt nbt* (2) *I(tn) nb pt nb tꜣ ḥry-ib qd.f ꜣḫt* (3) ... *m Itn* ....

Fig. 136. NK 42, facsimile drawing

NK 43 (FIG. 137)

Not catalogued

Illustrated in line drawing in Silverman, "The So-called Portal Temple of Ramesses II at Abydos," in *Akten des vierten internationalen Ägyptologen-Kongresses, München,* vol. 2 (Munich, 1985), fig. 2.1

Limestone

23 x 27 cm

Corner fragment. On one face: remains of part of a large cartouche of the Aten, facing right, followed on left by a column of text within dividers, signs facing right: *Ỉ(tn) nb pt nb tꜣ ḥry-ib qd[.f ꜣḫt].* On the other face: two columns within dividers of larger scale hieroglyphs facing left:

(1) … *Ỉ(t)n ꜥnḫ* … (2) … *t Ỉtn* ….

Fig. 137. NK 43, facsimile drawings

NK 44 (FIG. 138)

Not catalogued

Limestone

24 x 54 cm

Royal figures within a pavillion. Three pairs, each with the king followed by a queen on a smaller scale. The two pairs on the left face right and the pair on the right faces left. For a parallel to this frequent scene, cf. N. de G. Davies, *The Rock Tombs of El Amarna* 3, pl. 8 (Huya).

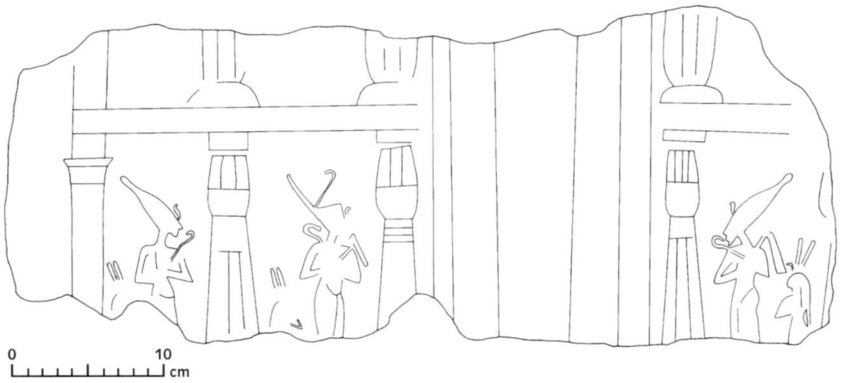

Fig. 138. NK 44, facsimile drawing

NK 45 (FIG. 139)

Not catalogued

Limestone

23 x 54 cm

Royal head, facing left, with streamer, to which a ray of the sun presents an ankh held in a hand. Illustrated in D. O'Connor, *Expedition* 12, no. 1 (fall, 1969), p. 34.

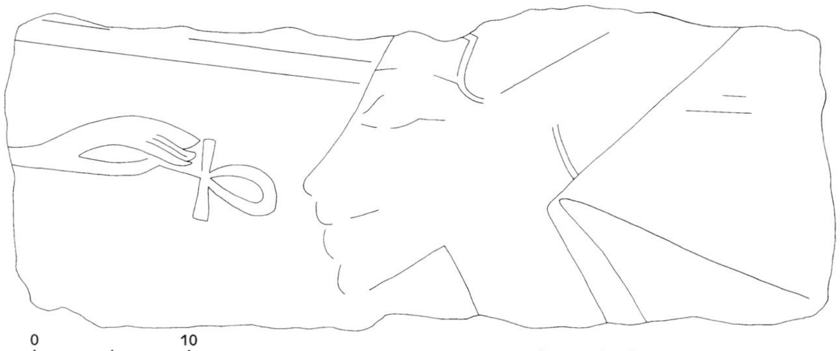

Fig. 139. NK 45, facsimile drawing

NK 46 (FIG. 140)

Not catalogued

Limestone

23 x 51 cm

Lower part of bending figure of man with staff on right, facing right.

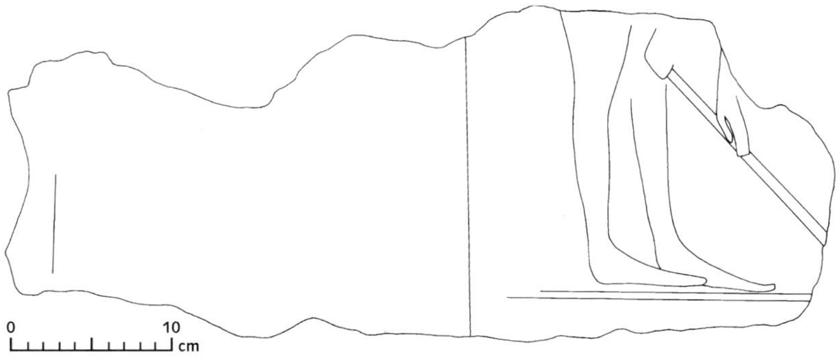

Fig. 140. NK 46, facsimile drawing

NK 47 (FIG. 141)

Not catalogued

Limestone

20 x 25 cm

Lower part of standing man with double garment and hands at side, facing right.

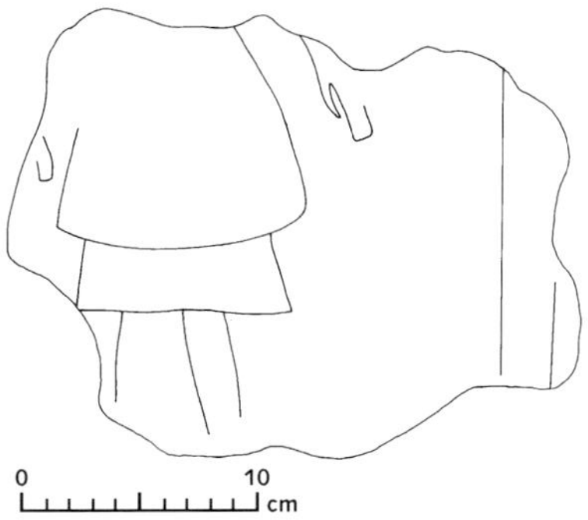

Fig. 141. NK 47, facsimile drawing

Stamped Bricks and Seals

On stamped bricks, cf. A.J. Spencer, *Brick Architecture in Ancient Egypt* (Warminster, 1979), and Erno Gaál, *Stamped Bricks from TT 32,* Studia Aegyptiaca 15 (Budapest, 1993).

SBS 1 (fig. 142)

Cairo JdE 91224. Expedition 67.94 (Cairo). UM 69–29–900, 906–909, 913. Expedition 67. 14, 122, 123, 124, 125, 273, 631
Various locations: RP 6 F (E) 36, 4 F (5 ex.), G 5 N (4 ex.), G 6 E (2 ex.), 5 F N (2 ex.), 5 E W (2 ex.), 5 E S+W , 5 F S + W, 5 F S, 5 F W, 4 D N+W (1 example each); not recorded: 8 examples
33 x 16 x 9 cm, 31 x 15 x 8 cm, 32 x 15.5 x 9 cm. Stamp area 14 x 6 cm
Approximately 30 mud bricks stamped with title and name: *ỉmy-r pr ḥḏ Ỉmn-ḥtp mꜣꜥ-ḫrw,* "the overseer of the treasury Amen-hotep, vindicated."

SBS 2 (fig. 143)

UM 69–29–914, 915, 919. Expedition 67.274, 467, 541, 542
Various locations, including RP 6 F (S+E) 37 (67.274), RP 6 E N, 6 F S, 7 F S 7, E
37 x 18 x 11 cm. Stamp area 12.5 x 6 cm
Dynasty 19, Ramesses II. Five stamped mud bricks of *Wsỉr ṯꜣty ỉmy-r niwt Pꜣsr, mꜣꜥ-ḫrw,* "The Osiris, vizier and overseer of the city, Paser, vindicated." Cf. V.A. Donohue, *JEA* 74 (1988), p. 111. For monuments of the vizier, see Kitchen, *KRI* 3, pp. 1–36, including a stamped brick from Theban Tomb 106 on p. 9.

SBS 3 (fig. 144)

UM Uncatalogued 699, 620
RP 5 F W, 5 F S+W, 7 F N+E, 8 E or F E
33 x 15 x 10 cm. Stamp area 14.5 x 6.5 cm
Five mud bricks stamped with title and name: *sš mšꜥ(?) n nb tꜣwy Mnty,* "scribe of the army(?) of the lord of the two lands, Mentjy." The title is an important one in the New Kingdom.

SBS 4 (fig. 145)

UM Unnumbered. Uncatalogued 696
RP J 6 N, H 7 S, H 7 E (1 example each), H 6 N, G 6 W, H 6 W (2 examples each), 3 examples with location unrecorded
27 x 18.5 (12) x 10 (8) cm. Small square stamp, area 6.5 x 6.5 cm
Twelve mud bricks stamped with title and name: *ḫrt*(?) *gnwty*(?) *Ḏsr*(?)*-Nb-by mwt.f Mr(t)* (?) *Mn-ḫꜣ* .... The text is abraded and continued study unsuccessful.

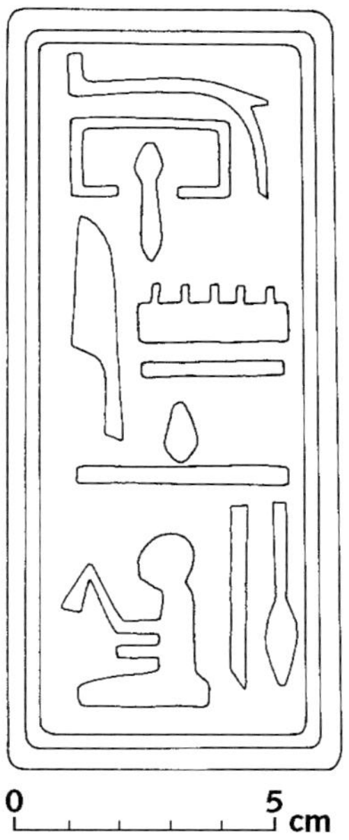

Fig. 142. sbs 1, facsimile drawing

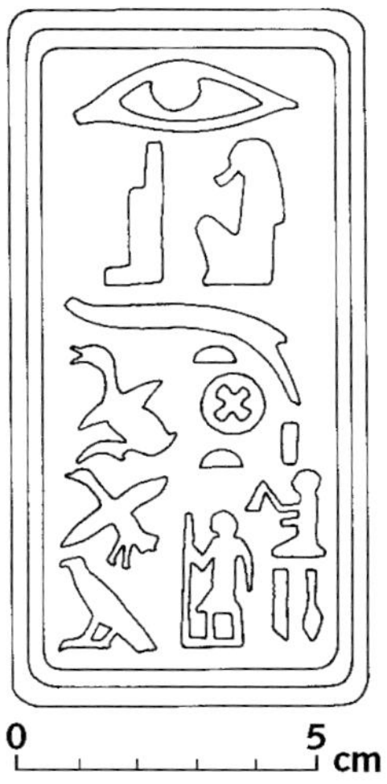

Fig. 143. sbs 2, facsimile drawing

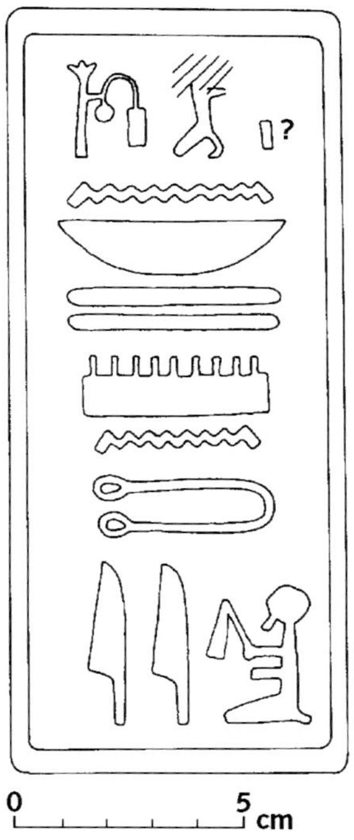

Fig. 144. sbs 3, facsimile drawing

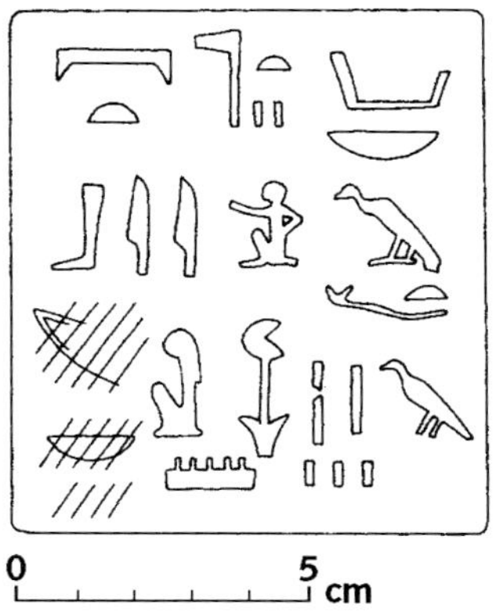

Fig. 145. sbs 4, facsimile drawing

SBS 5 (FIG. 146)

UM Uncatalogued 697
RP 4 F 9, G 3 E
31 x 15.5 x 9 cm. Stamp area 10 x 5.5 cm
Thirteen mud bricks stamped with title and name: *Ṯꜣy sryt ... mry tꜣwy Pꜣ-ḫw*(?), "fan-bearer of the beloved of the two lands, Pahu(?)." The text must be collated before an understanding is achieved.

SBS 6 (FIG. 147)

UM Unnumbered. Expedition Uncatalogued 698
RP J 7 (N), J 8 (E)
38 x 18 x 14 cm. Stamp area 13 x 5 cm
Two mud bricks stamped with the name *Mꜣꜥt-kꜣ-Rꜥ* in cartouche (of Hatshepsut).

SBS 7 (FIG. 148)

UM Unnumbered. Expedition Uncatalogued 6915
RP G 7 N
36 x 17 x 13 cm. Stamp area 13.5 x 5.5 cm
One mud brick stamped with the name: *Ḥr Nṯrt/Wsrt-kꜣw* in cartouche (of Hatshepsut).

SBS 8 (FIG. 149)

UM 69–29–934. Expedition 67.616
RP 8 F 4
12.3 x 12.3 x 5.6 cm. Stamp area 8.5 x 4 cm
Mud jar stopper with sealing of Horemheb: *Ḏsr-ḫprw-Rꜥ stp n Rꜥ*. (twice). Curiously, the text seems to end with a redundant *Rꜥ*.

SBS 9 (FIG. 150)

UM 69–29–932. Expedition 67.526
RP 7 F (N) 56
8 x 6 cm
Unbaked gritty mud brick jar stopper. Text in oval(?) ending in: ... *tꜣ* ... *m ꜣbḏw*.

SBS 10 (FIG. 151)

UM 69–29–1012. Expedition 68.17
RP 4 E (N)
3.5 x 2 x 1 cm
Baked gray mud seal with text in cartouche surmounted by double plume: *mḥt nb ꜣbḏw (wbn?)*.

SBS 11 (FIG. 152)

UM 69–29–930. Expedition 67.235
RP 6 E (W) 64
14 x 14 x 6.5
Unbaked mud seal with two impressions in an oval (3 x 5 cm) In center: *ꜥnḫ* with falcon over basket facing the sign on either side.

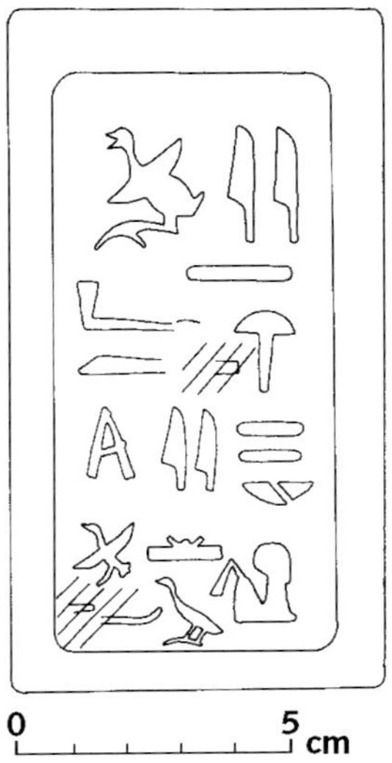

Fig. 146. SBS 5, facsimile drawing

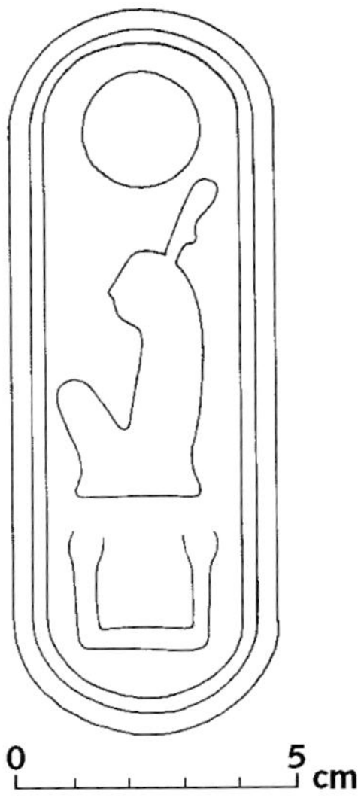

Fig. 147. SBS 6, facsimile drawing

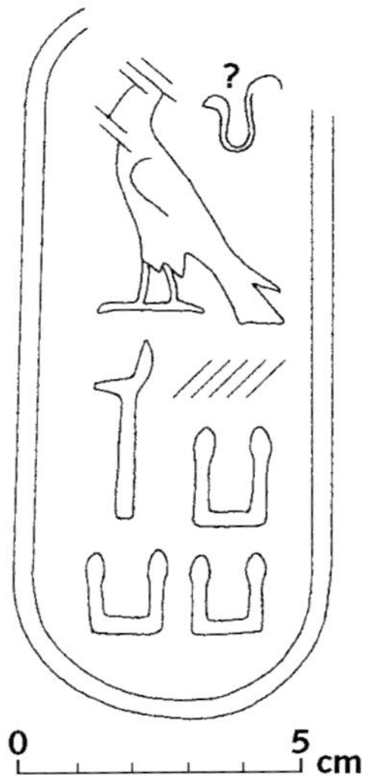

Fig. 148. SBS 7, facsimile drawing

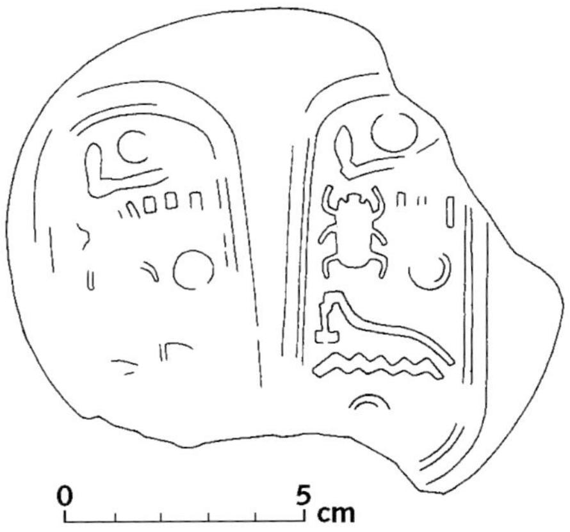

Fig. 149. SBS 8, facsimile drawing

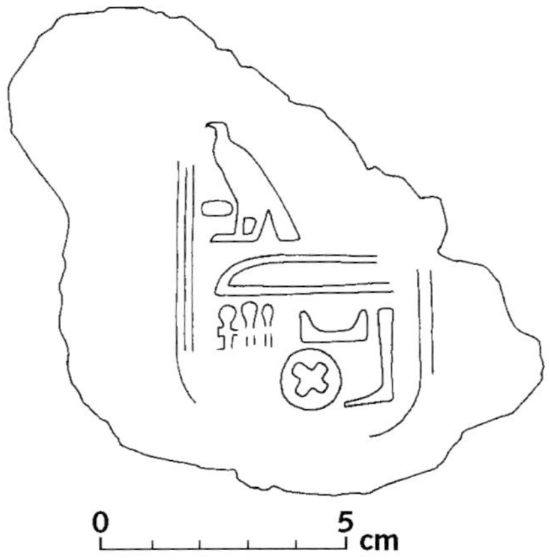

Fig. 150. SBS 9, facsimile drawing

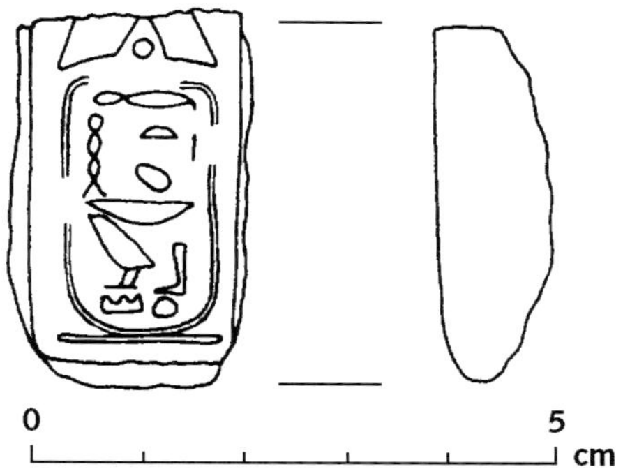

Fig. 151. SBS 10, facsimile drawing

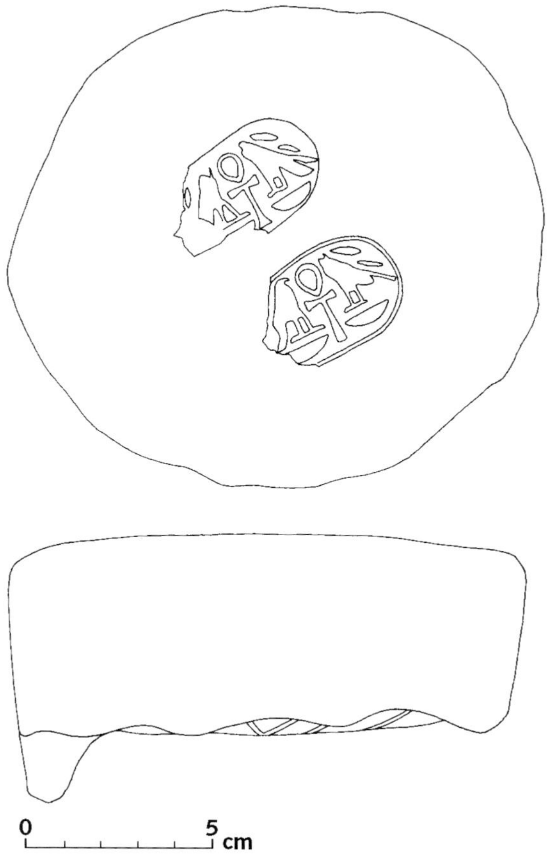

Fig. 152. SBS 11, facsimile drawing

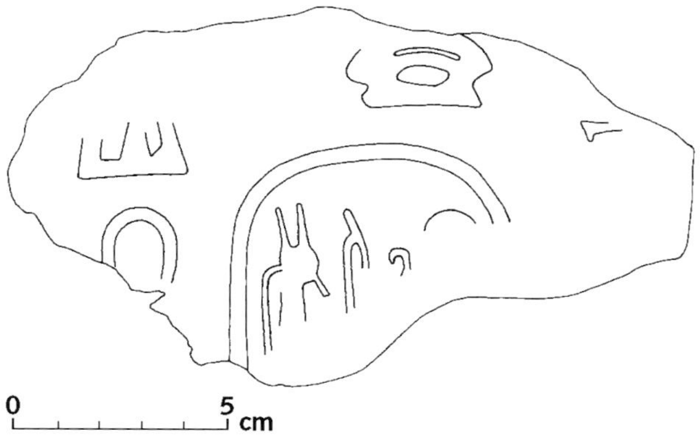

Fig. 153. SBS 12, facsimile drawing

SBS 12 (FIG. 153)

UM 69–29–941. Expedition 67.673
RP 16 x 10 x 5.5 cm
Impression on coarse, gritty plaster with titulary: *[nb] ḫꜥ[w]* followed by beginning of Ramesside cartouche and *dỉ ꜥnḫ*.

SBS 13 (FIG. 154)

A) UM 69–29–927. Expedition 67.21
4 x 7 x 2 cm
B) UM 69–29–929. Expedition 67.204
6.5 x 2 cm
C) UM 69–29–928. Expedition 67.22
3.5 x 2.5 x 1.5 cm
Gray clay sealing with fine impressions:

ḥm nṯr sḫnwt ḥm nṯr nrw n(?) … *ḥm nṯr ḥmt*

SBS 14 (FIG. 155)

UM 69–29–1014. Expedition 69.145
Kom Sultan TR 1
4.5 x 3 x 1.5 cm
Four scarab impressions on gray clay.

SBS 15 (FIG. 156)

UM 69–29–935. Expedition 67.632
RP
Mud sealing on jar stopper(?) with impressed writing(?).

SBS 16 (FIG. 157)

UM 69–29–1013. Expedition 68.20
RP 5 D (N)
Diameter 3.5 cm, thickness 2.3 cm
Baked gray mud seal with design and impressed writing(?).

SBS 17 (FIG. 158)

UM 69–29–931. Expedition 67.307
RP 7 C (W) 33
Diameter 1.8 cm, thickness 1.3 cm
Mud sealing with writing(?).

SBS 18 (PL. 23D)

UM 69–29–396. Expedition 69.45
RP H 7 (E)
3.5 x 2.3 x 5.7 (deep) cm
Limestone seal with "Horsiese" in oval at end.

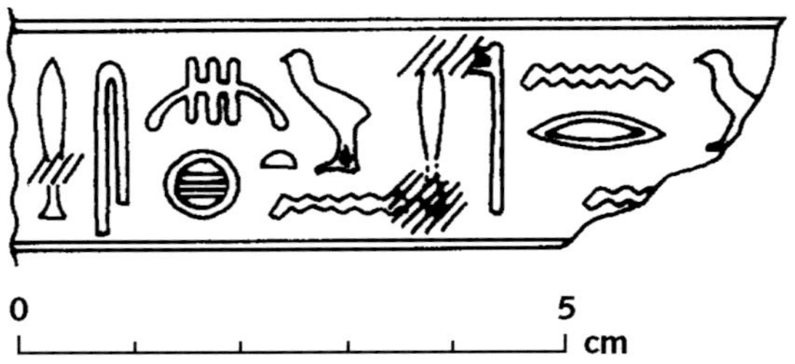

Fig. 154. sbs 13, facsimile drawing

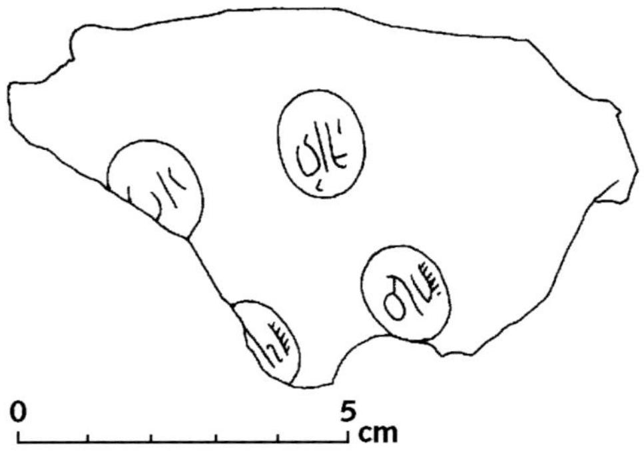

Fig. 155. sbs 14, facsimile drawing

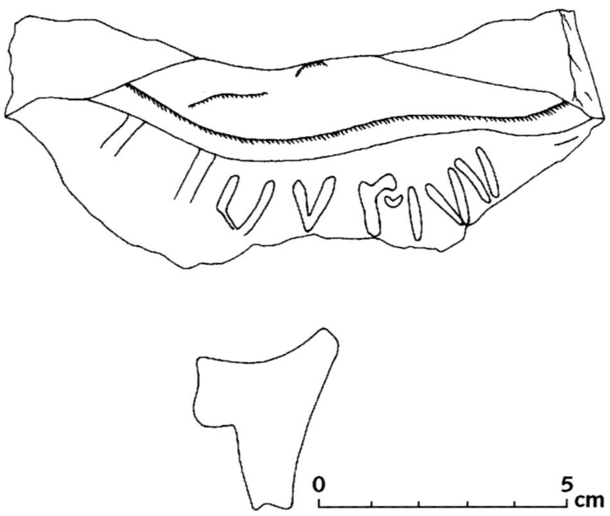

Fig. 156. sbs 15, facsimile drawing

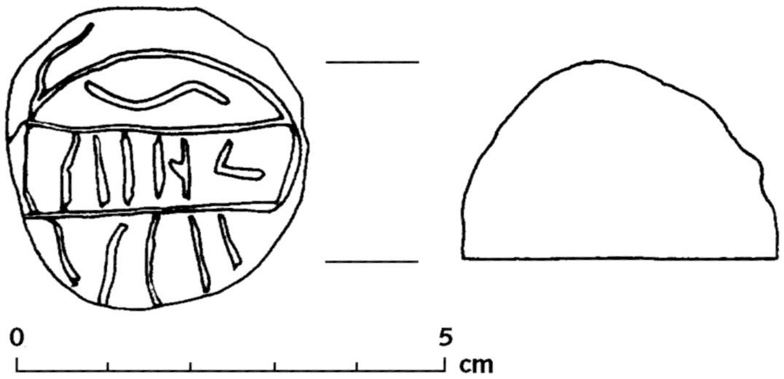

Fig. 157. sbs 16, facsimile drawing

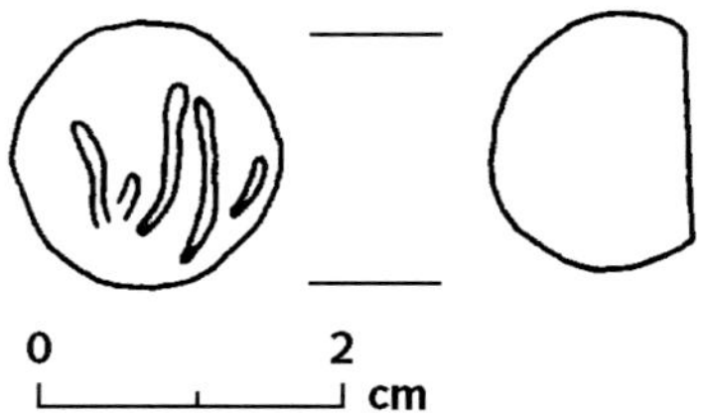

Fig. 158. sbs 17, facsimile drawing

Third Intermediate Period Objects

I am indebted to Prof. David O'Connor for drawing my attention to notes taken on this material by Prof. Anthony Leahy, whose comments and information about these texts have been utilized with his permission. The stela NK 4 above (Cairo JdE 91274) is dated by Leahy to the Third Intermediate Period, and it is likely that several of the stela fragments listed under NK (New Kingdom) actually belong to the Third Intermediate Period. The objects listed below, however, are specifically datable to this period. For a discussion of Abydos in this time, see: Anthony Leahy, "Abydos in the Libyan Period," in Anthony Leahy, ed., *Libya and Egypt c 1300–750 BC* (London, 1990), pp. 155–200. Several titles and personnel at the site are discussed by H. de Meulenaere, *Orientalia Lovaniensia Periodica* 6–7 (1975/1976), pp. 133–51. Several of the names represented in de Meulenaere's corpus are also attested in the following material, but specific identifications are improbable.

Inscribed Objects from the Tomb of Redi-Anhur (Tomb 3)

Dated by Leahy 700–650 B.C., Late Dynasty 25–Early Dynasty 26

TIP 1A (fig. 159, pls. 24–26a)

Cairo JdE 91219. Three fragments. Expedition 67.313 (left); 67.315 (right); 67.215 (small fragment on extreme right)
RP 7 C (W) 39 Tomb 3, NW of forecourt of temple
67.313+315, exclusive of 67.215: length 1.38 m
Height without moulding above: ca. 52 cm (= 1 cubit)
Lintel in three fragments of *Rdi-ỉnḥr* with torus moulding above. Left side illustrated by O'Connor, *Expedition* 10, no. 1 (1967), p. 16; *Expedition* 11, no. 1 (1968), p. 28. Traced by V. Pigott.

On the left, facing right, the owner sits on a chair with lion-foot terminals on cups, a low back, holding a napkin in his right hand and extending his left toward a table of breads. He wears a shoulder-length wig, broad collar, sash with leopard head(?) insignia, and beard. The offering table on a stand with breads has a tray above with offerings and pottery jars below on stands, a spouted ewer to the left on its own high metal or wood stand. Above the tray with offerings are the figure 1,000 four times above (right to left) the designations for bread, beer, cattle, and fowl. Between the offerings and the figure of the owner are four horizontal lines of text and a fifth vertical: "for the ka of the one honored before Osiris, foremost of the westerners, *Rdit-ỉnḥr,* united with every fine product, offerings."

To the right of the scene and text are two vertical columns of text:

> (1) Recitation: your water belongs to you, your abundance belongs to you, your plant growth belongs to you—which(?) comes forth from Osiris.
> (2) Recitation: your offerings (*ʿḫ*) belong to you, which come forth from Nephthys, O' *Rdi-ỉnḥr,* take to yourself your bread.

Facing this section to the right and facing left is a figure of the owner's son, largely damaged by the break, wearing a kilt ending just above the knee and pouring a libation from a vessel with his right hand. In front of him are five partly preserved horizontal lines:

> (1) *šd* ...... (2) *sꜣ.f smsw* ... (3) *ỉmn-mn* ... (4) *rḫ nsw mꜣʿ sp sn* (5) *ẖry-ḥꜣb Wnn-nfrỉ*
>
> (1)(?) ... (2) his eldest son ... (3) Amen-men(?) ... (4) very true king's acquaintance (5) the lector priest Wenen-nefer.

On the adjoining right side of the broken lintel is the head and left shoulder of this figure followed by two registers with figures and text.

The upper register consists of five standing figures, each with short kilt ending above the knee, shoulder-length wig, broad collar and sash. The first holds a staff with a mace-like terminal in his right hand, a napkin in the left; the second and fourth with hands at the side empty, and the third and fifth (partly damaged and missing) the right arm bent across the breast. The five men are captioned vertically in front of each:

> (1) *sꜣ.f smsw mr.f ḥm-nṯr Wn*(?)(*n-nfr*) (2) *sn.f Ḏd-ỉnḥr-ỉw.f-ʿnḫ* (3) *sn.f šps nsw ỉmn-ỉr-dỉ-sw* (4) *sn.f Ḏd-Ḏḥwty-ỉw.f-ʿnḫ* (5) *sn.f ḥsk ʿnḫ-Wsrkn*

The first is evidently the same man as the large standing figure to the left, followed by four brothers, also the sons of the tomb owner and each called his brother:

> (2) Djed-Anher-iuf-ankh, (3) the king's noble Amenerdisu,
> (4) Djed-Djehuty-iuf-ankh, (5) and the *ḥsk* Ankh-Osorkon.

This last figure is partly completed on the small third fragment (67.215) to the right of which the head of the owner faces right. On the reading of the name with initial ankh, see A. Leahy, "The Libyan Rulers in the Onomastic Record," in Alan Lloyd, ed., *Studies in Pharaonic Religion and Society in Honour of J. Gwyn Griffiths* (London, 1992), pp. 146–63, esp. p. 148, citation A 3 (this example).

The lower register consists of a seated harper leaning forward on his harp (damaged) and five standing women (the last missing but inferred from the caption). Each of the four preserved is identically represented with tripartite wig and close-fitting sheath dress from above the breasts to just above the ankles. The first also wears a broad collar.

> (1) *sꜣt.f wrt mr.f Ḏd-Mwt-ỉw.s-ʿnḫ* (2) *sn(t).s mry.f nt st ỉb.f Sꜣt-Nwbt* (3) *sn(t).s mr.f Tꜣ-šr(t) n(t) Mḥt* (4) *sn(t).s mry.f Mry-ỉt.s* (5) *sn(t).s mry.f Rnpt-nfrt*
>
> (1) His eldest daughter whom he loves Djed-Mut-ius-ankh,

(2) her sister whom he loves, of the place of his heart, Sit-Nubt, (3) her sister whom he loves Tasherit-net-mehet, (4) her sister whom he loves Meretyotes, (5) her sister whom he loves Renpet-nefret.

Note that the first son is designated as son while the others are called his (the son's) brothers, and similarly the eldest daughter is so designated and followed by her sisters. On the under surface of the lintel is the partly preserved column *Ḏd-mdw Ỉn-....*

Color notes: Much of the scene and text has been outlined in red before carving and shows traces of this color. The stone carver only approximately followed these directions, so that the carved hieroglyphs are frequently to the right or left of the red outlines. A blue border between thin red lines encloses the scene and is preserved along the top, left side, and bottom. On the left half the two columns of text have a dark yellow, ochre background. The necklaces of the second and fourth standing males in the upper register are painted blue. There are also traces of yellow outlines, particularly in the water flowing from the libation jar. For reference to this tomb, see Leahy and Leahy, *JEA* 72 (1986), p. 145, n. 26. The large head on the right, facing right, indicates that perhaps the length of the lintel was considerably larger. The extensive listing of family is perhaps indicative of the Libyan tribal system. References to the proper names on the lintel are as follows.

Ỉmn-mn ...	*PN* I, p. 29.6
Wnn-nfrỉ	*PN* I, p. 79.20
Ḏd-Ỉnḥr-ỉw.f-ꜥnḫ	*PN* I, p. 410.4 (frequent)
Ỉmn-r-dỉ-sw	*PN* I, p. 26.24
Ḏd-Ḏḥwty-ỉw.f ꜥnḫ	*PN* I, p. 412.8 (frequent)
Ḏd-Mwt-ỉw.s-ꜥnḫ	*PN* I, p. 410.16
Sꜣt-Nwbt(?)	not in *PN*
Tꜣ-šrt-nt-Mḥt	*PN* I, p. 369.4
Mry-ỉt.s/Mryt-ỉt.s	*PN* I, p. 161.17
Rnpt-nfrt	*PN* I, p. 224.11
Rdỉ(t)-Ỉnḥr	not in *PN*

TIP IB (FIG. 160, PL. 26B)

Cairo JdE 91261. Expedition 69.127 (or 921?)
RP F 7 (W)
Limestone
32 x 40 x 9 cm

Part of relief lintel(?), with head of tomb owner facing right, short wig, short beard, holding staff at diagonal in right hand and staff ending in a hand in his left hand, probably from a seated figure. The figure is painted red. For this type of staff, usually used to hold a fly-whisk, see C. Sourdive, *La main dans l'Egypte pharaonique* (Berne, 1984), pp. 134–73. In front of the head is the name Redi-Anhur. Above are six short columns of text separated by thick dividing lines:

(1) *ḥꜣty-ꜥ smr wꜥty* (2) *ḫrp ꜥḥ ỉmy ỉb nb.f* (3) *ỉry kꜣt nb n nsw* (4) *ḫry-ḥꜣb ḥry tp sḫm* (5) *ḥm(w) nṯrw ḥm-nṯr ꜣst ḥm* (6) ... *Rdỉt-Ỉnḥr*

(1) Hereditary prince, sole companion, (2) controller of the palace who is in the heart of his lord, (3) supervisor of all the construction works of the king, (4) chief lector priest, controller (5) of the priest(s) of the gods, priest of Isis, (6) ... Redit-Anhur.

I am not certain that I have understood the order of the title elements at the end of the text beginning with the end of column 4. Note the alternation of the name as *Rdỉt-Ỉnḥr* and *Rdỉ-Ỉnḥr.* A fragment of inscribed relief from the tomb was seen around 1972 on the Antiquities Market in Cairo but has not been located.

TIP IC (PLS. 27A–B)

UM 69–29–964. Expedition 67.661
Tomb 3, NW of forecourt of portal temple of Ramesses II
Wood coffin fragments with horizontal and vertical texts of the *Nbt pr špst Sꜣt-nwb,* daughter of the *ḥm-nṯr Ỉmn sš ḥtpw nṯr Ỉmn m Ỉpt-swt ... X.* Another fragment mentions the ... *nsw nṯrw ỉmy-r Šmꜥt wr ḥꜣt*(?) *Wsrkn. Sꜣt-nwbt* is presumably the same person represented as the second of the women relatives in the lintel TIP IA = Cairo JdE 91219 above. Dated by Leahy to 650–630 B.C.

Wooden coffin support with tenon at base, hieroglyphs (vertically) in white, facing left
79 x 7 x 7 cm

Ḥtp dỉ nsw Ỉtm nb tꜣwy(?) *Ỉwnw dỉ.f ḫt nb nfr wꜥb n kꜣ n Sꜣtt-Nwbt mꜣꜥ-ḫrw* (pl. 27B right)

Similar coffin support, hieroglyphs (vertically) in white facing left with tenon at base
76 x 7 x 7 cm

Ḥtp [dỉ nsw] Ỉnpw nb tꜣ ḏsr ...(?) *dỉ.f ḥtpwt nb n kꜣ n nbt pr Sꜣtt-Nwbt ....* (pl. 27B left)

Similar fragment
96.5 x 9 x 2.5 cm
Horizontal text, left to right: *ḏd mdw ỉn Ws-ỉr ḫntt ỉmntt ...*

Similar fragment
33 x 8 x 3 cm
Horizontal text: *ỉmꜣḫ ḫr Nbt-Ḥwt ...*

Similar fragment, horizontal text right to left: ... *Rꜥ Ḥr ꜣḫty*(?) *nṯr ꜥꜣ Ḥr ....* (pl. 27A)

Similar fragment
40 x 8 x 2.5 cm
Horizontal hieroglyphs right to left: *dỉ.f*(?) *ḥtpt nb ...*

Other Third Intermediate Period Objects

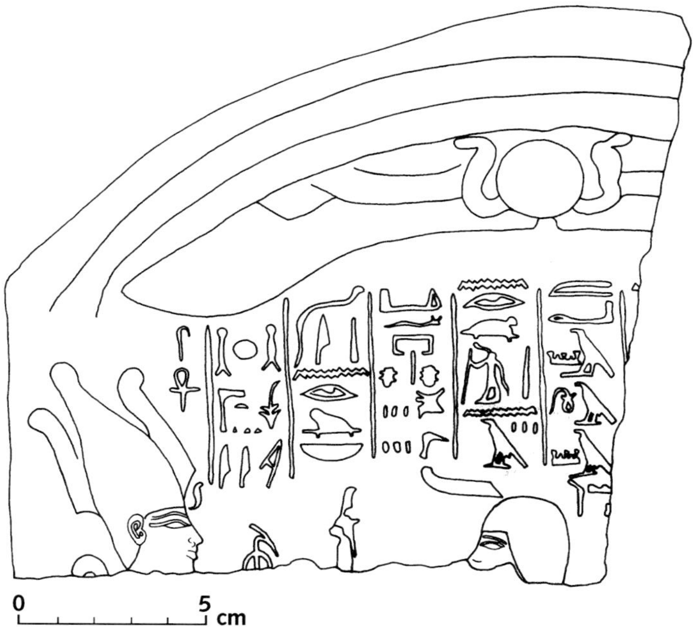

Fig. 162. TIP 3, facsimile drawing

TIP 2 (FIG. 161)
UM 69–29–1018. Expedition 68.90
RP 5 (E) 5
A) 11.5 x 14 cm
B) 4.3 x 5.5 cm
C) 4 x 5.3 cm
Three cartonnage fragments, black text on red varnished surface with spear-carrying divinity with Ibis(?) head, four columns of text to right, and two fragments, unplaced, each with three columns of text, mentioning the *ỉmy-ỉs, ḥsk Ḏd-ỉst-[ỉw.s ʿnḫ],* on one of the smaller fragments, and the *ỉmy-ỉs [Ns-pꜣ]-qꜣ-šwty* on the main fragment. For the titles *ḥsk* and *ỉmy ỉs,* see Leahy, *SAK* 8 (1980), p. 174, with reference to de Meulenaere, *CdE* 29 (1954), pp. 227–28. H. de Meulenaere points out that the title sequence is very common at Abydos in the Late Period and provides an extensive series of examples. Leahy indicates that *ỉmy ỉst* and *ḥsk* were cult officials of Shu-Tefnut and Osiris respectively.

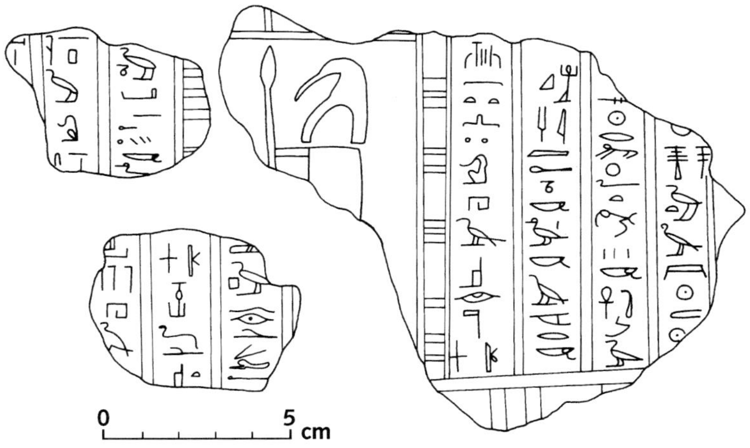

Fig. 161. TIP 2, facsimile drawing

TIP 3 (FIG. 162, PL. 27C)
Cairo JdE 91272 . Expedition 67.216
RP 6 E (W) 45
Upper left corner of smoke-blackened limestone stela
16 x 18 x 4 cm
Below a winged sun disk with uraei, Osiris with *atef* crown and uraeus, standing(?) on left, facing right, is presented with the figure of Maat by the dedicator, facing left, wearing a horizontal feather. Four columns of text with dividers on left, facing right read:

> (2) *ḏd mdw ỉn Ws-ỉr nb* (3) *nḥḥ mry nsw nṯrw* (4) *ḥqꜣ ʿnḫ*
> (1) *dỉ.f prt ḫrw tꜣ ḥnqt kꜣw ꜣpdw*
>
> (2) Recitation by Osiris, Lord (3) of eternity, beloved (sic) of the king of the gods, (4) ruler of life, (1) may he grant a voice invocation of bread, beer, cattle, and fowl.

On the right three columns of text, facing left, continue:

> (1) *n Ws-ỉr wr ʿꜣ nꜣ* (2) *Mšwš* (3) …
> (1) for the Osiris, great chief of the (2) Meshwesh, (3) ….

For another Abydene stela citing a great chief of the Meshwesh, see G. Daressy, *ASAE* 5 (1904), p. 93.

TIP 4A (FIG. 163, PL. 27D)
Cairo JdE 91259. Expedition 67.475, 592
RP 4 F (E) 5
Limestone
5 x 11.7 x 1.9–3.7 cm
Five horizontal lines of a stela. Incised hieroglyphs:

> (1) *[ḥqꜣ] ḏt Ḥr nḏ ỉt.f* … (2) … *tꜣwy ꞽIwnw psḏt ʿꜣt ỉmy* … (3) *Nmrtỉ* … (4) *sš mnḫt mrḥt kbḥ mw ỉrp ỉrtt(t)* … (5) *dd n pt qmꜣ tꜣ* …

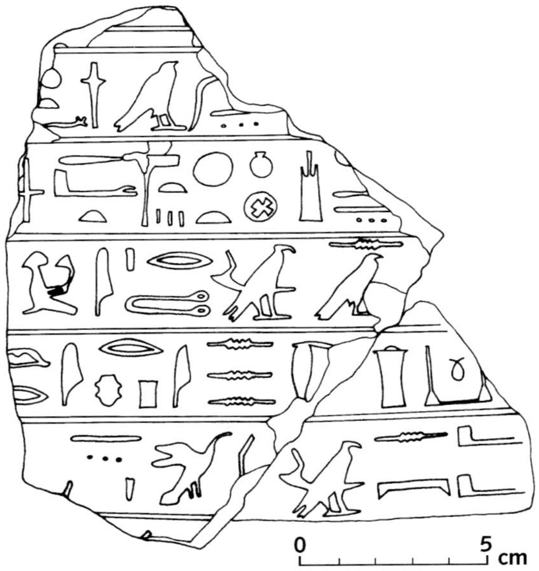

Fig. 163. TIP 4A, facsimile drawing

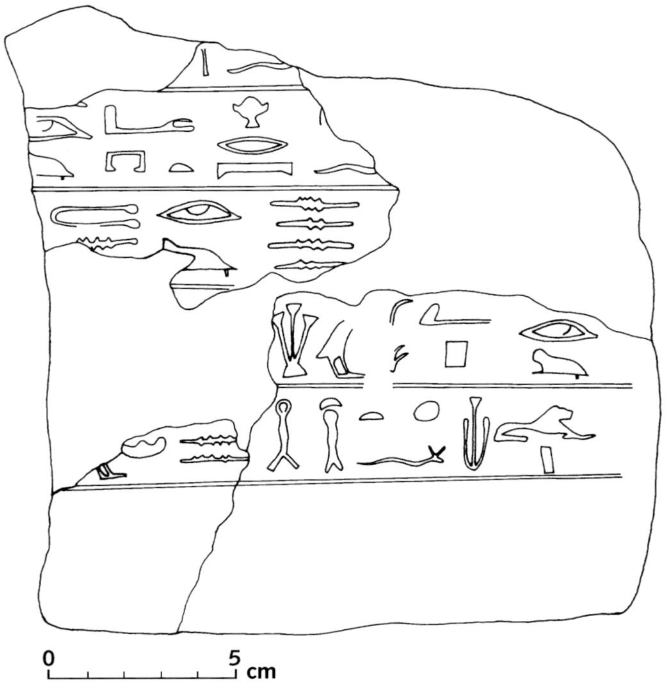

Fig. 164. TIP 4B, facsimile drawing

> (1) [ruler] of eternity, Horus, avenger of his father ... (2) ... the two lands, Heliopolis, great Ennead which is in ... (3) ... Namlot ... (4) alabaster, linen, oil, libation, water, wine, milk ... (5) which the sky provides and earth creates ....

TIP 4B (FIG. 164, PL. 27E)

UM 69–29–51. Expedition 69.174 A, B, C
RP G 6 (W)
Limestone
A (lower left) 10.5 x 5.5 x 5 cm
B (upper left) 15 x 11 x 7 cm
C (lower right) 16 x 13 x 7 cm

Five fragmentary lines on three pieces, possibly of the same stela as TIP 4 A found two years later. Although many of the hieroglyphs are clear, it is difficult to make connected sense of the context. Note in the second line of B the phrase *ḫry ꜥt,* "overseer of the chamber(?)." A singular orthographic characteristic of 67.475 and 69.174 A, B is the curious writing of *n* ﹏ (Sign List N 35) as a horizontal with two to four "bumps" in the middle.

TIP 5 (FIG. 165, PL. 28)

Cairo JdE 91251. Expedition 67.341
RP 7D (N) 28
Limestone
28.8 x 22.5 x 3.5 cm

Stela of Nephthys-tekhti. O'Connor, *Expedition* 10, no. 1 (1967), p. 16; *The Egyptian Museum Cairo in Ten Years (1965–1975)* (Cairo, 1976), no. 85, pl. 7. In the lunate under a winged sun disk is the *nfr* sign flanked by *wedjat* eyes and recumbent jackals. In the register below, the owner is represented standing, arms raised in adoration, before a table of offerings, wearing a long fringed garment, short wig, and incense cone. On the left, facing right, is a falcon-headed god standing on a podium with sun disk with uraeus on his head holding a *wꜣs* scepter with both hands in front. In front of the podium is a lotus flower with stem standing on a *shen* sign and topped by the figures of the four sons of Horus. The vertical caption to the god reads "Re," the horizontal caption to the dedicant, from left to right, reads *imꜣḫt (ḫ)r Ws-ir Nbt-ḥwt-tḫti,* "honored before Osiris, Nephthys-tekhti." For a similar (same?) name, see *PN* I, p. 189.5, with reference to G. Daressy, *Rec Trav* 24 (1902), p. 161, no. cxci, reading *Nbt-ḥwt-tꜣḫt.* Hornung points out that parents rarely gave children names compounded with that of Nephthys; cf. E. Hornung, in A.B. Lloyd, ed., *Studies in Pharaonic Religion and Society in Honour of J. Gwyn Griffiths* (London, 1992), pp. 186–88.

Three lines of text below the scene read:

> (1) *Ḥtp di nsw Ws-ir ḫnty-imntyw nṯr ꜥꜣ nb ꜣbḏw* (2) *di.f qrst nfr(t) m ḫryt-nṯr Nbt-ḥwt-tḫti sꜣ*(?) (3) ... *Ḥr-wḏꜣ*(?) *ms n Tꜣ-ḫrrt mꜣꜥ-ḫrw*
>
> (1) May the king grant an offering to Osiris, foremost of the westerners, the great god, lord of Abydos, (2) that he may grant a fine burial in the necropolis (for) Nephthys-tekhti, son/daughter of (3) ... Hor-wedja(?), born to Tahereret, vindicated.

For the name *Tꜣ-ḫrr(t),* see *PN* I, p. 366, 3, with reference to *British Museum Guide* (London, 1924), p. 65. Leahy suggests a date in the middle of the sixth century B.C.

TIP 6 (FIG. 166. PL. 29A)

Cairo JdE 91258. Expedition 67.473
RP 7 F (N) 3
Limestone
17 x 14 x 5 cm

Fragment of stela. Scene in sharply cut sunk relief, hieroglyphs sharply and neatly incised. Traces of red paint on winged disk, *wedjat* eye, *wesekh* vessel, and male figure; traces of blue paint in water

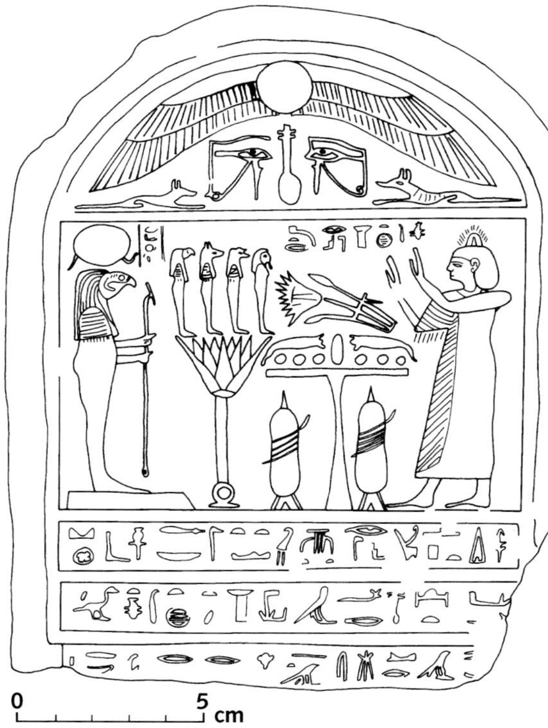

Fig. 165. TIP 5, facsimile drawing

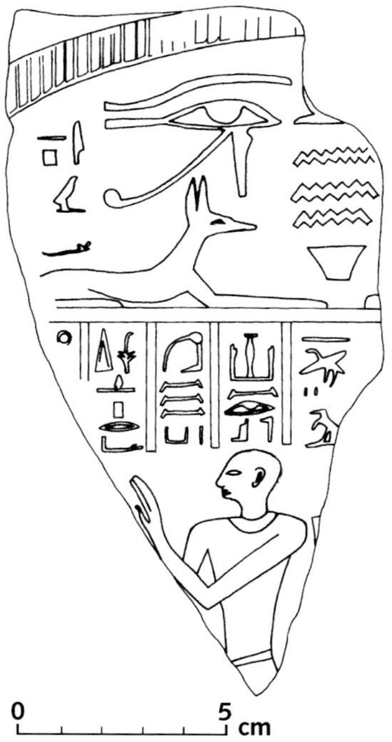

Fig. 166. TIP 6, facsimile drawing

sign in lunate. Below the *shen* sign, the water sign, and a *wesekh* vessel, and to the left a *wedjat* eye and a recumbent Anubis with the vertical text, *Ỉnpw tpy ḏw.f*, "Anubis upon his mountain." Of the scene beneath all that remains is the figure of a standing male facing left with upraised arm(s) in praise toward a missing figure of the divinity. To the left are two columns of text facing right:

(1) *ḥtp dỉ nsw Rꜥ* (2) ...

(1) May the king give an offering (to) Re, (2) ....

Above the figure of the dedicant three columns are preserved, facing left:

(1) *wꜥb kꜣ* (sic) (2) *ḥsk n Ws-ỉr n Pꜣy-nḥsy*

(1) *weeb* priest of the ka (sic), (2) *ḥsk* official of Osiris, (3) Paynehsy.

For the title *ḥsk n Ws-ỉr*, see references under TIP 2 above. Dated by Leahy to early sixth century B.C.

TIP 7 (FIG. 167, PL. 29B)

UM 69–29–91. Expedition 67.538
RP 7 F (E) 68
Limestone
31 x 20 x 5 cm
Fragment with remains of four columns of text facing right, the last with the titles *ỉt nṯr, ḥsk, ḥry sštꜣ ꜥr[q ḥḥ].*
UM storage photograph 15–27 or 33.

TIP 8 (FIG. 168, PL. 29C)

UM 69–29–126. Expedition 69.155

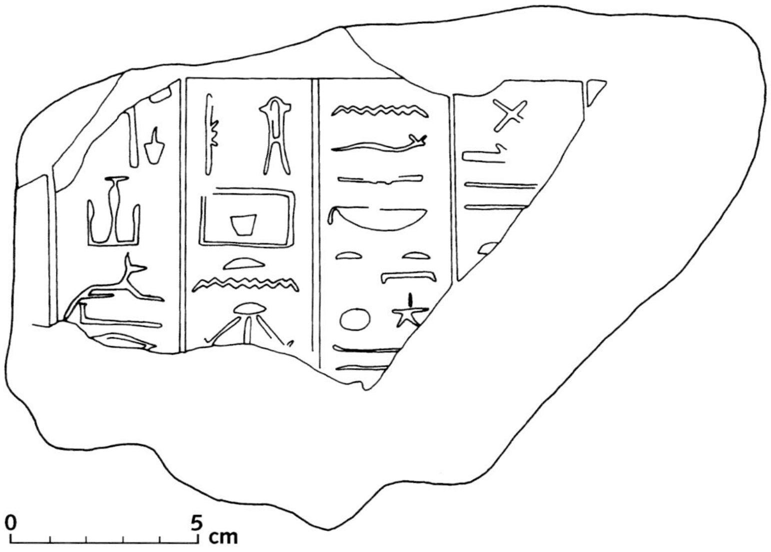

Fig. 167. TIP 7, facsimile drawing

RP T.T. 8
Limestone
35 x 32 x 8.5
Round-top stela fragment in three pieces with incised scene of dedicant before Abydene triad and members of family below, crude workmanship. In spite of the clarity of the photograph, the original is pecked out so crudely that the text is frequently unintelligible.
Upper register: On the left, the Abydene triad faces right toward the Abydene standard. Osiris is captioned (1) *Ws-ỉr nb Ḏdt* (2) *Wnn-nfr*

ḫnty imntyw; (3) *nṯr ꜥ3 nb 3bḏw.* Isis is captioned (4) *3st,* and Horus (5) *Ḥr-nḏ-it.f.* Osiris wears the *atef* crown with ram's horns and holds a *w3s* scepter, Isis extends her left hand forward, wears the disk and horns with vulture headdress, a long garment, and holds an ankh sign in her right hand. Hornedjyotef holds the *w3s* scepter in his left hand, an ankh in his right, and wears the double crown. Facing this group on the right, facing left, are eight crudely carved columns of text, an offering stand with a bouquet above it to the right of the Abydene symbol, and a dedicant with upraised arms, facing left on the extreme right. He wears a long pleated skirt. The text is almost incomprehensible.

(1) *Dw3 Ws-ir* (2) *Ḏd-mdw inḏ-ḥr nṯr ꜥ3* ... (3) *Wn-nfr s3 Ḥr*(?) (4) .... (5) *Ws-ir ḥsq*(?) ...... *s wr* ... *mwt.f Nwt* (6) ...... (cartouche) *Ḏd rdit n.f t3*(?) *nb ḏd* (7) .... *ḏd* ...... *ḥr* ... (8) *mrty*(?)*.f Wrdt*(?)

Perhaps this unsatisfactory reading can be improved upon.

Lower register: On the right below the dedicant in the register above is the text *iw wrr.* To the left are eight standing figures facing right, four pairs of a man and wife. All wear funerary cones on their heads, the men with short kilts and horizontal sashes across the shoulder, the women with long garments. All have their hands at the side. The first is captioned (?)*-nfr* followed by *ḥmt.f* .... The third is captioned *it* ..., followed by *ḥmt.f.* The fifth is captioned *it,* followed by *ḥmt.f Tik* .... The seventh is captioned *it Ḥr m3ꜥ-ḫrw,* followed by *ḥmt.f Tiḫnt.* Possibly this procession reflects the parents, and more remote grandparents for five generations including the dedicant.

UM storage photograph 22–34 or 18–1

Fig. 168. TIP 8, facsimile drawing

Late Period Objects

Under this heading several texts are included which are post-New Kingdom and Third Intermediate Period.

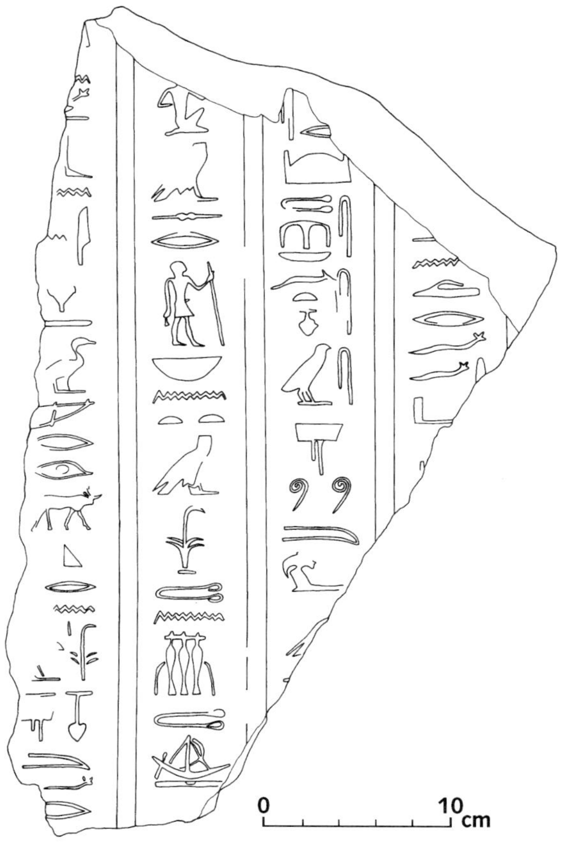

Fig. 170. LP 2, facsimile drawing

LP 1 (FIG. 169, PL. 30A)

UM 69–29–181. Expedition 69.204
RP
Limestone
28 x 32 x 5 cm
Inscription in five columns of text, top and bottom missing, left edge recessed. Enough is preserved on sides to indicate that there were only five columns.

> (1) *[Ws]-ỉr tꜣ ḥꜣt m ẖry … ḏf ḥn …* (2) *ỉmỉ.k dkn r ḥꜥt nṯr n.k …* (3) *[sbỉ]w.k sꜣw ỉꜣ ꜥꜣ …* (4) *sbỉw sp 4 ỉ sd … nỉwty ỉ h…* (5) *… 4 ỉm …*

UM storage photograph 18–4.

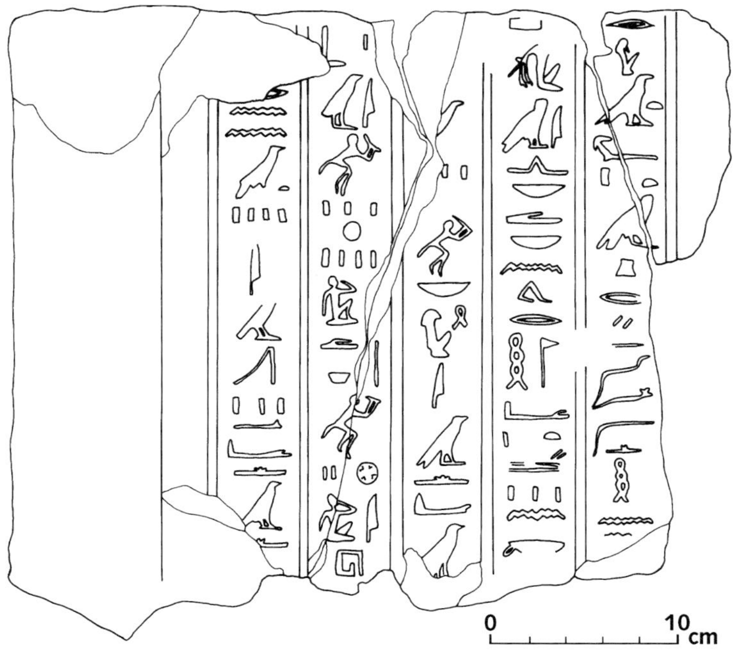

Fig. 169. LP 1, facsimile drawing

LP 2 (FIG. 170, PL. 30B)

JdE 91278. Expedition 67.272
RP 6 F (S+E) 35
45.6 x 29.2 cm
Four columns of text:

(1) *n dr.f ỉf ꜥ* (2) *[q]rs sṯ ḥb sft sw 200 m ḥꜣt ……* (3) *… m sr nb ntt m šmꜥw ṯn ḫnṯ …* (4) *… ỉn ḥry-tꜣ sꜣ mr ỉr ỉḥw qr.n sw smꜣ gs(?).f r …*

Egyptian Museum photograph in 1994.

LP 3 (FIG. 171, PL. 31)

UM 69–29–6, 31. Expedition 67.96
RP 5 E W 27
30 x 16 x 16 cm
Expedition 67.569
RP 8 C S 15
22 x 15 x 16 cm
Limestone with red paint
Dimensions of fragments joined: 44 x 19 x 17 cm
Tubular statue fragment, with belt and sash on front, hands at side, and two columns of text:

> (1) *… ỉrt-Rꜥ ỉmy-ḥꜣt ………… šps* (2) *… wḏꜣt r st.s …*

UM storage photographs: smaller fragment: 22: 23–25; larger fragment: 22: 28–30.

Fig. 171. LP 3, facsimile drawing

Summary

As indicated on the map, the area excavated consists of the front part of the ruined temple provisionally designated as the Ramesside Portal Temple and the area to its local west (to the rear of the preserved portion of the temple). For the temple, see D.P. Silverman, "The So-called Portal Temple of Ramesses II at Abydos," in *Akten des vierten internationalen Ägyptologen-Kongresses, München,* vol. 2. (Munich, 1985), pp. 271–77, and the map on p. 271, fig. 1. The blocks from the temple, both those in place and scattered fragments, will be published by Silverman and his associates. These include some of the blocks and fragments used either in earlier buildings at the site and/or blocks reused from other temples. The portal temple faces local east toward a large opening/gateway in the great enclosure wall of the area to the east, and the enclosed corner within this enclosure to the north of the gateway is known as Kom el Sultan.

Below the floor level of the temple is an area once extensively utilized by the memorial chapels of the Middle Kingdom, an area described in some detail in the preliminary report of O'Connor and designated by him as cenotaphs, since the chapels are evidently not connected with actual burials (D. O'Connor, "The 'Cenotaphs' of the Middle Kingdom at Abydos," in *Mélanges Gamal eddin Mokhtar,* Bibliothèque d'Etude 97/2 [Cairo, 1985], pp. 161–77). A single large stela (C 5) and several smaller stelae, mainly in hieratic, derive from this level, the most interesting being the large hieratic stela (C 1) with the names of thirty-two individuals, including several "doctors."

There are several significant indications of buildings/temples predating the Ramesses II temple. These include fragments of Old Kingdom blocks, perhaps from a temple, one with the name of Djedkare (OK 2), a large limestone lintel of Amenemhet III, perhaps from a brick chapel, several stamped bricks of Hatshepsut (SBS 6–7), a relief with a figure holding a naos with the name of Horemheb (NK 9) and a mud jar stopper with the same ruler's name (SBS 8). As even bricks can be reused, these indications suggest but do not prove the existence of earlier temples at the same site, although this seems to be likely. A case in point is the series of blocks of the Amarna Period, originally thought by me to have been brought from Amarna as building material, but more recently ascribed to a small building early in the reign of Akhenaten at Abydos by Silverman on the basis of the epithets used and a place name not otherwise attested at Amarna or on the blocks taken across the river to Hermopolis from Amarna.

Among the more interesting monuments of the New Kingdom are the lower part of a statue of the adjutant of the army Iamu under Amenhotep II (NK 1) and a stela of the royal scribe Si-Mut (NK 2).

Note should also be taken of the few literary texts on ostraca of the Ramesside period, The Instruction of Amenemhet and the Satire on the Trades and an unidentified story (A 1–3), as well as the figured ostracon (FO) with a scene of a brothel(?).

In connection with the building of the Ramesside temple, there are the relatively large number of bricks stamped with the name of the well known vizier of Ramesses II, Paser (SBS 2), and the large series of bricks of an overseer of the treasury named Amenhotep (SBS 1), presumably of the same reign. Of particular interest is the series of ostraca of accounts of building, which certainly relate to the Ramesside temple (B 1–18). The mention of the open court of Isis (B 1) may even provide us with the designation of the temple as a temple of Isis, and this and the other ostraca in the series provide us with the names of parts of the temple, the source of stone and gypsum, the account of deliveries of blocks of stone and gypsum, and the names of several officials: Neb-Amun and Shed-Hor (B 8–9).

The series of items from the Third Intermediate Period is of interest, particularly the once imposing tomb of Redi-Anhur (Tomb 3), with its lintel and extensive list of his family. The title *wr ꜥꜣ nꜣ mšwš* without the name preserved (TIP 3) is intriguing, especially in view of the celebrated stela Cairo JdE 66285: A.M. Blackman, *JEA* 28 (1942), pp. 83–95, which draws attention to the importance of Abydos in the Libyan Period. Note also the mention of a Namlot in TIP 4A. For the typically Libyan titles *ỉmy-ỉs, ḥsk, ꜥrq ḥḥ*, see TIP 2, 6, 7, and 8. For the Late Period, note the curious tubular statuette with a belt and sash (LP 3).

Bibliography

This bibliography consists of monographs and articles on Abydos relating to the Pennsylvania-Yale Excavations, references cited in the text of this volume, and selected recent work at Abydos by various scholars. It is not intended to be a comprehensive bibliography of the site, for which reference may be made to Kemp's 1972 article in the *Lexikon der Ägyptologie.*

Abu Bakr, Abdel-Moneim. *Excavations at Giza 1949–1950.* Cairo: Government Press, 1953

Adams, Matthew Douglas. "Community and Societal Organization in Early History in Egypt." *NARCE* No. 158/159 (1992), pp. 1–9

Andreu, Guillemette. "Polizei." In *LÄ* 4, cols. 1068–71. Edited by W. Helck and E. Otto. Wiebaden: Otto Harrassowitz, 1982

Andreu, Guillemette. "La stèle Louvre C. 249: Un complément à la reconstitution d'une chapelle abydénienne." *BIFAO* 80 (1980), pp. 139–48

Arnold, Dieter. *Building in Egypt: Pharaonic Stone Masonry.* Oxford: Oxford University Press, 1991

Ayrton, C.R., Currelly C.T. and Weigall, A.E.P. *Abydos,* Part 3. London: The Egypt Exploration Fund, 1904

von Beckerath, Jürgen. *Handbuch der ägyptischen Königsnamen.* MÄS 20. Berlin: Deutscher Kunstverlag, 1984

Blackman, A.M. "The Stela of Shoshenk, Great Chief of the Meshwesh." *JEA* 28 (1942), pp. 83–95

Boehmer, Rainer M., Dreyer, G. and Kromer, Bernd. "Einige frühzeitliche 14C-Datierungen aus Abydos und Uruk." *MDAIK* 49 (1993), pp. 63–68

Borchardt, Ludwig. *Denkmäler des Alten Reiches* II. Catalogue général des Antiquités Egyptiennes du Musée du Cairo. Cairo: Organisme Général des Imprimeries Gouvernementales, 1964

British Museum. *A Guide to the British Museum.* London: Trustees of the British Museum, 1924

Brovarski, Edward. "Abydos in the Old Kingdom and First Intermediate Period. Part I," pp. 99–121. In *Hommages à Jean Leclant,* Cairo: Institut Français d'Archéologie Orientale, 1994

Brovarski, Edward. "Abydos in the Old Kingdom and First Intermediate Period. Part II," pp. 15-44. In *For His Ka: Essays Offered in Memory of Klaus Baer.* Edited by David P. Silverman. Chicago: Oriental Institute, 1994

Bull, Ludlow. "Two Egyptian Stelae of the XVIII Dynasty." *Metropolitan Museum Studies* 2, part 1 (1929), pp. 76–84

Černý, Jaroslav. *Notebook* 101 (unpublished)

Chevereau, P.-M. "Contribution à la prosopographie des cadres militaires du Moyen Empire." *RdE* 43 (1992), pp. 11–34

Daressy, G. *Le mastaba de Mera.* Cairo: Mémoires de l'Institut Egyptien, 1898

Daressy, G. "Note sur un fragment de stèle d'Abydos." *ASAE* 5 (1904), p. 93

Daressy, G. "Notes et remarques." *Rec Trav* 24 (1902), pp. 160–67

Daressy, G. *Ostraca, Nos. 25001– 25385.* Catalogue général des Antiquités Egyptiennes du Musée du Caire. Cairo: Institut Français d'Archéologie Orientale, 1901

Dreyer, Günter. "Horus Krokodil, ein Gegenkönig der Dynastie 0," pp. 259–64. In *The Followers of Horus. Studies dedicated to Michael Allan Hoffman.* Egyptian Studies Association Publication No. 2. Edited by R. Friedman and B. Adams. Oxford: Oxbow, 1992

Dreyer, Günter. "A Hundred Years at Abydos." *Egyptian Archaeology* 3 (1993), pp. 10–12

Dreyer, Günter. "Recent Discoveries at Abydos Cemetery U," pp. 293–99. In *The Nile Delta in Transition: 4th– 3rd. Millennium* B.C. Edited by Edwin C.M. van den Brink. Jerusalem: The Israel Exploration Society, 1992

Dreyer, Günter. "The Royal Tombs of Abydos," pp. 55–67. In *The Near East in Antiquity.* Vol. 3. Edited by Susanne Kerner. Al Kutba: Amman, Goethe Institut, German Protestant Institute for Archaeology, 1992.

Dreyer, G., Hartung, U., and Pumpenmeier, F. "Umm el-Qaab." *MDAIK* 49 (1993), pp. 23–62

Edwards, I.E.S. *Hieroglyphic Papyri in the British Museum.* Fourth Series. London: British Museum, 1960

Edwards, I.E.S. *Hieroglyphic Texts in the British Museum* 8. London: British Museum, 1939

n.a. *The Egyptian Museum Cairo in Ten Years* (1965–1975). Cairo: Egyptian Museum, 1976

Erman, A., and Grapow, H., eds. *Wörterbuch der ägyptischen Sprache* 1–7, and *Belegstellen.* Leipzig and Berlin: Akademie Verlag, 1926–63

Fakhry, Ahmed. *The Monuments of Sneferu at Dahshur.* Vol. II: T*he Valley Temple.* Part II: *The Finds.* Cairo: Government Printing Offices, 1961

Fischer, Henry G. "The Inspector of the *Šḫ* of Horus, *Nby.*" *Orientalia* 30, (1961), pp. 170–75

Fischer, Henry G. "Two New Titles of the Old Kingdom," pp. 91–102. In *Aegyptus Museis Rediviva. Miscellanea in Honorem Hermanni de Meulenaere.* Edited by L. Limme and J. Strybol. Brussels: Musées Royaux d'Art et d'Histoire, 1993

Franke, Detlef. "Der Fundort der Statue Amenemhets III. auf der Qubbet el-Hawa, oder: Wer fand mit wem wann was wo?" *GM* 134 (1993), pp. 35–40

Frankfort, Henri. "The Cemeteries of Abydos: Work of the Season 1925–26. I. Stelae." *JEA* 14 (1928), pp. 235–45

Gaál, Erno. *Stamped Bricks from TT 32.* Studia Aegyptiaca 15. Budapest: Innova Press, Ltd., 1993

Gardiner, Alan H. *Ancient Egyptian Onomastica.* 3 vols. London: Oxford University Press, 1947

Gauthier, Henri. *Dictionnaire des noms géographiques contenus dans les textes hiéroglyphiques* IV. Cairo: Société royale de géographie d'Egypte, 1927

Germer, Renate. *Flora des pharaonischnen Ägypten.* Mainz am Rhein: Philipp von Zabern, 1985

Gessler-Löhr, Beatrix. "Zum Schreiben vom *mꜣʿ-ḫrw* mit der Blume." *GM* 116 (1990), pp. 25–43

Ghalioungui, Paul. *The Physicians of Pharaonic Egypt.* Mainz am Rhein: Philipp von Zabern, 1983

Gomaà, F. *Ägypten während der Ersten Zwischenzeit.* Beihefte zum Tübinger Atlas des vorderen Orients, Reihe B (Geisteswissenschaften) Nr. 27. Wiesbaden: Ludwig Reichert, 1980

Hari, Robert. *Répertoire onomastique amarnien, Aegyptiaca Helvetica* 4. Geneva: Editions de belles-lettres, 1976

Harvey, Stephen P. "The Monuments of Ahmose at Abydos." *Egyptian Archaeology* 4 (1994), pp. 3–5

Hayes, William C. "A Selection of Tuthmoside Ostraca from Der el-Baḥri." *JEA* 46 (1960), pp. 29-52

Helck, Wolfgang. *Materialien zur Wirtschaftsgeschichte des Neuen Reiches.* Abhandlungen der Geistes- und Sozialwissenschaftlichen Klasse, Jahrgang 1963, Nr. 3. Wiesbaden: Akademie der Wissenschaften und der Literatur; in Kommission bei F. Steiner, 1963

Hölzl, Regina. *Die Giebelfelddekoration von Stelen des Mittleren Reichs.* Beiträge zur Ägyptologie, Band 10. Vienna: Afro-Pub, 1990

Hölzl, Regina. "Round-Topped Stelae from the Middle Kingdom to the Late Period. Some Remarks on the Decoration of the Lunettes," pp. 285–89. In *Sesto Congresso Internationale di Egittologia Atti*, vol. 1. Turin: Tipografia Torinese, 1992

Hoffmann, Inge. *Indices zu W. Helck, Materialien zur Wirtschaftsgeschichte des Neuen Reiches.* Wiesbaden: Akademie der Wissenschaften und der Literatur; in Kommission bei F. Steiner, 1970

Hornung, Erik. "Versuch über Nephthys," pp. 186–88. In *Studies in Pharaonic Religion and Society in Honour of J. Gwyn Griffiths.* Edited by Alan Lloyd. London: Egypt Exploration Society, 1992

Hornung, Erik and Staehelin, Elisabeth. *Studien zum Sedfest.* Aegyptiaca Helvetica 1. Geneva: Editions de belles-lettres, 1974

James, T.G.H., and Apted, M.R. *The Mastaba of Khentika called Ikhekhi.* London: Egypt Exploration Society, 1993

Jéquier, Gustave. *Tombeaux de particuliers contemporains de Pepi II.* Cairo: Institut Français d'Archéologie Orientale, 1929

Jonckheere, Frans. "Le cadre professionnel et administratif des médecins égyptiens." *CdE* 52 (1951), pp. 237–68

Jones, Dilwyn. *A Glossary of Ancient Egyptian Nautical Titles and Terms.* London: Kegan Paul International, 1988

Junker, Hermann. *Giza* 7. *Der Ostabaschnitt des Westfriedhofs.* Vienna and Leipzig: Hölder-Pichler-Tempsky, 1944

Kaiser, W. and Dreyer, G. "Umm el-Qaab. Nachuntersuchungen im frühzeitlichen Königsfriedhof (2. Vorbericht)." *MDAIK* 38 (1982), pp. 211–69

Kemp, B.J. "Abydos," cols. 28–41. In *LÄ* 1. Edited by W. Helck and E. Otto. Wiebaden: Otto Harrassowitz, 1972

Kemp, B.J. "Abydos and the Royal Tombs of the First Dynasty." *JEA* 52, (1966), pp. 13–22

Kemp, B.J. "The Egyptian 1st Dynasty Royal Cemetery." *Antiquity* 41 (1967), pp. 22–32

Kemp, B.J. "The Early Development of Towns in Egypt." *Antiquity* 51 (1977), pp. 185–200

Kemp, B.J. "Large Middle Kingdom Granary Buildings (and the Archaeology of Administration)." *ZÄS* 113 (1986), pp. 120–36

Kemp, B.J. *Ancient Egypt: Anatomy of a Civilization.* London and New York: Routledge, 1989

Kitchen, Kenneth A. *Ramesside Inscriptions. Historical and Biographical* 3. Oxford: B.H. Blackwell Ltd., 1980

Kitchen, Kenneth. *Ramesside Inscriptions. Historical and Biographical* 7. Oxford: B.H. Blackwell Ltd., 1989

Leahy, Anthony. "Abydos in the Libyan Period," pp. 155–200. In *Libya and Egypt (c 1300– 750 BC).* Edited by Anthony Leahy. London: SAOS Centre of Near and Middle Eastern Studies and the Society for Libyan Studies, 1990

Leahy, Anthony. "Kushite Monuments at Abydos." In *The Unbroken Reed. Studies in the Culture and Heritage of Ancient Egypt in Honour of A.F. Shore,* pp. 171–92. Edited by Christopher Eyre, Anthony Leahy and Lisa Montagno Leahy. London: Egypt Exploration Society, 1994.

Leahy, Anthony. "The Libyan Period in Egypt: An Essay in Interpretation." *Libyan Studies* 16 (1985), pp. 51–65

Leahy, Anthony. "The Libyan Rulers in the Onomastic Record," pp. 146–63. In *Studies in Pharaonic Religion and Society in Honour of J. Gwyn Griffiths.* Edited by Alan Lloyd. London: The Egypt Exploration Society, 1992

Leahy, Anthony. "A Protective Measure at Abydos in the Thirteenth Dynasty." *JEA* 75 (1989), p. 59

Leahy, Anthony. "Two Late Period Stelae in the Fitzwilliam Museum." *SAK* 8 (1980), pp. 169–80

Leahy, Lisa Montagno and Leahy, Anthony. "The Genealogy of a Priestly Family from Heliopolis." *JEA* 72 (1986), pp. 133–47

Leclant, Jean. Archaeological survey articles in the annual journal *Orientalia*

Legrain, Georges. *Répertoire généologique et onomastique du Musée du Caire.* Geneva: Société anonyme des arts graphiques, 1908

Lesko, Leonard H. *A Dictionary of Late Egyptian* IV. Providence: B.C. Scribe Publications, 1989

Lieblein, Jens. *Dictionnaire des noms hiéroglyphiques en ordre généalogique et alphabetique, Supplément.* Leipzig: J.C. Hinrichs, 1892

Manuelian, Peter Der. *Studies in the Reign of Amenophis II.* Hildesheim: Gerstenberg Verlag, 1987

Marciniak, Marek. "Quelques remarques sur la formule IR NFR, IR NFR." *Etudes et Travaux* II. Travaux du Centre d'Archéologie Méditerranéenne de l'Academie Polonaise des Sciences 6 (1968), pp. 26–31

Marciniak, Marek. "Une formule empruntée à la sagesse de Ptaḥḥotep." *BIFAO* 73 (1973), pp. 109–12

Mariette, Auguste. *Abydos. Description des fouilles d'Abydos* II. Paris: Franck, 1880

Mariette, Auguste. *Catalogue général des monuments d'Abydos.* Paris: L'Imprimerie nationale, 1880

Mariette, Auguste. *Les Mastabas de l'Ancien Empire.* Reprint of 1889 edition. Darmstadt: Georg Olms Verlag, 1976

Martin, Geoffrey T. *The Memphite Tomb of Horemheb, Commander-in-Chief of Tutᶜankhamun* I. London: Egypt Exploration Society, 1989

Meeks, Dimitri. *Année Lexicographique* 2 (1978). Paris: author's copyright, 1981

de Meulenaere, H. "Le clergé abydénien d'Osiris à la Basse Epoque," pp. 133–51. In *Miscellanea in Honorem Josephi Vergote. Orientalia Lovaniensia Periodica* 6–7 (1975/1976). Leuven: Department Oriëntalistiek, 1976

de Meulenaere, H. "Une famille de prêtres thinites." *CdE* 29 (1954), pp. 221–36

Mostafa, Doha M. "A propos d'une particularité dans la décoration des tympans des stèles cintrées du Nouvel Empire," *GM* 133 (1993), pp. 85–96

O'Connor, David. "Abydos: A Preliminary Report of the Pennsylvania–Yale Expedition, 1967." *Expedition,* vol. 10, no. 1 (fall, 1967), pp. 10–23

O'Connor, David. "Field Work in Egypt." *Expedition,* vol. 11, no. 1 (fall, 1968), pp. 27–30

O'Connor, David. "Abydos and the University Museum, 1898–1969." *Expedition,* vol. 12, no. 1 (fall, 1969), pp. 28–39

O'Connor, David. "Abydos: The University Museum–Yale University Expedition." *Expedition,* vol. 21, no. 2 (winter, 1979), pp. 46–49

O'Connor, David. "The 'Cenotaphs' of the Middle Kingdom at Abydos," pp. 161–77. In *Mélanges Gamal eddin Mokhtar.* Bibliothèque d'Etude 97/2. Cairo: Institut Français d'Archéologie Orientale, 1985

O'Connor, David. "The Earliest Pharaohs and The University Museum." *Expedition,* vol. 29, no. 1 (1987), pp. 27–39

O'Connor, David. "New Funerary Enclosures (Talbezirke) of the Early Dynastic Period at Abydos." *JARCE* 26 (1989), pp. 51–86

O'Connor, David. "Boat Graves and the Pyramid Origins; New Discoveries at Abydos, Egypt." *Expedition,* vol. 33, no. 3 (1991), pp. 5–18

O'Connor, David, "The Status of Early Egyptian Temples: An Alternate Theory," pp. 83–98. In *The Followers of Horus. Studies dedicated to Michael Allan Hoffman.* Egyptian Studies Association Publication No. 2. Edited by R. Friedman and B. Adams. Oxford: Oxbow, 1992

Omlin, Jos. A. *Der Papyrus 55001 und seine Satirisch-erotischen Zeichnungen und Inschriften.* Turin: Edizioni d'Arte Fratelli Pozzo, 1973

Patch, Diana Craig. *The Origin and Early Devlopment of Urbanism in Ancient Egypt: A Regional Study.* Ph.D. Dissertation, University of Pennsylvania. Philadelphia, 1991

Peterson, Bengt. *Zeichnungen aus einer Totenstadt.* Stockholm: Medelhavsmuseet, 1973

Petrie, W.M. Flinders. *Abydos,* Part 1. Egypt Exploration Fund Memoir no. 22. London: Egypt Exploration Fund, 1902

Petrie, W. M. Flinders. *Abydos,* Part 2. Egypt Exploration Fund Memoir no. 24. London: Egypt Exploration Fund, 1903

Petrie, W.M.F. *A Season in Egypt.* London: Field and Tuer, 1888

Posener, Georges. "Les richesses inconnues de la littérature égyptienne." *RdE* 6 (1951), pp. 27–48

Posener-Kriéger, Paule. *Les Archives du temple funéraire de Néferirkarê-Kakaï.* Cairo: Institut Français d'Archéologie Orientale, 1976

Ranke, Hermann. *Die ägyptischen Personennamen* 1, 2. Glückstadt: J.J. Augustin, 1935, 1952

Richards, Janet. *Mortuary Variability and Social Differentiation in Middle Kingdom Egypt.* Ph.D. Dissertation, Department of Anthropology and Asian and Middle Eastern Studies, University of Pennsylvania. Philadelphia, 1992

Schulman, Alan R. *Military Rank, title and organization in the Egyptian New Kingdom.* MÄS 6. Berlin: B. Hessling, 1964

Sethe, Kurt. *Urkunken des ägyptischen Altertums* IV. Leipzig: J.C. Hinrichs, 1906–1907

Silverman, David. P. "The So-called Portal Temple of Ramesses II at Abydos," pp. 269–77. In *Akten des vierten internationalen Ägyptologen-Kongresses, München,* Band 2. Hamburg: Helmut Buske Verlag, 1985

Simpson, William Kelly. "The Lintels of Si-Hathor-Nehy in Boston and Cairo." *RdE* 24 (1972), pp. 169–75

Simpson, William Kelly. *The Offering Chapel of Sekhemankhptah in The Museum of Fine Arts, Boston.* Boston, 1976

Simpson, William Kelly. "Studies in the Twelfth Egyptian Dynasty: I The Residence of Itj-Towy. II The Sed Festival in Dynasty XII." *JARCE* 2, 1963, pp. 53–63

Simpson, William Kelly. *The Terrace of the Great God at Abydos: The Offering Chapels of Dynasties 12 and 13.* Publications of the Pennsylvania–Yale Expedition to Egypt No. 5. New Haven and Philadelphia: The Peabody Museum of Natural History of Yale University & The University Museum of the University of Pennsylvania, 1974

Sourdive, Claude. *La main dans l'Egypte pharaonique.* Berne: Lang, 1984

Spencer, A.J. *Brick Architecture in Ancient Egypt.* Warminster: Aris & Phillips, 1979

Spencer, Patricia. *The Egyptian Temple: A Lexicographical Study.* Studies in Egyptology. London: Kegan Paul International, 1984

Spiegelberg, Wilhelm. "Beiträge und Nachträge zu Daressys Publikation der hieratischen Ostraca des Museums von Gizeh." *OLZ* 5 (1902), cols. 307–35

Spiegelberg, Wilhelm. "Bemerkungen zu den hieratischen Amphoren-inschriften des Ramesseums." *ZÄS* 58 (1923), pp. 125–36

Spiegelberg, Wilhelm. *Hieratic Ostraka and Papyri found by J.E. Quibell, in the Ramesseum, 1895-6.* London: B. Quaritch, 1898

Stadelmann, Rainer. "Tempel und Tempelnamen in Theben-Ost und-West." *MDAIK* 34 (1978), pp. 171–80

Vernus, Pascal. *Le surnom au Moyen Empire.* Rome: Biblical Institute Press, 1986

van de Walle, B. "Une tablette scolaire provenant d'Abydos." *ZÄS* 90 (1963), pp. 118–23

Ward, William A. *Index of Egyptian administrative and religious titles of the Middle Kingdom.* Beirut: American University in Beirut, 1982

Wegner, Josef. "Old and New Excavations at the Abydene Complex of Senwosret III." *KMT* 6:2 (summer, 1995), pp. 58–71

Yoyotte, Jean. "Un corps de police de l'Egypte pharaonique." *RdE* 9 (1952), pp. 139–51

Indices

Titles without names

Title	Object	Accession no.	Expedition no.
ỉmy-r pr	C 31	69–29–138	67.90
ỉmy-r pr ḥḏ	NK 30	JdE 91266	67.635
ỉmy ḫt	OK 1	JdE 91218	69.95
ỉmy-ḫt sꜣ pr	OK 1	JdE 91218	69.95
ỉry ꜥt n ꞽImn	NK 37	69–29–61	67.26
ỉt nṯr	TIP 7	69–29–126	67.538
wꜥb	FO	JdE 91286	67.6
wbꜣ nsw	NK 25	69–29–159	67.264
wr ꜥꜣ nꜣ Mšwš	TIP 3	JdE 91272	67.216
rḫty	C 28	69–29–172	68.11
ḥm nṯr ꞽImn	TIP 1C	69–29–964	67.661
ḥry ꜥt	TIP 4B	69–29–51	69.174
ḥry sštꜣ ꜥr[q ḥḥ]	TIP 7	69–29–126	67.538
ḥry gnwty(?)	SBS 4	Uncatalogued	696
ḥsk	TIP 7	69–29–126	67.538
sš	FO	JdE 91286	67.6
zš wt(w)	OK 1	JdE 91218	69.95
sš pr ḥḏ	NK 33	JdE 91276	67.121
sš ḥwt-nṯr n…	NK 23	69–29–113	69.8
sš ḥtpw ꞽImn m ꞽIpt-sw	TIP 1C	69–29–964	67.661
sš qd(t)	C 22	JdE 92179	67.268
sšm ḥꜣb n Ws-ỉr	NK 33	JdE 91276	67.121
sḏm ꜥš	NK 27	69–29–40	67.636

Royal names

Royal name	Object	Accession no.
Ahmose	NK 3 (in personal name)	JdE 91260
Akhenaten	NK 41–47 (blocks of the Amarna Period)	not catalogued
Amenemhet II	C 3	UM 69–29–131
Amenemhet III	MK lintel (C 5)	Peabody Museum Yale, Egypt 7227 JdE 91243
Amehhotep II	NK 1	JdE 91221
Amenhotep III	NK 16 (NK 10)	UM 69–29–38 UM 69–29–54
Djedkare Isesi	OK 2	UM 69–29–50
Hatshepsut	SBS 6 SBS 7	UM Unnumbered UM Unnumbered
Horemheb	NK 9 SBS 8	Uncatalogued 69.5 UM 69–29–934
Mery-Re	OK 5	UM 69–29–119
Ramesses II	(B 2) B 13 (SBS 2) passim	Private collection UM 69–29–231 UM 69–29–914, 915, 919
Sekhem-Re-...	C 21	UM 69–29–180
Sesostris	C 24	UM 69–29–149
Sesostris I	C 13	Cairo or Abydos storeroom
Sesostris II	C 34	not catalogued
Seti I	D 9 NK 36 NK 38 NK 39	JdE 91282 UM 69–29–70 UM 69–29–152 UM 69–29–153

Object Concordance in Alphanumeric Order

Object	Accession no.	Expedition no.
A 1	JdE 91283+	67.560
A 2	JdE 91283+	69.43
A 3	JdE 91283+	67.457
A 4	JdE 91283+	67.266
A 5	JdE 91283+	67.32
B 1	JdE 91283+	69.128
B 2	Private Collection	
B 3	JdE 91283+	69.167
B 4	JdE 91283+	69.215 (Left)
B 4	JdE 91283+	69.48 (Right)
B 5	JdE 91283+	67.530
B 6	JdE 91283+	69.26
B 7	JdE 91283+	69.42
B 8	JdE 91283+	67.65
B 9	JdE 91283+	67.639
B 10	JdE 91283+	67.446
B 11	JdE 91283+	67.437
B 12	JdE 91283+	69.156
B 13	JdE 91283+	67.529
B 14	JdE 91283+	67.688
B 15	JdE 91283+	67.380
B 16	JdE 91283+	69.115
B 17	JdE 91283+	69.137
B 18	JdE 91283+	67.170
C 1	JdE 91253	67.234
C 2	JdE 91245	69.212
C 3	UM 69–29–131	69.208
C 4	JdE 91283+	69.86
C 5	JdE 91243	69.207
C 6	UM 69–29–135	69.214
C 7	UM 69–29–147	69.216

Object	Accession no.	Expedition no.
C 8	UM 69–29–122	69.150
C 9	JdE 91244	69.211
C 10	UM 69–29–56	69.203
C 11	JdE 91283+	69.191
C 12	JdE 91249	69.151
C 13	J. R. Survey	Square 725 / 940
C 14	JdE 91248	69.219
C 15	JdE 91220	69.205
C 16	JdE 91242	69.218
C 17	JdE 91283+	69.193
C 18	JdE 91247	69.196
C 19	UM 69–29–128	69.195
C 20	UM 69–29–215	69.103
C 21	UM 69–29–180	69.169
C 22	JdE 91279	67.268
C 23	JdE 91279	68.76
C 24	UM 69–29–149	67.3
C 25	UM 69–29–141	67.355
C 26	UM 69–29–166	67.549
C 27	UM 69–29–114	69.24
C 28	UM 69–29–172	68.11
C 29	UM 69–29–397	69.88
C 30	UM 69–29–92	67.540
C 31	UM 69–29–138	67.90
C 32	UM 69–29–117	69.40
C 33	UM 69–29–103	67.676
D 1	JdE 91282+	69.83
D 2	JdE 91283+	67.447
D 3	JdE 91283+	67.444
D 4	JdE 91282+	69.161
D 5	JdE 91282+	68.65
D 6	JdE 91282+	69.15
D 7	JdE 91282+	69.79
D 8	JdE 91282+	67.452
D 9	JdE 91282+	67.112
D 10	JdE 91282+	69.105
D 11	JdE 91282+	69.116
D 12	JdE 91282+	69.70
D 13	JdE 91282+	67.523
D 14	JdE 91282+	67.354
D 15	JdE 91282+	67.349
D 16	JdE 91282+	67.355
?D 17	JdE 91282+	67.343
FO 1	JdE 91286	67.6
LP 1	UM 69–29–181	69.204
LP 2	JdE 91278	67.272

Object	Accession no.	Expedition no.
LP 3	UM 69–29–6, 31	67.96
MK Lintel	Peabody Anthro. Egypt 7227	67.97 / 128 / 64 / 165
MK 1	JdE 91221	67.291
NK 2	JdE 91252	67.237
NK 3	JdE 91260	67.472
NK 4	JdE 91274	67.4
NK 5	JdE 91254	69.153
NK 6	UM 69–29–116	69.39
NK 7	UM 69–29–60	67.25
NK 8	JdE 91280	69.154
NK 9	Uncatalogued 69.5	Abydos Magazine
NK 10	UM 69–29–54	69.201
NK 11	UM 69–29–127	69.172
NK 12	JdE 91263	67.684
NK 13	UM 69–29–80	67.382
NK 14	UM 69–29–79	67.357
NK 15	JdE 91290	69.152
NK 16	UM 69–29–38	69.200
NK 17	UM 69–29–8	67.118
NK 18	UM 69–29–69	67.173
NK 19	UM 69–29–62 (L)	67.31 (L)
NK 19	UM 69–29–84 (R)	67.463 (R)
NK 20	UM 69–29–74	67.238
NK 21	JdE 91269	67.384
NK 22	UM 69–29–95	67.559
NK 23	UM 69–29–113	69.8
NK 24	UM 69–29–148	67.2
NK 25	UM 69–29–159	67.264
NK 26	UM 69–29–170	67.687
NK 27	UM 69–29–40	67.636
NK 28	Uncatalogued	
NK 29	UM 69–29–65	67.98
NK 30	JdE 91266	67.635
NK 31	JdE 91265	67.608
NK 32	JdE 91250	67.278
NK 33	JdE 91276	67.121
NK 34	UM 69–29–58	67.15
NK 35	UM 69–29–67	67.169
NK 36	UM 69–29–70	67.175
NK 37	UM 69–29–61	67.26
NK 38	UM 69–29–152	67.87
NK 39	UM 69–29–153	67.88
NK 40	JdE 91273	67.84

Object	Accession no.	Expedition no.
NK 41	UM 69–179	No number
NK 42	Uncatalogued	Abydos Magazine
NK 43	Uncatalogued	Abydos Magazine
NK 44	Uncatalogued	Abydos Magazine
NK 45	Uncatalogued	Abydos Magazine
NK 46	Uncatalogued	Abydos Magazine
NK 47	Uncatalogued	Abydos Magazine
OK 1	JdE 91218	69.95 / 69.889
OK 2	UM 69–29–50	69.165 (or 166)
OK 3	UM 69–29–178	69.164
OK 4	UM 69–29–48	69.163
OK 5	UM 69–29–119	69.67
SBS 1	UM 69–29–900 / 906–909 / 913 JdE 91244	67.94 / 67.14 / 122–125 / 273 / 631
SBS 2	UM 69–29–914 / 915 / 919	67.274 / 467 / 541 / 542
SBS 3	UM Uncatalogued 699 / 620	
SBS 4	UM Uncatalogued 696	
SBS 5	UM Uncatalogued 697	
SBS 6	UM Uncatalogued 698	
SBS 7	UM Uncatalogued 6915	
SBS 8	UM 69–29–934	67.616
SBS 9	UM 69–29–932	67.526
SBS 10	UM 69–29–1012	68.17
SBS 11	UM 69–29–930	67.235
SBS 12	UM 69–29–941	67.673
SBS 13	UM 69–29–927	67.21
SBS 14	UM 69–29–1014	69.145
SBS 15	UM 69–29–935	67.632
SBS 16	UM 69–29–1013	68.20
SBS 17	UM 69–29–931	67.307
SBS 18	UM 69–29–396	69.45
TIP 1A	JdE 91219	67.215 (Fragment)
		67.313 (L)
		67.315 (R)
TIP 1B	JdE 91261	69.127 (or 921)
TIP 1C	UM 69–29–964	67.661
TIP 2	UM(?)	68.90
TIP 3	JdE 91272	67.216
TIP 4	JdE 91259	67.475
TIP 5	JdE 91251	67.341
TIP 6	JdE 91258	67.473
TIP 7	UM 69–29–91	67.538
TIP 8	UM 69–29–126	69.155

Plates

1a. General view of the Pennsylvania–Yale excavations, looking southwest, with the facade of the Ramesses Portal Temple in the foreground and cenotaphs behind

1b. Cenotaph F5–8, looking southwest

2. ok 1 in situ

3A. OK 1 front

3B. OK 1 side

4a. OK 2

4b. OK 3

4c. OK 4

4d. OK 5

5A. Dynasty 12 lintel

5B. C 1

6a. c 3

6b. c 5 in situ

7a. c 5

7b. c 5, field photograph

8a. c 6

8b. c 7

8c. c 8

8d. c 10

9a. C 21

9b. C 24

9c. C 25

9d. C 26

9e. C 27

9f. C 28

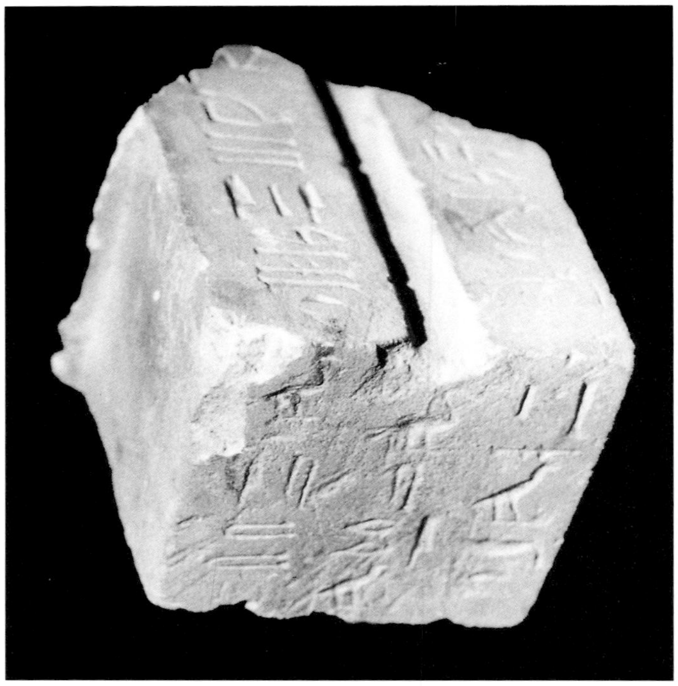

10a. c 29 side

10b. c 29 side

10c. c 29 top

10d. c 30

10e. c 31

11a. c 32

11b. c 33

11c. nk 1 back

12a. nk 1 right side

12b. nk 1 left side

13. NK 2

14A. NK 3

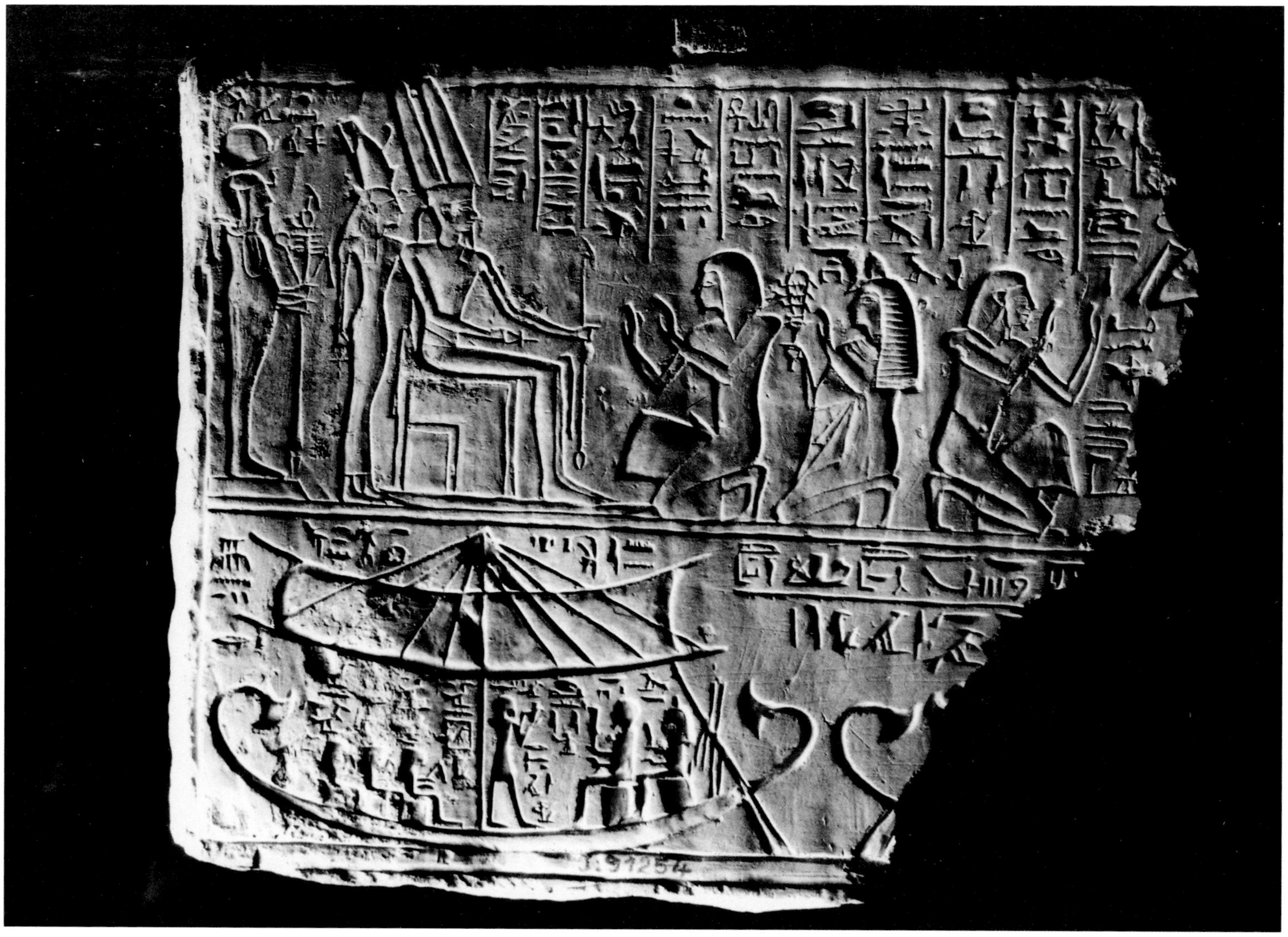

14B. NK 5

15a. NK 6

15b. NK 7

15c. NK 8

16a. NK 10

16b. NK 11

16c. NK 12

17a. NK 13

17b. NK 14

17c. NK 16 front

17e. NK 17 front

17d. NK 16 back

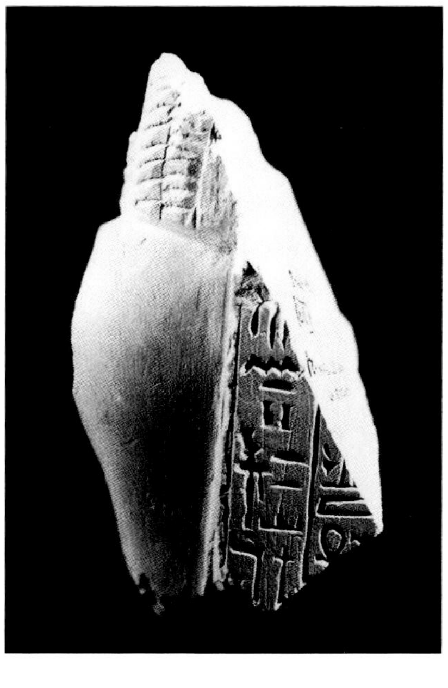

17f. NK 17 back

18a. NK 18

18b. NK 19 left and right

18c. NK 20

18d. NK 22

19A. NK 23

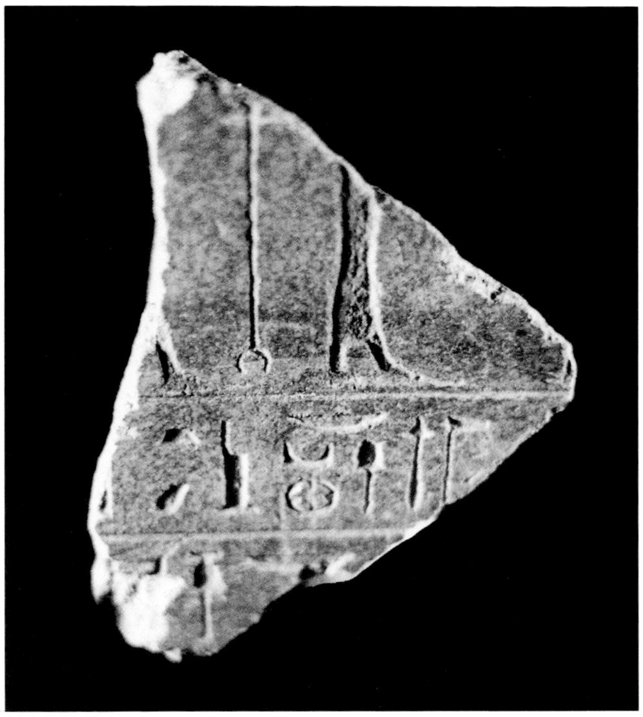

19B. NK 24

19C. NK 25

19D. NK 26

19E. NK 29

20a. NK 31

20b. NK 32

21. NK 33

22a. NK 34

22b. NK 35

22c. NK 36

22d. NK 37

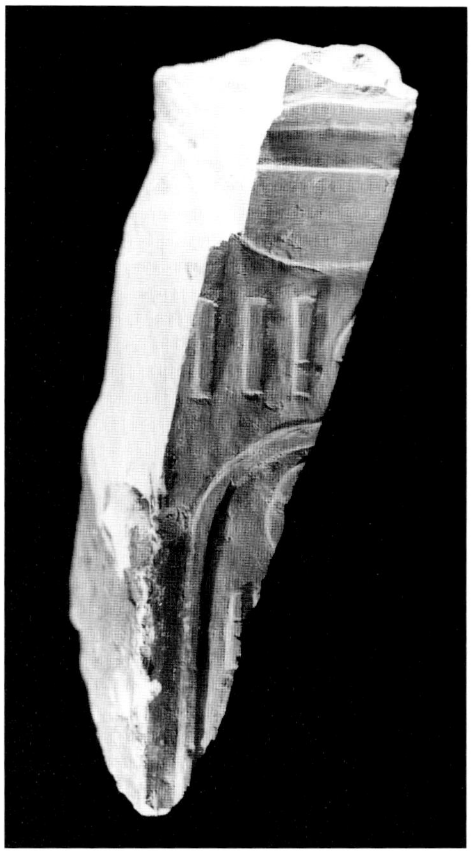

23a. nk 38

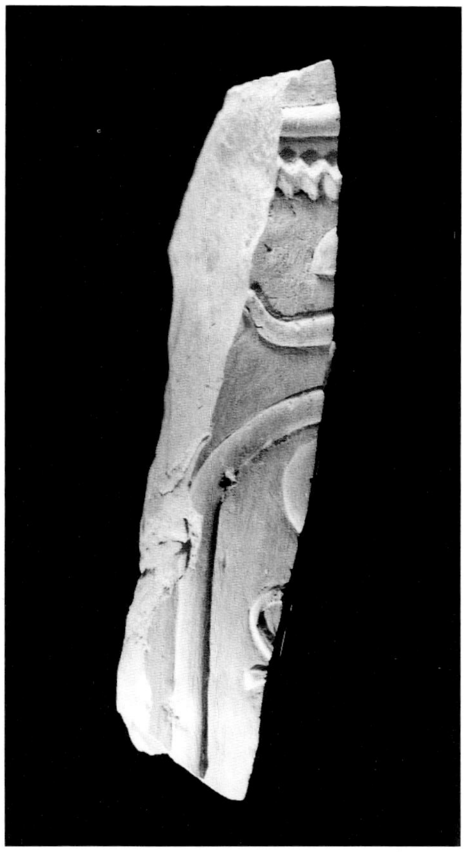

23b. nk 39

23c. nk 41

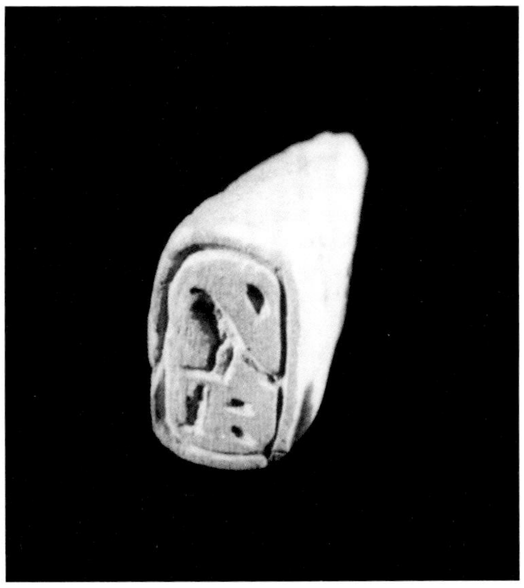

23d. sbs 18

24A. TIP IA left, after discovery

24B. TIP IA left, after cleaning

25a. tip ia right, after discovery

25b. tip ia right, after cleaning

26a. tip ia extreme right

26b. tip ib

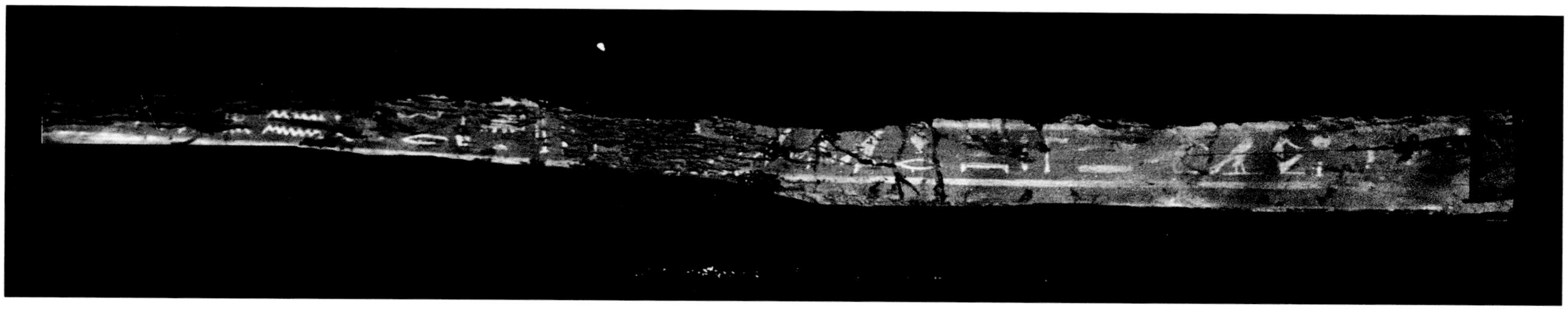

27A. TIP 1C

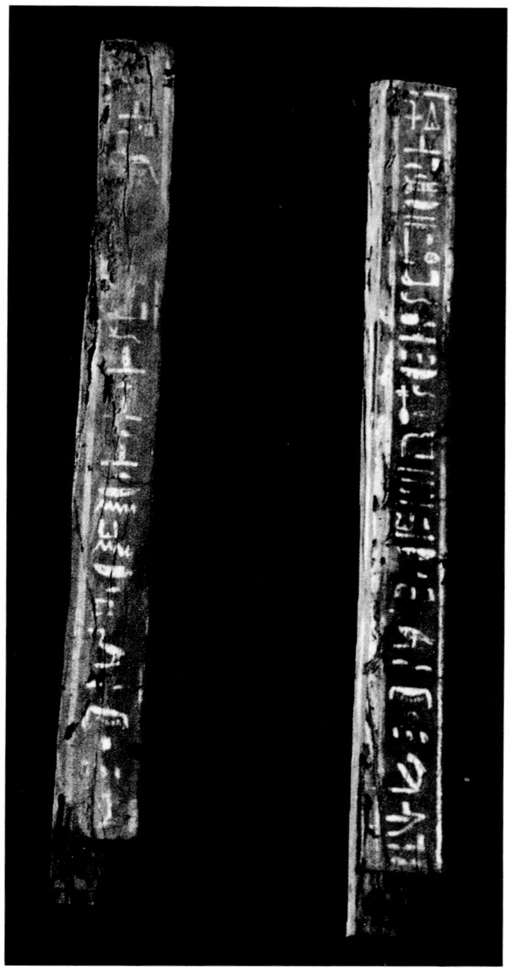

27B. TIP 1C

27C. TIP 3

27D. TIP4A

27E. TIP 4B

28. tip 5

29A. TIP 6

29B. TIP 7

29C. TIP 8

30A. LP 1

30B. LP 2

31a. lp 3 top, front

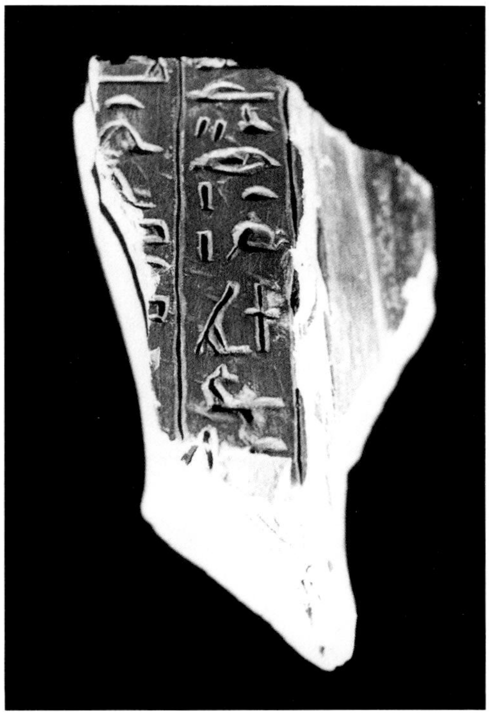

31b. lp 3 top, back

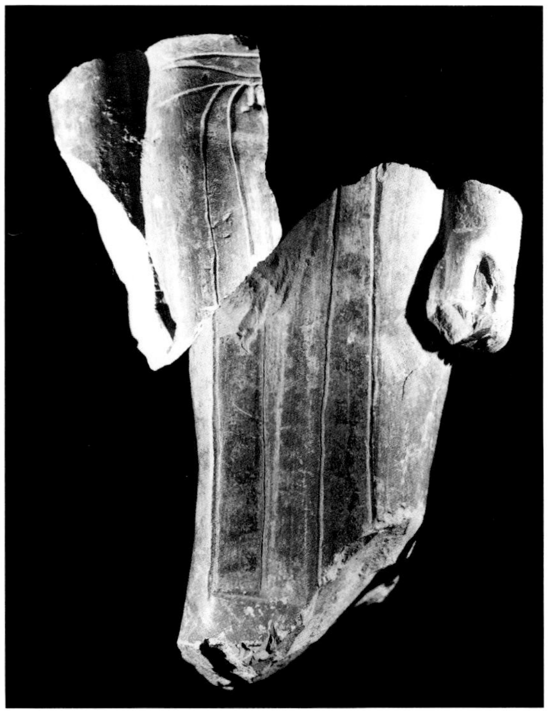

31c. lp 3, top and bottom, reunited

31d. lp 3 bottom, front

31e. lp 3 bottom, side

31f. lp 3 bottom, back